Rock 'n' Roll

RADICAL

The Life & Mysterious Death of Dean Reed

By Chuck Laszewski

Beaver's Pond Press, Inc.
Edina, Minnesota

ISBN-13: 978-1-59298-115-1
ISBN-10: 1-59298-115-1

Library of Congress Catalog Number: 2005930098

Photographs courtesy of Patricia Reed Wilson
Translation of German by Gayle Carlson

Printed in the United States of America

First Printing: September 2005

09 08 07 06 05   5 4 3 2 1

Beaver's Pond Press, Inc.

7104 Ohms Lane, Suite 216
Edina, MN 55439
(952) 829-8818
www.BeaversPondPress.com

To order, visit www.BookHouseFulfillment.com
or call 1-800-901-3480. Reseller discounts available.

This book is dedicated to my wife, Cindy,
with all my love.

Chuck,
always love your
work. Hope you enjoy
mine.
Rock on!
Chuck
3/2013

Contents

Acknowledgments

This book could not have been written without the help of two talented and extraordinarily generous women. Gayle Carlson was a young German teacher when I slid into her classroom at Alexander Ramsey High School in 1972, and although we both left that school, I would periodically contact her when I needed help with all things German. That was the case in 1992 when I contacted the German Embassy and learned only immediate family could ask for the Stasi files from the former German Democratic Republic. I requested the forms, Gayle translated them and Dean Reed's mother filled them out. When the four volumes arrived some months later, Gayle worked long hours, balancing her teaching load and family responsibilities to translate them into English. Those documents provide the rich detail of Reed's days in East Germany that would otherwise be unavailable to me, his friends or his relatives.

Patricia Reed Wilson, Dean's gorgeous and delightful first wife, early on recognized what a unique man she married and the storybook life they were leading. As a result, she kept every letter, every photo, every diary entry related to him. She graciously submitted to five different interviews and invited me to her home in Los Angeles. When I arrived, she opened the treasure house, answered all my questions, let me rummage through all the files and made me lunch. I also am indebted to all of Dean Reed's friends and relatives who took the time to answer my questions and provide insights. They did not read the book before its publication, but I hope the man I've depicted is close to the man they knew and loved.

Several colleagues and editors at the *St. Paul Pioneer Press* were instrumental in the development of the book and the newspaper story that was the basis for it. Walker Lundy, the paper's editor throughout the 1990s, immediately granted my request to use the paper's phones and letterhead to make the calls and write the Freedom of Information requests. After the story was published in 1996, he generously paid Gayle Carlson for some of her time spent on the translations. "I like to encourage my reporters in their interests, even when I don't understand them," Walker said in granting the permission, and that seemed pretty darned enlightened to me. Blake Morrison made suggestions on the rough draft and set me up with his agent. Bruce Orwall and Michele Cook gave me a free room and an entertaining death trip through Los Angeles, pointing out where big stars died. John Camp, better known as John Sanford, provided encouragement and the words on the cover. Jeff Kummer helped hone my investigative and document-gathering skills. Joe Soucheray was probably the only one who read the *Pioneer Press* piece buried in the Saturday edition two days after the Fourth of July, but he approached me in the newsroom the following Monday and said, "There's your book." He was right.

My friends Kent Anderson, Jim Schoessler and Karl Vick, all read drafts and commented freely, some of which I took to heart. John and Mary Adams encouraged me and I leaned on Mary's Spanish skills to translate some documents. My neighbor and broomball commissioner, Randy Gustafson, printed at least a dozen copies of my manuscript in his print shop, taking the time to format it and catch any spelling errors. Vick, of the *Washington Post* and Morrison, of *USA Today*, backed me financially in this venture. So have Bill Norton, David Smith, Dan Jarl, John Hallberg, Steve Hard, Tom Collins, my parents Roy and Joanne Laszewski and through the years, my father-and mother-in-law, Q.T. and Nadine Smith. Without their help, a reporter's salary would not have stretched far enough to bring this book to light.

Thanks, too, to the fine folks at Beaver's Pond Press, including editors Catherine Friend, Teresa Hudoba, owner Milt Adams and his assistants Kellie Hultgren and Judith Palmateer.

I've spent parts of the past fourteen years working on this book, using vacation time to drive to Colorado for interviews or to pound away on the computer. I tried not to let it interfere with family time, but, of course, it did. So, to my children Denise and Rick, here's to your patience. Now you can see what Dad has been up to all this time. Finally, my lovely and wise wife, Cindy, has heard me propose some new idea at least once a year. She gently steers me away from the worst of them and, like this book, does all she can to help the others to fruition. I love you always.

The Body in the Water

Sven Bosener was searching for a body. A gruesome task, sure, but strangely exciting for the young East Berlin police officer. For Bosener was searching Zeuthener Lake for the body of an American, and not just some tourist who had slipped through Checkpoint Charlie for a day. This American was as familiar in communist East Germany as President Ronald Reagan. Bosener knew if he found the body it would have national, and probably international, implications. He liked the idea that it might even make him famous, if only for a few days. Bosener had been patrolling the lake for less than thirty minutes, not enough time to get bored. It was pleasant duty on this sunny, warm, late spring morning. He slowly maneuvered his small boat northward, his gaze alternating between the open water before him and the shoreline to his right. It was 8:20 a.m. when Bosener thought he saw something floating near the weeds, about seventy feet from the shore.

The policeman brought the small boat around and opened the throttle slightly, turning the putt-putt-putt of the motor to the higher pitched, steady growl of a propeller churning through the water. As he neared the weed bed, Bosener could make out hair and then a blue jeans jacket with a fur collar. The police officer cut the throttle and eased his craft alongside the body, his heart racing slightly as he realized that he was about to touch a piece of history. At the same time, he was saddened by the death

of a man he had never met but who had touched him nevertheless. For Bosener knew he had found what he, his fellow officers
and the East German secret police had been seeking.[1]

It was the body of superstar Dean Reed, a movie actor and
rock 'n' roll singer known and mobbed throughout South America, Eastern and parts of Western Europe and the Soviet Union.
Reed was one other thing. He was an American living in Communist East Berlin, something as unusual during the Cold War as
Kevin Costner doing slapstick comedy. Bosener's discovery of
Eastern Europe's equivalent of Elvis Presley occurred on Tuesday,
June 17, 1986. But East German government officials, aided by
the secret police, had been working on a cover-up ever since
Reed stormed out of his house the previous Thursday evening
and missed his Friday appointments at the DEFA film studio in
nearby Potsdam.

Bosener grabbed the boat hook and pulled the body aboard.
He radioed for other officers and together they laid the fully
clothed body out on the shore. An investigator took several pictures of the tall, athletic star. Even in death, and after spending
several days in the water, his handsome features were still mostly
intact, features that had made millions of girls swoon and the
luckiest ones fall into his bed. Orders moved quickly down the
ranks. The officers were to say nothing of their discovery to anyone. Bosener sighed. It was hardly a surprise, since secrets were
the currency of the communist life. Still, just this once, he had
hoped Reed's stature would be enough to rip away the curtain of
silence and provoke a public demonstration of mourning and re-
membrance of the man, his music and his movies. And just maybe
there would be a little something extra for the cop who found
the body. The bureaucrats had other plans. Within hours, the official government media was reporting that Reed had died from a
"tragic accident" in the lake, but revealed few details. The lack of
information quickly prompted rumors and speculation on both
sides of the Atlantic that Reed was murdered.

The most likely suspect was the Stasi, East Germany's notorious secret police. Those rumors were fueled by Reed's increasing
disenchantment with the Communist government and a longing

to resume his career in the United States, where he had minor success twenty-five years earlier. At a time when President Reagan was publicly calling the Soviet Union and its satellite nations an evil empire and Soviet Premier Mikhail Gorbachev was loosening some of the restrictions in the day-to-day lives of citizens in the tightly controlled country, it was always a great propaganda coup to trot out Reed. Until recently, he could be counted on to criticize American policies and speak fondly of the Socialist life he had been living since moving to East Germany in 1972. Just two months earlier, Reed had been interviewed on CBS's *60 Minutes*, and he had defended the East German government. But cracks had appeared in the interview when the singer acknowledged that he disagreed with some of the government's restrictions on people's lives. Worse, he told interviewer Mike Wallace that he wanted to come home.

The Stasi had its own concerns. Dean Reed had been a spy for them. Maybe the CIA knew, maybe it didn't. Maybe Reed would tell the United States spy agency everything he knew about their methods and maybe he wouldn't. It was quite possible the spymasters in East Berlin did not want to gamble with their operative, who they knew was erratic and undependable.

But the Stasi was hardly alone. There were plenty of people who would feel much better knowing Reed was dead. In 1978, Reed had traveled to Lebanon and lived with Palestinian soldiers as they waged a guerrilla battle with Israel. He spent an evening with Israel's most hated enemy, Yasser Arafat, spoke glowingly of the Palestinian struggle and roundly condemned Zionism. Could the Israeli Mossad have silenced an outspoken ally of Arafat's drive for an independent nation? The Mossad had a long record of slipping into other countries to arrest or kill men they viewed as enemies of Israel and they were not overly concerned with the niceties of whether it was legal or illegal. Or perhaps it was agents of the brutal right-wing dictatorship of General Augusto Pinochet in Chile. For more than a decade, Reed had raised money and awareness throughout the world in an attempt to topple the general. Just three years earlier, the American had recklessly traveled to Santiago in the middle of a vicious crackdown by Pinochet and participated in demonstrations by students and miners. It had ended with Reed's arrest and expulsion, but perhaps the vindictive dictator had tired of the singer's constant attacks and dispatched his killers to silence him. After all, Pinochet's operatives had once brazenly murdered an exiled Chilean critic as he got into his car in Washington, D.C.

Some friends and family even suggested the CIA killed Reed. During his *60 Minutes* interview, Reed renewed his attack on the United States, harshly criticizing Reagan and worse, defending the Berlin Wall as necessary to keep the United States out rather than East Berlin citizens in. He had traveled to Nicaragua, met with President Daniel Ortega and entertained his troops in the field as they fought the U.S.-backed Contras, who had direct connections with the CIA. Ronald Reagan's unwavering support of the insurgency against Ortega's government had recently been exposed as illegally thwarting the will of the Congress and included selling arms to Iran to continue financing the Contras. Still, American viewers were outraged at Reed's comments on the newsmagazine and sent him hundreds of scathing letters.[2] Perhaps the CIA decided to follow the popular mood and killed this traitorous native son. Or maybe it was as pedestrian as a jealous husband or boyfriend who killed the sexy film and rock idol. Reed had lived the star's lifestyle on three continents and while he steered clear of illicit drugs, he had indulged heavily in sex and rock 'n' roll. He was married three times, but those vows had never diminished his passion for beautiful and willing women.[3] A man enraged by his wife's dalliance with the star could easily have followed the accessible Reed, forced him off the road by the lake, killed him and dumped the body in the water.

The East Berlin Police would investigate Reed's death and provide answers to many of the questions, answers that only recently, with the reunification of Germany, have become available. But as mysterious as his death was at age 47, it was his life that enthralled and intrigued all those who knew him. Reed had a knack for injecting himself into the historical action of the 1960s, 1970s and early 1980s, wherever in the world it was happening. Frequently, he was a minor player, but sometimes he was very much at the forefront. Occasionally, he even managed to make the newspapers and magazines back home. In 1978, Reed was arrested in Buffalo, Minnesota, while protesting with farmers over the siting of a high-voltage power line. He spent twelve days in jail and spurred an international incident that flooded President Jimmy Carter with telegrams from all over the world. The wire services wrote stories about him and *People* magazine showed up for his trial.

At heart, Reed's story is a uniquely American tale. Like thousands of men of his day, Reed wanted to be a star and fell under the spell of the guitar and the rhythms of rock music. He toiled at his craft and eventually counted some of the biggest stars in Hollywood as his friends. He acted in films with the likes of Yul Brenner and sang with Phil Everly. But his artist's heart was always open to the emotions and struggles of others. Those struggles, and the counsel of friends and mentors, changed Reed in fundamental ways so that it became impossible for him to ignore what was happening in the world. Soon he was working as hard for social change as he had for a hit record or a box-office smash. Eventually, he willingly put his career and his life on the line to stand with people from South America to Minnesota if he thought they were being trampled by the rich and powerful.

"A basic principle of Dean, he stood for what he believed," said Phil Everly, who with his brother Don formed one of the most popular duos in rock history. "I guarantee he would stand for you. If he gave his word, he would do it. That's a rare commodity."[4]

During the funeral service for Reed, his mother, Ruth Anna Brown, told the hundreds gathered in East Berlin that she would no longer attempt to bring her son's ashes back to the United States for burial. Instead, the ashes would stay in East Germany where he had lived happily and loved two women.[5] But in 1991, after Germany was unified, Brown changed her mind and the ashes were brought back and buried in the Green Mountain Cemetery in Boulder, Colorado, not far from where his journey began. A simple headstone marked the spot.

DEAN CYRIL REED
DENVER 1938–BERLIN 1986
AMERICAN REBEL

Mobbed

The flight from New York took all day and Reed arrived in Santiago, Chile, with that peculiar fatigue common to anyone who has spent the day sitting still and tricking the mind into thinking about anything but what lies ahead. When the plane finally touched down, the excitement and anxiety of his new venture sent a jolt through him. Reed was alert as he descended the stairway from the plane, the warm setting sun reflecting off the Andean peaks beneath which the city was comfortably tucked. He quickly took in his surroundings before focusing his eyes straight ahead as he tried to make out the Spanish signs. Unable to read the language, he looked for pictures or an English word, anything that could direct him to customs. It took him a moment, but he found it and fell in line with the other foreign visitors. He chewed his nails as he waited for the queue to move. The agents were curt with their questions and meticulous as they ran their hands over the clothes in suitcases. So Reed was surprised when the agents gave his luggage a cursory look and treated him with a diffidence not afforded the other passengers. Reed strode through the airport doors with his guitar and luggage to a waiting car, but stopped short on the sidewalk.

"Señor Dean, Señor Dean," was all he could understand of the language. No one was carrying on a conversation anyway, not with the shrieks and screams of a thousand women drowning out every other intelligible sound. His moment's hesitation was interpreted as invitation and the whole mass surged forward. The crowd wanted to see him, touch him, devour him. Reed squeezed into the car, but despite having a motorcycle escort, they could barely move. Reed smiled broadly in the back of the cab, but it was the stunned smile of a lottery winner. He had no reason to expect this, had not been prepared for it. After all, back in Los Angeles he was just another struggling singer and acting student. He had a standard contract with Capitol Records, the kind they hand out dozens of times a year, hoping to strike gold or platinum with one or two of them. He had one minor hit, "Our Summer Romance," and his career was moving so slowly it could be mistaken for stagnate. Some of the folks at Capitol had mentioned that "Our Summer Romance" was selling very well in parts of South America and finally the twenty-two-year-old singer decided he had nothing to lose. He borrowed money and hopped on the only flight leaving LaGuardia Airport for Santiago on March 9, 1961. His driver spoke only Spanish, so Reed could only murmur "Damn" as he squirmed in his seat, looking out the side windows, then the back window and finally the windshield.

It was the view out the front that Reed kept coming back to. A van from a Santiago radio station stayed just a few feet ahead of the taxi, broadcasting live the arrival of the American star. The station had done a superb job in the days preceding Reed's trip of whipping up the fans and they were not about to quit now that the man himself had landed. The radio announcer reported Reed's every wave to the crowd and called out the streets the caravan was traveling so more people could line the roadway and wave from the open apartment windows. Capitol Records and its local people had provided Reed all the accouterments of a superstar. The hotel was the city's finest, used by diplomats and other VIPs because of its location across the street from the Moneda, the presidential palace. Another crowd of thousands had formed by the hotel, all of them pushing and screaming to see their idol. Reed plunged through the crowd and finally, after nearly losing his shirt, tumbled into the hotel lobby. Once in his room, which overlooked the plaza, he opened his window and waved to the fans, his fans. The adrenaline rush that had kept him going for the past hour began to fade and sleepiness overtook him. But Reed was ecstatic.[1]

This was the success, the love that he had been dreaming of since he left the University of Colorado. This was the kind of adulation Elvis and Reed's buddies, the Everly Brothers, received in the States. He wanted nothing less. He was, at last, a rock star.

The next day was more of the same. The teenagers, especially the girls, were gathered outside his hotel. This time, however, his driver aggressively pushed the car through the throng, bruising several who did not get out of the way fast enough.

"Hey, what are you doing?" Reed yelled. The driver said nothing, staring straight ahead and laying on the horn. Another girl banged hard off the right front fender and was spared from falling under the car by the sea of arms that grabbed her. Reed punched his driver in the shoulder.

"What the fuck are you doing? You're going to kill somebody. Slow down, they'll move."

This time, the driver glanced at his passenger and rattled off an explanation but Reed understood not a word of it. The driver slowed some, but Reed's anger grew as they neared the radio studio, where he was to be interviewed and pose for publicity shots. Once inside, he was greeted by the station owner, a translator and the publicist from Capitol Records.

"Dean, good to see you," the Capitol man started, but Reed cut him off.

"Where the fuck did you get that driver? He's a menace. He damn near killed fifteen people out there."

"Well, it's a bit of a mob scene, isn't it?" the Capitol man said with a grin. "He just wanted to make sure you got here okay."

"Don't give me that shit. There's no excuse for that. Those people just want to see me and they're the ones buying my records. You can't treat'em like trash. I'm not riding with that man again. He's gone."

"Dean, we hired him for the day, we can't get anyone else."

"Fine, I'll walk back."

The man from Capitol snorted. "You'll never make it back. They'll tear your clothes off and make you sing every song you ever learned and then they'll make you sing'em again."

But Reed would not be moved and told them to make whatever arrangements they thought necessary. He did the interview, posed graciously for all the publicity shots and a few impromptu photos with radio staff members, handed out autographs and then headed for the door and the five-block walk back to the hotel. The decision was a good one for Reed and even better for his fans. The Santiago police officers, however, had witnessed better ideas. For the next thirty minutes it took more than fifty police officers, sweating profusely and pushing hard, to clear the way for Reed and keep his fans from crushing him.[2]

At night, Reed performed in large theaters and clubs. Everywhere, his shows were sellouts and he played before packed houses. The front of one theater was adorned with a ten-foot high picture of the American singer. "Every town had a dancing hall and millions of teenagers," said Patricia Reed, his first wife. "He would be totally mobbed."[3] His days were not unlike those he spent in Los Angeles. He traveled around with his publicity photos, talked to agents, radio station managers, club owners, anyone who could pump up his record sales and renown. He sat for newspaper and magazine interviews. He was booked on television variety shows, some of which lasted for five hours. The difference here was that the booking agents, radio and television people wanted to talk to him. Instead of being turned down eight times out of ten, suddenly it was Reed who had to say "no." There were more possible bookings than the performer had hours in his seventeen days there.

The young American was falling under the spell of South America and especially Chile. Santiago's restaurants and cafes reminded him of Los Angeles, but without the perpetual hustle and phoniness. Or maybe it was because here he was on top, not just another struggling artist. Every day was another nice hotel, exclusive nightclub, swimming pool with waiters, limousine, and more beautiful women and enthusiastic fans for whom he happily signed his autograph a hundred times a day.[4] The tour also sharpened Reed's performing skills, both on and off stage. The shows often lasted two hours and he was learning how to work the crowed, how to pace the show and himself.

"In person, he could make you cry, he could make you laugh," said Patricia Reed. "The voice went beautifully with the looks. If you listen to the record, it wasn't that good. He didn't have the salesmanship on a record. He didn't have a specialty. He copied others: Elvis. In person, he had his personality. Older women wanted to screw him; young girls wanted to be with him. It was his innocence, his romanticism."[5]

His concerts were mostly rock 'n' roll songs and light ballads that he had been recording for Capitol. "Our Summer Romance," was the one the audience came to hear and they were thrilled by his covers of other American hit songs. But he would throw in a few Broadway show tunes, the kind he had worked on with his teacher Marge Raitt back in Los Angeles. To ingratiate himself with the crowd, he would take a song like "Maria" from *West Side Story* and substitute a popular girl's name from the country in which he was performing. It rarely failed to connect with the audience. His first few shows, Reed was understandably nervous. His American experience had been small clubs with maybe two hundred people, many half-listening. In Chile, he was playing theaters with thousands of people, all focused on the man with his guitar. The thought of a two-hour show was unnerving. He wasn't even sure he knew two hours worth of songs. How would he talk to them between numbers? But he had developed a natural ease on stage and once the lights came up and the MC had finished the introduction with the only words the singer understood, "Dean Reed," the nervousness floated out through his guitar pick and he was off improvising. Reed was an energetic singer, gyrating on stage, jumping down into the audience and pulling women out of their chairs to dance with him. Reed would sprinkle in the few phrases he had learned during the day. "Muy bonita chicas," ("my beautiful girls"), he would tell the audience as he left his dancing partners and climbed back on stage. The crowd roared with appreciation and that applause kept the clock ticking and conserved his bag of songs for a few more minutes. It was working. The reviews were glowing. His friend Phil Everly knew Reed's act and gave it good grades. "He was a cross between Buddy Holly and Pat Boone," Everly said. "He was not enough of a rocker for the Holly thing. But he was more rock than Pat. Dean could out-sing 50 percent, 60 percent of the singers. He could out-perform a lot of them. He was great onstage."[6]

Because Reed never put together his own band, a chunk of nearly every day was devoted to rehearsal. The band had to be sharp enough to give Reed the freedom to spend time in the audience, repeating a chorus over and over to different women, or dancing with whomever he pulled from a seat. Each new town or even each new venue meant teaching his music to new people, to help them anticipate his moves. "Of course I had stage fright," Reed said. "The routine, which you can acquire in my profession like in every other, didn't help." It didn't help because it had been developed around a minor league career of playing a club until about midnight, schmoozing with the owner and perhaps talent scouts for another hour or so and then heading home in his convertible. This was like suddenly being dropped into a sold-out Yankee Stadium. After the rehearsals, he could relax for a few hours before plunging into the long, energy-sapping show. Reed poured every atom of energy and personality into his fans, and he wanted nothing more than to fall into bed and sleep for a week. But his night had just begun. "The managers have organized a party where you must make an appearance," Reed recalled. "A well-known actress has announced that she is coming, or an important man in show business. You must smile into the cameras, must clink the champagne glasses."[7]

Reed refined his performances at these parties, improving on the natural charm that had propelled him this far. It was always, "Hola, yo Dean Reed," as though he was the waiter, rather than the star of the party. That bit of modesty was invariably disarming, but he was quick to follow that with "Como se llama?" a sincere wish to know the name of whomever he was speaking to. He resisted the temptation to survey the room, looking for someone bigger, prettier or more interesting. Instead, he locked his gaze on his new friend, not only to let them know they were the only person in the room, but to gauge them, plumb their depths. "Eyes are the mirror into the soul," he would tell his friends, but it was the skin that was the transmitter to the heart. Dean would touch a hand, cradle the speaker's elbow or pat his companion on the shoulder. The effect was always the same. Each person believed she was becoming a Dean Reed intimate, and few could, or wanted to, resist. The shows in Chile, Argentina, Peru, Brazil and Uruguay were wildly successful. So were the parties, where radio executives and record distributors were often among the invited. Record sales jumped, making the folks back at Capitol happy. The seventeen days flashed by and Reed packed his gear and headed back to Hollywood. The tour injected him with even more confidence. He knew now how it felt to be a huge star. Dean was sure it would take only fifteen or twenty minutes to repeat that success in the States. For now, surely, everybody must have heard how he had conquered Latin America. It was a much more pleasant plane ride home. Reed slept peacefully much of the way.

The truth was, he craved fame the way plants crave the sunlight. The feeling awakened in him shortly after he got his first guitar in 1950. After his family had moved several times, they settled again in the Denver suburb of Wheat Ridge. Reed's father, Cyril, gave his son a guitar for his twelfth birthday. The boy fooled around with the gift, teaching himself how to play and copying two of his favorite singing cowboys, Roy Rogers and Gene Autry. Rogers, in particular, was near the peak of his popularity with movies and eventually a weekly program on the televisions that were multiplying in the living rooms around the country. "Soon, I could play so well that at parties or during school vacations, often people said, 'hey Dean, play something.' Actually, what I wanted to do was impress the girls," Reed recalled.[8] Cyril liked to recount a story of his son on the stage for a junior high school show. "He was called Slim Reed then and he was scared to death."[9]

By the time he was attending Wheat Ridge Senior High School, his guitar and singing were bringing him the attention he needed. Reed performed at shows in school and sometimes at local events. Best of all, the girls were responding the way he had hoped. There was something about a guy who could work the frets and sing in key that touched the heart of young women. Elvis Presley had discovered that, and the reaction of women to his breakthrough hit, "Heartbreak Hotel," in early 1956 just reinforced what Reed already had discovered on his own. Playing other people's songs worked fine, but the teenager found a way to inflame the passion. He wrote some of his own songs and one of the first was about his sweetheart, Linda. The song worked its magic better than giving her his class ring. Dean and Linda went steady for months and were often seen around town holding hands or slipping away to neck. Even after they broke up, Reed did not forget her and recorded the song a few years later. Unfortunately, the American public was less enthralled than his former girlfriend and the song went nowhere.[10] A few months later, Reed had an accidental brush with national recognition that hooked him forever.

Reed graduated from Wheat Ridge Senior High School in June 1956 and spent the summer working at the VC-Bar dude ranch about two hundred miles southwest of Denver. He worked the ranch during the days and at night entertained the guests as a cowboy singer. The day work was hard, the kind his tough father was happy to know his son was doing. But it was the nighttime singing that eased the young man's sore muscles and kept him from quitting. Bill Smith was one of the wranglers on the ranch and he had a gift for needling his young hands.

"Reed, you still feeding the horses? Get over here and carry these saddles into the barn."

"But I just started feeding and watering the horses. After that trail ride they need it, and maybe a brushing, too."

"Dang it, boy, I told you to feed them five minutes ago. I've got mules that move faster than you."

"Shoot, Bill, I outrun those raggedy old mules of yours every day. And I carry a ton more than they do. 'Dean, carry the saddles, Dean, hay the horses, Dean, grab those bags.' "

"The mules are faster than you and they don't give me near as much backtalk. Yes, sir, give me those mules any day over you summer cowboys."

"Does your wife know how you feel about those animals? Anyway, where'd you get the idea they're fast? I've never seen them move faster than a trot and that was only when they saw you coming to the corral with the packs. I could beat any one of them over any distance."

Smith let out a hoot. "I know you were a big track man in high school, but over ten miles your sneakers and little cotton shorts wouldn't stand a chance. Those mules have more stamina than a drunk on a barstool."

"Oh, yeah, and they never stop just because they're ornery," Reed replied. "When that old mule takes a notion to stay put, I wouldn't even have to run. I could stroll to the finish line as easy as walking to the bunkhouse."

"Crawling would be more like it. Those mules have hoofs. They can take the pounding of the road all week, but those dainty little feet of yours would turn to hamburger, assuming your lungs don't burst first."

"Big talk, my friend. Are you willing to put some money behind it?"

Smith loved the idea. They hiked up to the ranch house and asked the owner for his permission to settle the wager. The owner was amused, but more than that, he saw the makings of cheap entertainment for his staff and guests. He not only approved the race, he also threw in the supplies they would need. Smith, on a big mule named Speedy, would race Reed in his tennis shoes and running shorts. The race would begin at the VC-Bar's rodeo arena and proceed to Gunnison and back, a distance of 110 miles. The ranch cook drove a truck to fix their meals. Each would keep careful track of time-outs for meals and sleeping. If one reached a designated spot five minutes ahead of the other, that person got a five-minute head start on the next leg. The conditions could not have been harder for a man. The race was run during the first hot days of August and while the pine trees provided some shade along the way, most of the time Reed trotted and walked under the sun's brilliance. Within an hour, his shirt was soaked through and Reed sipped water constantly to head off dehydration. Despite his persistence, the damn mule was always just ahead of him. With nine miles left, Reed faced the prospect of losing, a prospect his pride would not allow. He ditched his walk-and-trot strategy and ran to the finish. Forty-seven hours after the race began, Reed limped into the rodeo arena and collapsed in front of the guests and ranch hands who had gathered to watch. Three minutes later, Speedy crossed the finish line. Reed was right about the animal's temperament. The animal had balked several times, including at a small stream bridge within sight of the finish line. The actual racing time was twenty-two hours, or an average speed of five mile per hour. Dean was exhausted and Smith's warning about what would happen to his feet proved accurate. They were blistered and raw. His lips were cracked and encased in a white ring of dried salt, giving him the look of a woman with a peculiar shade of lipstick. "I'll be darned, Deano," Smith started as he dismounted from Speedy and walked over to the grimacing teenager. "When I saw you running I thought for sure I had you. I didn't figure there was any way you could keep up that pace, and even if you did, I didn't think you could make up the lead Speedy and I had. You're all right, kid. Not too bright, but all right. Here's what I owe you."

Smith dug into his jeans, pulled out a quarter and handed it to Reed.[11] For all their big talk, they were small bettors. The race was pure Reed. "He was always stubborn and tough," according to his older brother Dale.[12] The race provided a bigger payoff for Reed and the VC-Bar. A week later, Reed was plunking down that quarter and thumbing through the *Newsweek* he purchased with it. He stopped at the National Affairs section. There, tucked in between columns about a minor controversy at the Republican Party convention and a military trial over a sergeant who slapped a recruit, and in the same issue as the sinking of the luxury liner *Andrea Doria,* was a story headlined, "Triumphant Man." Reed relished the publicity and years later, when people would ask him about his life, he rarely failed to mention the race, nor the fact that *Newsweek* wrote about it. For Reed, it was the first time he was exposed to a national audience. As he stepped off the plane from South America, he wondered if his triumphant tour would spark a return visit from the good people at *Newsweek.*

Three

Wandering the West

Dean Reed was born September 22, 1938, the second of three sons born to Ruth Anna and Cyril Reed. Cyril was a tough, commanding figure. He lost a leg in a farm accident growing up in Illinois and from the time he was sixteen, he got around with the help of a wooden leg.[1]

Cyril migrated west after college and taught history and math at Denver's West High School. There, one of his students, Ruth Anna Hansen, caught his eye. Even though he was eleven years older than Ruth Anna, they dated, fell in love and were married after she graduated from high school in 1931. Cyril continued teaching until 1942, a year after the birth of their third and last child, Vernon. Now thirty-nine and prevented from serving in World War II because of his leg and his age, but tired of teaching, Cyril began a series of ventures that would take the family throughout the West. At first, he started a chicken farm, building the chicken houses himself and selling eggs and the birds. But he soon tired of that enterprise and the family settled into a new routine of moving every couple of years.[2] There was El Monte, California, just southeast of Pasadena, where Cyril briefly returned to teaching. Then it was on to Salt Lake City, towns in Arizona, back to the Los Angeles area in Pomona where he had a lawnmower dealership. Dale, who was the eldest by four years, and Dean would assemble the rotary lawnmowers and demonstrate them for customers. Los Angeles had not yet sprawled far from the ocean and dairy farmers and orange growers dominated the countryside.

"We had a lot of fun there, playing in the orange orchards," Dale said. "The bums would live in the concrete ditches. Dean was forever getting me in trouble. He would get me to sneak up on the bums and steal their comic books. He couldn't run as fast, so they would get him and he'd yell, 'Dale, Dale.' "[3]

But those days ended like the others with another move, because "it's hard when you're a school teacher and you just quit your job," Ruth Anna said. None of Cyril's new businesses made him rich and he always was looking for the next big venture that might pay off. When Dean was ten, the family moved back to Denver. By now, Cyril not only didn't want to teach, but he had come to believe that the public schools didn't know what they were doing. So he pulled Dale out of the public school and enrolled him in the private Colorado Military Academy in the Denver suburb of Littleton. But Cyril didn't want Dale to go alone and he enrolled Dean as well.[4] For the Reed boys, the military academy was a tough place. Most of the boys who attended the school lived in the dormitory. The Reeds were considered "day boys" because they went home every night. The rest of the students were jealous, an envy that was fueled by the fact that many of them had been dumped there by parents who couldn't deal with their sons. Dale hated the academy and he knew it was a worse experience for his kid brother.

Only one thing made the school tolerable. At the military academy, Dean received weekly riding lessons in the more structured English riding style. The Reeds had messed around with horses from time to time, mostly when they visited their cousin in Grand Junction, Colorado. Their cousin gave them a few tips on riding western style and then they would be off, galloping around the pastures or picking their way through the foothills. Dean loved the academy's riding lessons and he had a good feel for the horses. Soon, he could ride easy in the saddle. He could make the horse go where he wanted with only a subtle pull on the reigns or change from a cantor to a gallop with a jab of his heel and cluck of his tongue. He also mastered the more dangerous feat of jumping his horse over steeplechase poles. "The only thing that this uniform has brought me is the joy of riding," Reed recalled years later. "I still have this love today. At the age of eleven, I bought my first horse, with my own money." The youngster mowed lawns, shoveled sidewalks and with his dad and brothers cut Christmas trees in the woods and sold them. When Reed finally scraped together $150, he bought Blondy, a flaxen with a yellow-white mane and tail. He rode her everywhere.[5] The military academy experiment ended after a year and the family moved again. They settled in another Denver suburb, Wheat Ridge, where Dean returned to the public school system for his junior high school days.

Cyril Reed gave his boys a fairly typical upbringing for the times. He would not tolerate sissies. He worked them hard and if they bawled, he meted out punishment or ridicule. But he also tried to instill in them his love of knowledge and books. In this, his middle son was happy to oblige. Dean enjoyed reading and sometimes would ride off on Blondy with a book in search of a cool place to lie down and read.[6] As he moved into high school, Reed was still a self-conscious kid. When he looked in a mirror, all he saw was a skinny boy with big ears. Still, any physical shortcomings he perceived could be overcome through personality and intelligence. High school was a buffet of new social treats and he was trying as many of them as he could pile on his plate.[7] The yearbook at Wheat Ridge Senior High School pictured Reed as a member of the student council, the social services club, the junior play and the boys' chorus. He also was a member of the track team and the gymnastics team, where he performed on the rings.[8] The skinny freshman disappeared into the well-muscled young adult. By his senior year, in 1956, he was 6-foot-1 and sporting the athletic build that would never desert him. The big ears had receded into his head, covered in part by a more stylish haircut for his brown hair, replacing the crew cut of his academy days. His blue eyes often lit up with the laughter of the good-time kid, but it could smolder with the romantic's flame as played his love songs.

After his blistered feet healed from racing the mule, Reed once again followed his older brother to school. But unlike the military academy, this time it was Dean's choice. The University of Colorado in Boulder, with the Rocky Mountains towering over the campus, was a beautiful place for the Reed boys to study science. Dale was about to begin his senior year as his younger brother fell into line at the registrar's office to sign up for his first classes. Cyril Reed, in yet another of his schemes, had built three apartment houses in Wheat Ridge and set himself up as a small landlord. The boys moved into one of the apartments, which was less than twenty-five miles from the college campus. Ruth Anna made fun of the apartments because she thought they looked like a chicken house, but for the two brothers it was the perfect first step to independence, even though it was Cyril who kept the cupboards filled with groceries.[9]

For the brothers, it was a chance to overcome the four-year gap in their ages and get to know each other better. Dale showed Dean the ropes of college life. Where the buildings were, of course, but he also got his brother into the gymnastics club with him. For Dean, it was back to bouncing on the trampoline, pointing his toes to the ceiling on the rings, making giant loops on the high bar and juggling. The rings and the high bar kept the freshman in shape and gave him the physical activity he craved to counteract the hours behind the books. Gymnastics was another place for Reed to succeed and perform before an audience. During his sophomore year, he finished fifth in the national gymnastics tournament at the University of Nebraska.[10] At half time of the Buffaloes basketball games, the club often entertained by doing juggling tricks. The slots were limited and Reed mostly just watched as Dale and the others performed, although he was there to sub when needed. Dale also owned the boys' transportation, a 1948 Dodge convertible that ferried them between the apartment and their classes. The other vital service the convertible performed was picking up their dates. And girls were one of the big contributions Dean made to the living arrangement. "He was always a ladies man and he got all the girls and I got to help him," Dale recalled. "We had a few girls over for dinner. Marilyn Vandeberg, Miss Colorado. He dated her. He always had very pretty women. He was a good-looking guy and he was a people person. People liked him."[11]

Both young men were pursuing difficult degrees that forced them to study hard. They were interested in the sciences and right after his graduation, Dale went to work for the National Bureau of Standards in electroengineering. He shipped out to conduct experiments in Antarctica. Dean was studying meteorology. His early grades, however, revealed a struggling student with a D in "Man in a Physical World," and Cs in literature and history classes. His only A came in physical education. The transition from high school was proving more difficult than Reed expected. He hit the books harder, spent more time in the library and by spring semester, the grades were improving. In the fall of his sophomore year, Reed was cited for "excellence in scholarship."[12] College was turning into a good time. From the beginning, Reed picked up tuition and spending money by convincing Boulder restaurants to let him stroll from table to table strumming and singing and collecting any tips the diners were inclined to give him.[13]

In the summer of 1957, Reed was back working a dude ranch, but this time in the Estes Park resort area, forty miles northwest of Boulder at the edge of Rocky Mountain National Park. By day, it was manual labor, including time as the lifeguard and cleaning the pool. But he lived for the nighttime work. A cowboy hat pushed back on his head and the guitar strapped across his shoulders, Reed would amble among the tables at a popular college beer joint. The manager paid him to sing ballads for the young lovers or flirt with tables of coeds. Reed's song selections were good and his patter genial and while it is unlikely many were going to the pub just to hear him, everyone seemed to linger a little longer and order more while he strummed his guitar. Other times, he would perform from the small stage and if the crowd was particularly boisterous and unlikely to listen to the young troubadour, Reed would sneak onto the darkened stage, turn the microphone up loud and burst into "Jericho" in full voice. It stopped the diners in midsentence and even the waiters and waitresses clattered the dishes less. He had their attention.[14]

When he returned to Boulder for his sophomore year, Reed was on his own. Dale had graduated and was in the Antarctic studying the ionosphere. Like his younger brother, Dale was destined for a small measure of fame when Reed Ridge in that frozen continent was named for him. Before heading to his new assignment, Dale tossed the Dodge convertible keys to his brother and told him to take good care of it. The rest of the family also headed south, although only as far as the warm weather. Cyril, Ruth Anna and Vernon left Colorado one more time and settled in Phoenix. Being on his own suited Dean just fine. He had the car, the apartment and the confidence of a second-year man and the feeling of invincibility that most nineteen-year-olds wear like psychic armor. The year passed quickly and Reed returned to Estes Park to work and perform the way he had the previous summer. But things were different this time. His singing and playing was beginning to develop a small following. A radio station in Denver talked to him about signing on with them and doing a show as the Denver Kid. It never quite panned out. At the same time, a local man who had been a singer in Hollywood approached Reed and offered to be his manager. Roy Eberhard, whose real name was Leroy Eberharder, convinced Reed that he could make it as a singer. Eberhard explained the hard facts to his protégé. Nothing came out of Colorado but mountain streams and cattle; if Reed were serious about being a singer, he would have to go where the record studios were. That meant places like Nashville, New York City or Los Angeles. Eberhard did not have to talk long.

Four

The Czech Chanteuse

"What is wrong with this damn town?" Reed muttered to himself as he drove away after being turned down by another club manager days after his return from South America. "I've got millions of people screaming for me in Chile and Argentina and that idiot owner is running out some kid nobody's ever heard of four night a week. I hope his fucking little club goes belly-up. Dammit, I hate this place."

Hollywood was no Santiago and waving to the other stars and his friends in a restaurant was not the same as being mobbed by adoring fans. He was back taking more acting lessons with his mentor Paton Price but he was baffled by the fact that his success in South America couldn't be thrown into his suitcase and carried back home. He cut some more records for Capitol, but they went nowhere. The record company made the decision to spend most of its time and money on other stars and when it came down to choosing between Dean Reed and Jack Jones, Capitol went with Jones. For Capitol, that decision would prove to be a wash, as Jones went on to enjoy a middling career as a second-tier singer who sold a respectable number of albums, but was never a big seller. Reed, meanwhile, landed a few concerts, but they were small clubs with a few hundred people watching, a jarring drop from the packed halls of just a few weeks earlier.

Dean was energetic, but that energy overwhelmed his patience. Even as a teenager, he had taken sleeping pills in order to slow down and get some rest. Now that energy was looking for an outlet and Los Angeles was a dam. By September, just six months after returning from Latin America, his meager patience was exhausted. His mother remembered the call he made to her.

"Mom? It's Deano."

"Hello, dear. How are you?"

"I'm fine. But I've had it with this place. Nothing's happening here. I'm going days, sometimes weeks, between shows and the records aren't going anywhere. I need to get back to South America. You think you could lend me $400?"

"I don't know, Dean. You know your father wasn't happy when you dropped out of college and went to Hollywood. Neither was I. Maybe it's time you came on back home. You gave it a good try."

"Mom, listen, I'm close to making a lot of money. I'll pay that $400 back and then some. You know how big I was down in Chile, Argentina. They'll pay me well down there and I'll push my record sales so high that they'll have to pay attention to me at Capitol, Decca, RCA and every other record company in America."

"Deano, you know I'd help you in anything you try. But your dad is still muttering about the money we've given you before. He keeps saying, 'if that boy wants to be a big shot singer, then he can get a job washing dishes until the money rolls in.' "

"Yeah, I can hear him. There's no way I can convince him, no way I ever could talk to him. I'm done trying. That's why I'm talking to you, Mom. You know I'm right. If you could just get me $400, I'll repay you before Dad even knows. Hey, maybe I'll even fly you down to Chile and you can come see me perform."[1]

Reed was persuasive and within a few days, a letter arrived from Ruth Anna, with a $400 check enclosed. But it's quite likely Cyril found out about the $400 because the repayment was not nearly as quick as Reed had promised. In October, he flew back to Chile, but authorities barred him from entering the country until he had a job. So Reed traveled to Buenos Aires, Argentina, and spent several weeks calling agents and club managers, trying to set up jobs in Chile so he could obtain a work visa. After his first tour of South America, Reed had enrolled in a concentrated Spanish course back in Los Angeles.[2] With time to kill, Reed started to pick up the Spanish language. Every day he would go to the park near his hotel and listen to people, sometimes trying out the phrases he learned. He had a knack for it. "He taught himself Spanish," Patricia Reed said. "When he got to a country, he would learn the language as quickly as he could so he could communicate. He had a musician's ear and picked it up easily."[3] After several weeks of sitting on the park bench, Reed received the necessary clearance to enter Chile and return to work singing his songs. He was back and so were the thousands of screaming fans, the television variety shows, the radio interviews and the hundreds of autographs. The commotion attracted the attention of another star, Nyta Dover. Dover was ten years older than Reed and it was a traumatic ten years. Born and raised in Czechoslovakia, Dover's family was politically prominent. When the Nazis marched in and took over the country in 1939, Dover and her family were rounded up and sent to prison. The family managed to escape, but not intact. The Germans killed her father and the family was forced to flee the country, eventually winding up in South America. Dover grew into a lovely woman. At 5-foot-10 inches, blonde hair and busty figure, she attracted attention and stares wherever she went among the predominately shorter and darker-haired people of Chile, Argentina and Uruguay. It was almost preordained that she would become an entertainer. She was a cabaret player, singing and dancing and leaving the stage only to return in a different outfit—sometimes no more than strategically placed feathers or short outfits with plunging necklines to show off her long legs and ample cleavage.

The act worked well and her standard of living had finally returned to what she vaguely recalled as a young girl before the German tanks rolled through her town. But even with the years on the run and starting over in a new land, Dover's mother never let her forget the family's aristocratic ways. Dover carried herself with a patrician air. She also was well established in the entertainment community, so when a newcomer created a stir, somebody who needed police escorts, it wasn't long before Dover found herself at the same party with Reed. As Marge Raitt had in Los Angeles, Dover decided to teach the talented, but green, young man the lessons he needed to make it in Latin American society. Dover got him an agent. She took him to Argentina and lined up shows for him and provided him more contacts. She checked him into the best resort hotels, the kind reserved for only the very wealthy or the very famous. And she got him a girlfriend—herself. They became lovers and being seen on Reed's arm, having her picture taken by news photographers covering Reed, did nothing to hurt her own career. Dover showed Reed how the entertainer, the rich entertainer, was supposed to live. "She had an apartment in Montevideo," Patricia Reed said. "She lived out of hotels and had servants with her. I met her in Argentina. She taught him the correct way to eat, she taught him about European paintings, how to be with wealthy people."[4]

It was an open relationship between Reed and Dover. When they were together, they would frolic on the sand beaches and make love in her hotel rooms. When they were apart, they would write each other frequently. While Dover adored Reed, she talked openly, if disdainfully, about the men she was seeing while Reed was touring. If Reed was seeing other women, it did not seem to bother her. Her reply letters were packed with tidbits about her performances and the arc of her career and suggestions on what he should do to further his. Reed had other women since coming to Hollywood, but Dover was different. This was the most intense and sustained love affair of his young life. How it affected Reed emotionally, whether he considered marrying her, is unclear. The way he treated the love affair in his life was contradictory. He kept most, if not all, of her letters. Yet, in later interviews and his own writings about his life, he makes no mention of Dover. But in the early 1960s, there was not such reticence.

"I love you I love you—I love you," she wrote in one typical note.

> So! I feel better! Thank you for your sweet letter...I do honestly think that bought [*sic*] of us are happy when we hear from each that it is difficult to express...! It's wonderful to be so close to each other and have so much love...

isn't it! Oh, I'd better shut up, because I miss you something awful! You don't know how low, worried I was when I got your letter…and everything seemed easier, rosier and I felt 100 years younger and all this just thanks to your letter and the love you made me feel and sent me in every line.

You must be back in Santiago since yesterday and I hope that everything went great and that even if you had that tremendous success you wrote me about that at least your "fans" did not get all your clothes! I had a good laugh reading about the radio station destruction and your forehead scratch but I know that it must have felt great!

You are making 1,000 for five days tour and how much did you do for the day they broke down the radio, nearly killed you and tore your suit? I hope that it is not included in the 1,000."[5]

Reed moved blissfully through his days with and without Dover, but even he was slowly coming to the realization that his treatment was unique. Throughout South America, people were becoming resentful of the United States. They saw their powerful neighbor to the north not as an ally, but as a colonial power, whose businesses were taking the raw materials of their countries for pennies a pound and selling the products for dollars an ounce. They saw the United States keeping military governments and corrupt civilian governments in power as long as they pledged to keep their markets open and pursue policies of free enterprise, policies that usually favored American businesses.

How they ran their countries, treated their people or the type of political system they maintained was of little importance to Washington. The anger went public in 1958. In late April, Vice President Richard Nixon toured several Latin American countries and he was jeered at every stop. In Montevideo, Uruguay, forty students pushed toward his car chanting, "Get out Nixon." In Lima, Peru, two thousand demonstrators pelted the vice president's party with eggs, oranges, bottle and stones and he was spat upon as he returned to his hotel. In Caracas, Venezuela, two hundred people attacked his motorcade, shattering the window of his car with rocks. The crowd tried to pull Nixon from the car. The television coverage back home, complete with shots of graffiti on the walls advising "Yankee, Go Home," surprised many Americans. But it made some of them realize for the first time that they were not universally loved.

Reed, at first, did not pay much attention. He was in love, with Dover, with his fans and with his fame. But Reed never shook the habits his father instilled in him. One of the most basic Cyril Reed dictates was always read, always learn. The daily papers helped Reed with his Spanish. One day, he came across a story about Chilean workers who had beaten the branch manager of an American business. While they punched and kicked him, they chanted, "Yankee, go home." The contradictions stopped Reed cold. Here was a man, a Chilean, pounded by his countrymen for the crime of running a business for Americans. Yet, every day, Reed, a real American, walked and sang among these same Chileans and the only danger he encountered was the possibility of being crushed by fans. He couldn't resolve the riddle and figured he needed more information. He decided to spend a little time away from the four-star hotels and exclusive nightclubs and visit the other Chile. Only this way could he solve the paradox.

"I remember exactly how I drove past the edge of the slums of Santiago on my trip to the beaches of the Pacific," Reed later wrote. "In this section, consisting of shacks, naked misery ruled. There, children stood on the edge of the street, barefoot, with torn shirts and bloated stomachs, the unmistakable signs of insufficient nutrition. Muggy emanations came through the open car window, iridescent green sewage trickled down between the dwellings. A dead dog lay on the edge of the street; swarms of flies hang in the air. I began to reflect at this time. There was the safe world of modern cities; there were the slums. There was the officially strong friendship with my homeland and there were the 'Yankee-go-home' calls. But more and more questions gnawed at me. And then I thought more frequently about my teacher Paton Price who had urged me to look for the truth. What was true in this world and what wasn't? I still didn't know."[6]

The Jungle and the Bomb

*T*he headlines blared from the newspapers in Argentina and Chile and were picked up by other ones around South America in early 1962. No one had seen the American for five weeks, and while the first few weeks were open anyway, in recent days he had missed a scheduled performance. The missed club date sent reporters to their typewriters to construct dispatches saying the popular artist was missing in the jungle. The reports sent more than one girl into tears and for a couple of days, the main topic of conversation among many teenagers was the fate of Dean Reed and whether he was dead or alive. Each day heightened the mystery and increased the odds that the star had met his end.

It had started out innocently enough. As 1961 bled into 1962, Reed was touring, but his restlessness overtook him. He was ready for a new adventure. In Chile, he met three other Americans who were planning to travel into the Amazon jungle. The three men had met a Catholic priest who regaled them with tales of a tribe of native people he had discovered. They had not been exposed to

Western culture or Christianity. The priest lived with the tribe, taught them the catechism and convinced them to wear clothes. At his urging, they built a small chapel where he could celebrate Mass. Eventually, the priest contracted malaria and had to leave the jungle for treatment. When he returned to his converts, he was devastated. The good new of Jesus Christ had failed to take root in the way the padre had hoped. Instead, the natives were back to their naked ways. Worse, they had torn down the chapel. The priest relayed all the details in a sad monotone, but his somber mood did not touch the Americans. They were intrigued by the tale and asked the priest if they could visit and film the people for a possible documentary. The man was too despondent to lead an expedition back to one of his great failings, but he was willing to provide them directions. The three men were freelance camera-men and they convinced NBC to bankroll their expedition. The cameramen were in a club in Chile when they struck up a con-versation with the American singer and before they finished their yarn, Reed was hooked. He asked to go along and the men, figur-ing Reed could finance some of the trip, readily agreed.

A hazardous journey into uncharted territory was the kind of daredevil stunt Reed had been drawn to ever since he was a boy. His wife Patricia attributed it to mild epilepsy he suffered as a child. Even though the seizures were effectively controlled by medicine, he developed a death wish, she said. Perhaps. Just as likely was Reed's relationship with his father, which he described as "not very good."[1] Older brother Dale said Dean was always try-ing to prove his grit and courage to his dad. Cyril's badgering of the three boys to be men, to be fighters, resonated with the mid-dle son and he yearned for the old man's approval "He was always showing off for Dad, showing he was a good as I was," Dale said. "He was Mom's boy and I was Dad's boy." Once, Cyril took all three boys up to Big Lake in the Rocky Mountains. It was early enough in the spring that a thin layer of ice still covered much of the lake even though the air temperature was near 70 degrees. Dean never hesitated. He peeled off most of his clothes and dived into the water. In the never-ending competition between the two oldest boys, Dale knew he had to do the same. The cold water felt like "getting hit with a sledgehammer," Dale recalled.[2] Cyril was thrilled by the display of toughness his boys showed and the arms he threw around them as they emerged from the lake pleased Dean as he waited for the goose bumps to disappear and for his jaw to regain control of his chattering teeth. A trip up the Amazon River into uncharted regions would be someting to tell old Cyril.

The four men traveled north and east from Chile into Brazil. They hired boats and a few river men to take them into the jungle. They laid in provisions of food and water and trinkets to present to the tribe if they found them. The big, heavy television cameras and the canisters of videotape took up practically one whole dugout canoe. Reed traveled relatively light. Except for some clothes and his share of the provisions, all he brought with him was his Martin guitar. The journey up the river was relatively uneventful. The boatmen worked hard on their poles and paddles as they battled the Amazon's current. The Americans helped some but were rather clumsy handling the boats. The heat and humidity also was a problem. It was the height of summer in South America and if this journey had any comparison, it would be paddling through the Florida Everglades in July. Reed had never done that and growing up in the dry and comparatively cooler climes of Colorado had not prepared him for the shirt-soaking heat and humidity of the jungle. With so little clothing, he was forced to hang his shirt on a branch and hope it would dry overnight. Worse were the mosquitoes, which seemed to hang like a black cloud over the boats. The men wore long pants, with their socks pulled over trousers so the bugs could not fly up their legs. But even with long-sleeved shirts, the mosquitoes were always biting their necks and faces. The men cursed loud and often at the high-pitched drone of the little biters and smeared themselves with various ointments the Brazilians offered. It was an uncomfortable ride and in the nearly undisturbed jungle, there was no guarantee their search would be successful.

After a couple days' journey they noticed a clearing along the river, about where the priest had predicted, and the men hoped they were getting close to the village. They disembarked, followed a barely visible trail through the trees and vines and soon found an opening and the huts. They were quickly surrounded by dozens of men and women, all considerably shorter than the Americans.

Their dark hair was worn straight down in a bowl cut that left the bangs about an inch above their eyes. And just like in the Tarzan movies he had watched as a kid, some of the men carried blow-guns. The men did not seem particularly alarmed, however, at the sight of the four white men, although the large camera carried by one of them aroused some anxiety. But hand signals and a few phrases the priest had taught Reed and the others quickly set everyone at ease. The white men brought out their gifts and passed them around. In return, the natives gave the Americans beautiful turquoise butterflies and colorful earrings made by the women. The men portaged in the rest of their belongings and sent the boatmen home with instructions on when to return for them.

The mosquitoes and humidity continued to take a toll on Reed, but he was enthralled with what he saw. The tribesmen taught Reed how to use a blowgun. Forcing a quick, hard breath through the tube to propel a poison dart a dozen feet or more seemed easy enough. But Reed's first few tries elicited laughter and pointing from the veterans as the dart barely made it out of the tube and stuck in the soil. He might bag a bug, they explained to him, if one happened to be crawling where the dart fell. They showed him what he was doing wrong and after a few more tries, Reed could shoot the dart ten feet. He did better with the bows and arrows, something he had at least a passing familiarity with from his childhood. But it was the day-to-day survival skills that impressed Reed the most. The people strung nets in the Amazon so they could swim and bathe without fear of attack by piranhas. At night they put hot coals under Reed's hammock to keep the mosquitoes away and ward off any chill. The hammocks were strung from poles and because of his greater height and weight, the natives had to string Reed's bed higher so that his butt wouldn't rest in the coals. As always, the women took to him, often trying to snuggle with him in his hammock. Reed was hardly above one-night stands, but a certain chivalry overtook him here and he would gently turn them out. He observed the custom of the men resting during the day and the women standing nearby, picking flies and other insects off their men. For his part, Dean would pull out his guitar and sing his songs. If the response wasn't exactly the wild adulation he had received elsewhere in South America, his strange instrument and foreign tongue intrigued his hosts.[3]

But as the days dragged on the Americans began arguing more amongst themselves. More accurately, Reed was growing more critical of his fellow travelers. Perhaps still reflecting on the ugly American images he had seen before he left Chile or perhaps feeling that the Americans were simply taking advantage of an open and friendly people, Reed began nagging his companions.

"Look guys, I think we ought to be a little more careful about how we handle ourselves here," Reed said.

"We're handling ourselves just fine. We're handling the women pretty good too."

"Yeah, they love the big white man. They've never seen cocks that big. They'll miss us when we're gone."

"That's what I'm talking about," Reed responded. "We don't know what they're thinking. Maybe they think we're gods and they have to please us. Maybe the men fear us and hope if they give us their women we won't hurt them. I don't know. But what if you knock one of them up? You'll never be around to help with the baby. It's not like you're going to take him every other weekend."

"Up yours, Reed. This is every man's fantasy. We can screw them all we want and there is no chance that one day they'll show up at our doorstep to embarrass us in front of our wives and girlfriends."

"Yeah, and who are you to tell us about fucking women. You've been bragging about your one-night stands and the women waiting for you after a show. Well, Mr. Rock 'n' roll, these are our fans."

"The difference is, I can speak the language of the women waiting for me after a show," Reed said. "I can spend some time romancing them, figure out what they want from me, whether they are too fragile for a one-nighter. You don't know shit about these women. You just get a little horny, point to one of them, drop your pants and expect them to jump your bones. You got the slam, bam down cold but you don't even know how to say 'thank you, ma'am.'"

"Dammit, Reed, we'll do whatever we want. If you want to be the saint and keep your pants on, be our guest. But we're going to screw the women, shoot parrots and take seconds on their food if we feel like it."

"The parrots are another thing," Red replied. "You are killing too many of them and the other animals. You're just killing them because you're bored and then stacking up the bodies. You're like the old Buffalo hunters…"

"You think you're so goddamned smart, Reed. Buffalo hunters. There's four of us here. The buffalo would still be trampling the prairies if there were only four buffalo hunters. We're not hurting a thing. It's sport. It's fun. It takes my mind off the heat. I'm done talking to you. I've got better things to do. But I'll tell you something. Get off my back or we'll leave you here."

The men continued their uneasy relationship for the remainder of the five weeks. Dean remained enthralled with everything he saw. Eventually, the river boatmen returned and the adventurers paddled back to the city life. Reed had missed a club date by staying so long in the jungle, but instead of tagging him with a reputation as an unreliable act, it turned into one of the best publicity ploys of his career.[4]

When he finally emerged from the jungle, guitar in hand and needing a shave, he was surprised to find the newspaper and radio journalists looking for him. When word reached folks in Argentina that Reed was alive and well and ready to perform again, it was front-page news. At the Buenos Aires airport, the photographers pushed and shoved near the bottom of the gangway, trying to position themselves for a good photo as Reed emerged from the plane. As he descended to the tarmac, the reporters whistled and shouted to get his attention.

"How did it go in the Amazon?"

"Why weren't there any signs of life from you?"

"Were you in the power of the Indios?"

Reed recounted his weeks in the jungle and all that he had seen and done there. He assured the reporters that he had not been tied up by the Indios, that they were friendly people and the adventure was not nearly as great as it seemed.

"What did the Indios think of you Americans?" one of the reporters asked.

"You have asked me whether the Indians have anything
against Americans," Reed said, his mind reflecting on the arguments he had with his traveling companions. "The jungle on the
Amazon is the only place in all of South America where I didn't
see signs with the words, 'Yankee, go home.' And it is the only
place where I didn't hear the shouts of 'Yankee, go home.' To the
Indians, the Americans are entirely normal people. They couldn't
have had any bad experiences with them, simply because they
have never gotten to know any of us. Now that they have
known us, they are probably putting up signs."[5]

Not that he needed much help, but the jungle adventure
landed Reed on all the television and radio shows and the exposure pushed him to the top. One of the leading teen magazines of
South America published a poll of its readers, asking them to list
their favorite performers. Number one, with 29,330 votes was
Dean Reed. Elvis Presley, without question the top attraction in
the United States, could only poll 20,805 among these kids, good
for second place. Paul Anka was third with 17,548 and the tallies
dropped off quickly to 7,000 for Ray Charles and fewer for others
such as Danny Chilean, Frank Sinatra and Reed's good friends, the
Everly Brothers.[6]

Reed decided it was time to use that popularity for something
other than selling tickets and records. The United States and the
Soviet Union were in the early stages of what would be a nearly
forty-year arms race. Each side was building up its arsenal of nuclear warheads, pointing more and more of them at the other's
military and civilian centers. Only sixteen years had passed since
the first atomic bombs were developed and detonated by the
United States over Japan during World War II. As each side rushed
to develop bigger and more sophisticated warheads, they would
test them. For years, those tests had been conducted in the atmosphere, generating enormous amounts of radioactive fallout that
was traveling around the globe and contaminating nearly every
person, water source and soil with low levels of tritium and other
radioactive isotopes. By the late 1990s, it would be revealed that
just the atmospheric nuclear bomb tests over Nevada from 1951

to 1962 exposed millions of children to large amounts of radioactive iodine. In fact, the U.S. studies showed that children were exposed to ten times the amount released in the nuclear power accident at the Chernobyl plant in Ukraine. The nuclear weapons testing accomplished something besides proving whether the bomb worked correctly. It was a bald show of force. When the United States conducted an atmospheric test, the Soviets could fairly easily monitor it and learn that its enemy had something new in its arsenal. Likewise, if the Red Army detonated one of its warheads, the leaders in Washington knew within hours what new firepower the Communist government had developed. It inevitably spurred a new round of research, development and detonation.

For a while, the two superpowers seemed to acknowledge the madness of the arms race and in 1958 they agreed to a moratorium on nuclear testing. However, in August 1961, negotiations amongst the United States, the Soviet Union and Great Britain to establish a permanent ban on testing nuclear weapons fell apart. The following month, the Soviet Union resumed underground tests of nuclear devices and within days, the United States followed suit. In March 1962, President John Kennedy upped the ante. The president went on national television and announced the United States would resume atmospheric nuclear tests in mid-April unless the Soviet Union agreed to an internationally supervised test ban when the two sides met in Geneva in two weeks. The two sides were unable to reach an agreement, so on April 25, the United States tested a nuclear bomb in the atmosphere above Christmas Island in the Pacific, the first such test since the 1958 moratorium. The detonation was sharply criticized by neutral countries and many Third World leaders. Reed still struggled with why the Chileans and others loved him but despised the United States. But as a pacifist convert of Paton Price, Reed harbored no doubts about nuclear weapons testing. He decided to join the criticism. Readers all across Chile woke up to find a large ad in their April 26, 1962, newspapers, paid for by Reed. Alongside a photo of himself, the singer wrote an open letter, in Spanish, to the people of Chile.

My Friends: In the name of humanity of all the countries in the world, I hope that all of you will send letters to President Kennedy, White House, Wash. D.C., U.S.A., begging him to stop the scheduled atomic tests. Each test of Russia or the United States of ten megatons of fission condemns 15,000 children not yet born to a life of crippleness or a premature death. Because of the past atomic tests thousands of children will be born with physical defects, or blind or invalid. Please send this letter and do your part to save the lives of the children of the future. Sincerely, Dean Reed.[7]

Protesting was an inherited trait for Reed. His dad had dragged him and older brother Dale to school board meetings when the family lived in Denver. Cyril didn't think the public schools knew what they were doing. He would rail against the progressive ideas and methods for educating the children. The former math teacher was particularly upset about the "new math" and urged the board to return to the basics, the math of computation, and get rid of the idea of sets and subsets. Cyril lost the argument but he had taught a lesson to his middle boy. This is America, and in America, we have a voice in decisions and you damn well better use it.

The reaction of the press in Chile was quick and could not have surprised Reed. Radio stations and newspapers all aired and published stories and interviews with Reed elaborating on his views, including his status as a conscientious objector. The coverage, at least in the eyes of the U.S. Embassy in Santiago, was slanted against the United States.[8] While it is unclear how many letters his advertisement generated for the White House, there is no question it generated even more publicity for the young singer. Reed told reporters he would make similar appeals in the coming weeks as he traveled to performances in Peru, Brazil, Argentina, Colombia and Venezuela. But in one corner, Reed's open letter was drawing poor reviews. The U.S. Embassy was not used to American citizens criticizing their country, especially in a foreign land. Protesting American policies in the fifty states was becoming more common, especially with the mass marches organized by Rev. Martin Luther King to end racial policies that denied black Americans the same rights to schools, buses, hotels and ballot boxes as white Americans. However, citizens visiting abroad still were expected to toe the official line on foreign affairs. Dean Reed was no exception.

"Embassy attempting locate Reed and caution him propriety public statements adverse United States," was how Ambassador Charles Cole in the embassy in Santiago put it in his telegram to the State Department.[9]

One of Cole's deputies, Philip J. Farley, put it more forcefully in a memo a week later. Farley said that Reed's "behavior is unacceptable if the facts as reported are true. Thus, I believe that Embassy Santiago should be instructed to contact Reed, and make it clear that his derogatory actions as an American traveling in such sensitive political areas are considered contrary to the best interests of the U.S. Because he is no doubt considered by others to be a representative of the U.S., although not official, I feel that, as a public personality, his actions cannot be condoned."[10]

On May 4, the State Department issued orders to the embassies in Santiago, Lima, Rio de Janeiro, Buenos Aires, Bogotá and Caracas, telling them to locate Reed and instruct him "his actions are considered by the Department as being contrary to the best interests of the United States" and then report if Reed persisted in his political activities.[11] Those instructions quickly backfired on the government. In Lima, Peru, an employee of the U.S. Information Service contacted the master of ceremonies of a popular Peruvian television show, Pablo de Madalengoitia, and told him about Reed's anti-bomb testing statements in Chile. The Lima newspapers learned of the meeting and reported that the U.S. government was attempting to kill Reed's appearance on the show. That gained even more credibility when the show was postponed from May 13 to May 20, officially because of equipment failure that knocked the television station off the air all day.[12]

The episode prompted a telegram by Reed's friends, led by Paton Price, to Ambassador James Loeb, Jr.

> Shocked by your reaction and Ambassador Cole's to Dean Reed's public statement against nuclear testing. Your attempts to silence him and bring pressure on foreign radio and concert producers to cancel contracts with Reed are intolerable interferences with inalienable rights of an American citizen and constitute dangerous attack on our traditional freedoms of speech and religion. Your unwarranted

interferences in internal affairs of Chile and Peru in violation Charter Organization American States will arouse justified resentment among Latin American People. We feel
obliged to bring these violations to attention American
people and in association with American Civil Liberties
Union are protesting to secretary (Dean) Rusk. We urge
you protect rights of American Citizens in Peru rather than
undermine them.

Thirteen people signed the telegram, including actor Roger
Smith, who had more than a half-dozen movies to his credit and
was seen regularly on television with *77 Sunset Strip*; Glen Cor-
bett, who was watched weekly in the series *Route 66*; Hope
Lange, who had been in movies ranging from *Bus Stop*, with
Marilyn Monroe to the recently released *Wild in the Country*, with
Elvis Presley; Miss America Marian MacKnight and anti-war ac-
tivist David Dellinger.[13]

The telegram also prompted a story in the May 22, 1962, *Los
Angeles Times* that quoted Reed's letter to his friends in which he
claimed that someone in the U.S. Embassy in Chile threatened to
take away his passport because of the paid advertisement. While it
was not a huge story, it did force State Department spokesman
Lincoln White to say, "we didn't demand of anyone that Reed's
passport should be pulled." However, he reiterated the department's
position that Reed shouldn't do anything to hurt his country."[14]
Reed decided to clear up any misunderstandings the embassy
might have and on June 4, he paid a visit on Ambassador Cole in
Santiago. He slid his right palm down his pants leg as he was led
down the corridor, trying to eliminate any perspiration. Reed reminded himself to throw his shoulders back, walk in erect and extend a strong, dry hand. He was not going to let the ambassador
know that his first trip to an American Embassy was intimidating.

"Come in, Mr. Reed," Cole said, rising from behind his desk
and extending a hand, but indicating the straight-backed chair for
Reed, rather than the couch. "I understand you've been making
some comments critical of your country."

"No, sir, I have not," Reed replied, looking straight into Cole's
eyes. "I've simply stated the scientific truths. Atomic weapons test-

ing is deadly to people born and those to come. And now your people have tried to silence me."

"Go on. What is it you think we have done?"

"You obviously contacted the embassy in Peru and they sent someone to threaten Pablo de Madalengoitia, told him he would be in trouble if he let me perform on his television show. And, in fact, he postponed my appearance, hoping the pressure would disappear. That's an outrageous action by the U.S. government and an abridgment of my free speech rights."

"It might be, Mr. Reed, if it happened as you say. But I find it hard to belie—"

"Oh, it happened all right, I—"

"Young man, if you will stop interrupting me, we'll get along a lot better." Reed started to say something, then nodded.

"Thank you. As I was saying, I find it hard to believe that an embassy employee had anything to do with the postponement. First of all, I have no authority over any other embassy, nor do I give them any orders. I just tell Washington what is happening here and it is up to them to decide how to proceed. So, I did not tell anyone in Lima to do anything to you. Furthermore, has anyone from this embassy harassed you?"

"No."

"Have they spoken to your agent, or any of the club owners or television station managers or in any way tried to make your life difficult?"

"No."

"So, if we did not bother you here, where you took out your ad and where you spend most of your time, why would you think that we would try to bother you in Lima, far from the center of the controversy?"

"Well, for one thing, it might be easier for you to intimidate people there," Reed said. "There might be less press coverage that far from Santiago and you would have a freer hand."

"That's a nice fantasy, but I'm telling you now, as the U.S. representative here that it did not happen. And let me ask you something else, Mr. Reed. Why weren't you critical of the Soviet Union and its tests?"

"As you know, Mr. Ambassador, the Soviets have not conducted any atmospheric atomic tests since 1958. In 1958, I was going to school in Boulder and was not as aware as I should have been of what was happening in the world. If they resume atmospheric tests, I will strongly consider taking out another ad. But for now, the danger is posed by President Kennedy's atomic tests, not Khrushchev's underground ones."

"Mr. Reed, I'm asking you, as a fellow American, please stop. This is a war we are engaged in with the Soviets. Thankfully, it is not yet one with bullets and bombs, but it is a war, nonetheless. You have a following here and these one-sided statements make the United States look like the villain. And by god, we are not the villain. Your comments give aide and comfort to the people here who are looking for an excuse, any excuse, to cast us in that role and disrupt the balance of power in Latin America and throughout the world. You must think before you speak. You must think of how your fans will interpret your remarks, how the press might misinterpret them and how the Communists here and elsewhere will twist them."

"I'm sorry, Mr. Ambassador, but I will not be silenced. I doubt you realize just how big my following is here. I was recently named the most popular singer in South America. When I have the power, I have to use it. And everything I have read and everything that I believe tells me President Kennedy is wrong. Only by the people rallying can we make the leaders understand that they must change. They must seek peace. They must destroy their weapons of mass destruction."

The two men parried for a few minutes more, but eventually Cole arose, walked from around his desk, shook the singer's hand and escorted him to the office door. In the language of diplomats, it was a full and frank discussion, with neither side budging from their positions. For his part, Reed was excited and replayed much of the conversation in his head as he walked through the embassy's gates and onto the city streets of Santiago. Just like a concert performance, his nervousness had disappeared almost as soon as he began talking. He made his points and he did not cower before the U.S. government. Nothing had happened to him. He still had his passport and even more, he had the official assurance that no one had tried to interfere with his performance and, it seemed to Reed, an unspoken acknowledgment that they would not try to do so in the future. He won. The government was at least a little afraid of him, and yet, there was apparently nothing they were willing to do, other than give him a stern talking-to. That brought a smile to his face. Cole could try all he wanted, but he was a weak second to his father Cyril when it came to a good tongue-lashing.

Cole came away with his own impressions of the young singer and their meeting. "My estimate of the young man is that he is very egocentric and conceited and not too intelligent," Cole wrote in his report to the State Department. "He is much impressed by the following he has among Latin American teenagers and thinks of himself as having much influence over them. It is my guess also that he is being made much of and flattered by the Communist elements in the entertainment profession, the newspapers, etc. I am not sure how much real harm he is doing, but I am confident he is doing no good. It is my guess that it will be impossible to influence him by rational argument and that he will greatly enjoy any publicity that his friends can get for him in the U.S. by attacking the State Department or otherwise."[15]

It was a fairly astute assessment of Reed after a single meeting but it contained one flaw. His denigration of Reed's intelligence was at odds with the twenty-three-year-old's life in and out of the classroom. Not only was Reed becoming fluent in his second language, but through the influence of his father, had always been a voracious reader. As a child, and even in the early years in Los Angeles, Reed would take a book and ride out on his horse or his car and find a quiet place and tree to sit against and read. By now, much of what he was reading was more idealistic than a middle-aged diplomat was likely to see as realistic or smart. Cole had confused what he perceived as Reed's ignorance with what, at worse, was naiveté. One of the books that had impressed Reed recently was *Jean Christophe*, by French author Romain Rolland. The title character happened to be a singer who saw the poverty of the world and sang ballads about it. Reed read the book as he was traveling through South America and touring its slums. The book became a field guide for him and like an avid bird-watcher, Reed took the tome with him wherever in the world he was calling home.

"That impressed Dean," his wife Patricia said of the book. "He also believed that what you saw, you always told the truth. He was not only a good-looking man, but an intellectual. He could talk about anything. The young Dean was a totally different human being than the older Dean. He was totally innocent, an idealist human. The young Dean was an adventurer and fun." Patricia said the young entertainer also was learning something else, something that Cole had suspected. "He saw he got publicity when he shocked people with his views. He felt important. He would cry at night and say he wanted to be important, to do something important."[16] In a newspaper interview, Dean elaborated on the point he made to Ambassador Cole. "But I think artists have an obligation to stand up for what they believe in, no matter where they are."[17] The same words, but different meaning for the two men, based on their roles and stations in life. Cole perceived a power-hungry, publicity-craving punk. Reed saw himself as a world citizen whose fame obligated him to speak out against the wrongs perpetrated by governments. That view of himself made him revise what happened in Chile when he told the story twenty years later. By then, he changed the details so that the ad in the paper urged the people of Chile to write not only to President Kennedy, but also Khrushchev.[18]

Back in the United States, the economy was still strong as it had been with little interruption since the end of World War II when the nation was the only one with its industries unscathed by the bombings and battles that damaged much of Europe and Asia. The strong economy, combined with powerful unions that pushed for higher wages as well as government policies that were friendly to the returning GIs, had produced one of the largest middle classes ever seen in the world. While poverty still existed in the United States, it was often hidden in the smaller towns and rural areas or black ghettos, places Reed was not likely to see. But in South America, the poverty was not nearly so well hidden. It was everywhere and Reed couldn't avoid it, even as Dover was teaching him how to mingle with the wealthy 2 percent.

"Dean took a serious look at what was going on in Latin America, and the two classes, the rich and the poor," his friend

Marv Davidov said. "The poor are oppressed terribly. So Dean, sensitized to a radical vision by Paton, and having an independent judgment, too, he was a bright guy, he took a look at reality and decided to do something about it. He tossed in with the left, which was usually Communist left and the trade unions and organized dissent. He sang at demonstrations and supported actions on behalf of oppressed people."[19]

In his public comments, Reed sounded like anything but a Communist sympathizer. His perception of the situation in many of the South American nations was that the United States treated them as colonies and, by tolerating or even encouraging dictatorships there, was forcing the people into the very arms American officials feared the most. "I feel that unless our government stops putting people and countries into only two classes, Communist or Fascist, and starts working along with people in South America who do want land reform and who may not believe 'Peru for the North Americans' but who also are not Communists, we will certainly lose all of South America to the Communists."[20]

Reed was not yet plunging headlong into politics and mass movements to improve the lot of the poor. Speaking to a church group back home, sometimes singing at leftist rallies in South America, even placing ads in the newspapers was no more than riding a bike with training wheels. It was a start and Reed experienced the same thrill a child feels when the bike tips to one side before the support wheels catch hold. But he was never in any danger and his primary concerns were Dean Reed and becoming a star, not only in South America, but back home.

"If someone asks me today what kind of person I was in those years that I traveled all over Latin America, the answer is simple," Reed reflected twenty years later. "I was a man who wanted to bring joy to the people and to boost their courage, who wanted to help them preserve the belief about the meaning of life with my songs and with my political position. At that time, I didn't sing songs like, 'We are the Revolutionaries.' Still, I believe that a simple little love song, a temperamental rock song or a cowboy song are good for the people."[21] It would not be long, however, until the training wheels came off.

The Everlys, Raitt, Rosenburg and Price

ack in Los Angeles several weeks after the showdown with Ambassador Cole, Reed couldn't help reflect on how little his situation had changed since he first arrived in that city in the late summer of 1957. It had seemed clearer then. Roy Eberhard, the Denver man who wanted to be Reed's manager, had suggested he drop out of college and head to Hollywood. He knew some people there, he told the boy, and that was where the recording companies were. It made sense to Reed and when his summer job had ended at the dude ranch in Estes Park, instead of heading to Boulder, he just kept going south to Phoenix. His mom, dad and younger brother Vernon were there and he owed them the courtesy of telling them his plans. He also knew the reaction he would get.

"Mom, Dad, you know the guy I've told you about, Roy Eberhard? Well, he knows a lot about the music business and he thinks I should go to Hollywood and try to get a recording contract. He thinks I'm good enough, thinks I should be able to sign on with RCA or Capitol or Decca."

"Sure, see if you can't take a couple weeks off from your job next summer and try your luck," Cyril said.

"Aww, Dad, this isn't something you can do in a couple of weeks. You've got to work at it full time, just like any other job. I'm headed there now."

"You can't go now, you've got school starting," Ruth Anna said.

"Nope. I'm dropping out."

This was more than Cyril could stand. He resorted to full bluster, yelling at his son.

"You're a real genius, you know that. Drop out of college and a chance to make something of yourself just so you can play that stupid guitar. Guitars are recreation. They're something to do after work, like a beer. IT'S NOT YOUR WORK! Meteorology, that's real work. It's using your brains. It's science. Look where science has gotten your brother. And it's worthwhile. People depend on weather forecasts sometimes for their very life. Nobody depends on a damn guitar. Why don't you just get a beret and become one of those beatniks. I hear they like guitars."

"I'm so sick of you criticizing everything I do, Dad. No matter what I do, it's never been enough. With you it's always, 'look at Dale.' Well, I'm not Dale, Dad. Dale's great, but I've got my own life to live. I've got a talent with the guitar. People pay to hear me. They applaud me, Dad. Do you know what it's like to have a room full of people listening to you, applaud—"

"I spent a good part of my life with a room full of people listening to me, Dean. It's no big deal."

"Those were children, Dad, and they had to listen to you. And that's another thing. It's pretty funny, you telling me not to quit school. You've quit just about every job you've ever had. I'm just following in your footsteps."

"God damn you, Dean. You and your smart little mouth. I've worked harder than you'll ever dream. I ran my daddy's farm after he died. I worked twice as hard as anybody so I could get through college early and support my younger brothers. You have no idea what hard work is. You have no idea what it is to sacrifice and worry, always making sure there would be enough money to keep your wife and kids with a roof over their heads, and maybe put a little away so the boys could go to college and maybe have it better than their old man."

"I appreciate that, but it's not what we're arguing about. We're talking about me doing what I think is right for my life."

"Cyril, maybe he could drop out for a year, see what happens with this music business and if it doesn't work out, he could go back to school," Ruth Anna suggested.

"He'll never go back. If he drops out, he'll never go back to school. I know my boys. He'll be too stubborn. And Hollywood will change him. He'll go soft out there. All those pretty boys running around, half of them homosexuals. There probably isn't anybody out there who knows how to plow a field or wire a house. They think singing songs and jumping on a horse in some movie is real life. No sir. He needs to stay in school."

"I don't know why I even bother talking to you, Dad. You don't listen to anybody. I should have just driven to L.A. and sent you a letter and signed it 'your dropout, Dean.' But I thought, I'm almost nineteen, maybe this time he'll treat me like a man and let me make my own decisions."

"I'll treat you like a man when you make decisions like a man."[1]

That last one stung. Reed pivoted, hugged his mom goodbye and slammed the door on his way out. Cyril stood there, still worked up and red-faced, but unsure whether to fling one more shot after his son or limp out and hug him goodbye. By the time his mind finally fired up again, his boy was gone.

Reed had sold his brother's old '48 Dodge and purchased his own car, a black 1957 Chevy Impala convertible. He climbed in behind the wheel and roared off down the road. With the top down, he let the wind blast the doubts and his dad's arguments out of his mind. It was a long and monotonous drive on the two-lane road that crossed the Arizona and California desert. Somewhere in the middle of that drive, Reed saw a man hitchhiking. Bored by the solitude and tired of the radio and the few stations it could bring in clearly, Reed stopped and offered him a lift. The passenger looked like a hobo with his worn trousers and his frayed shirt and a two-day beard on his face. Still, the man could tell a yarn and as the miles rolled by, Reed told the man he was headed to Hollywood with hopes of cutting some records and making it as singer. The hobo wanted to hear a little, so as the car sped along (and Reed always drove as fast as he could he sang some of the tunes he had performed in Estes Park. That night, as they ended the day's drive, Reed put his new friend up in the same motel. The next day they parted, but the hitchhiker told Reed that he, too, had been to Hollywood and tried to make it. He had some success fronting a country western band. Unfortunately, his life began to reflect his songs as booze became more important than the music. To repay Reed's kindness, he gave the driver the name of an artist & repertoire man at Capitol Records that he knew and wished the young man well. Reed carefully tucked the name into his pocket and when he arrived in Hollywood later that day, he stopped only long enough to clean up and change his clothes. Then he wheeled his convertible through the streets of Los Angeles until he pulled up at Capitol Records.[2]

The doors opened at Capitol and whether because of his hitchhiking friend or Roy Eberhard's old contacts, Reed was able to get past the receptionist and show what he could do for the men who made the decisions. They liked his looks, figuring they might be able to turn him into a teenage heartthrob. The guitar playing was fine, the voice pleasant. By his second day in town, Capitol had Reed posing for trial publicity photos. By the fifth day, he was singing for the president of the company.[3] The confidence Reed had developed over the years singing in restaurants and at the ranch did not desert him. His ten minutes with the president went well and he was signed to a standard seven-year contract with one-year renewal options. The contract guaranteed Reed eight master recordings each year and Capitol would pay him $45 for each master. Maybe he could eventually convince his dad this was a good decision after all.[4]

While the contract provided a little security, unless Reed and his records generated some excitement, Capitol could drop him at the end of any of those years. So Reed did the young star hustle. Eberhard proved he wasn't just flattering the kid, and moved his family to Los Angeles to handle the details of what they both hoped would be a quick ride to the top. Eberhard started by renting an old home in the San Fernando Valley that was once owned by Shirley Temple. Just around the hill was the ranch of Reed's idol, Roy Rogers.[5] Reed moved in with the Eberhards and his manager lined up gigs at the Troubadour and other clubs around

Hollywood. The singer was not content to rely on Eberhard, however. Reed's car became a mobile office and he made the rounds, knocking on the doors of clubs, handing out his publicity pictures, angling for performance dates and cutting singles. "He would spend his days riding around in his convertible with that greasy kid stuff, his guitar in the car, all his photos, papers all over the place, his songs, music," his wife Patricia recalled.[6]

Still, times were lean. Reed was just another good-looking guy with a guitar at a time when America was exploding with handsome guitar players. They all thought they could be the next Elvis, a guy who would burst on the scene and remake popular music in his own image. Reed shared the dream, but his music was not ground-breaking and Pat Boone, Paul Anka, Ricky Nelson and others already claimed the clean, handsome nonthreatening image Reed projected. More than once he had to swallow his pride and turn to his parents, usually his mother, for money to keep him going a little longer while he knocked on more doors, cut another 45 for Capitol or played another club.[7] His timing was not all bad. Record companies were caught by surprise at the popularity of rock 'n' roll. Teenagers were buying up singles and albums at a rate never before seen. They couldn't get enough and at times it seemed that just about anybody the record studios put on vinyl was snapped up by several hundred thousand kids. With that kind of seller's market, record executives were more willing to take a chance on unknowns. Those executives began to think it was so easy they could manufacture anyone into a star and tried to prove it with Fabian, a young man with little singing talent but a good body and photogenic face. With Presley drafted into the U.S. Army in 1958 and no longer recording, they thought Fabian could fill the void. While he had a couple of middling hits, Fabian did not last long and had to wait for a nostalgia wave in the 1970s to pick up a few of the dollars he and his handlers thought he would make in the 1950s and '60s. Reed also was encouraged by the success of guys like Marty Robbins and Johnny Cash. Like Reed, they were influenced by country western music and blended it with the up-tempo beat of rock to turn out hits like "White Sport Coat and Pink Carnation" and "Teenage Queen." As often as Reed tried to reassure himself by listening to those tunes, making it in Los Ange-

les was not nearly as easy as learning to ride a horse or even performing on the rings. His confidence fell with his bank account
and Reed confided to his mother that he was considering giving
up and going back to school. He might well have done so, had it
not been for Paton Price.

Price was a well-known figure in American acting circles. He
trained at the American Academy of Drama and roomed with
Kirk Douglas in New York City. He produced plays with Helen
Hayes, and Frank Lloyd Wright designed a theater for Price in
Hartford, Connecticut.[8] While not as well-known to the general
public, his acting and teaching abilities were recognized and ap-
preciated by his peers in the theater. Price also was a committed
pacifist and refused to serve in the military during World War II.
That was an enormously unpopular stance for anyone to take. In
the early days of the 1940s, Americans were scared and the world
seemed to be on the verge of a takeover by the devil himself. Hitler reigned supreme on the European continent and was close to
squashing Britain. Japan had unleashed a vicious attack on China
and other Asian counties and then successfully bombed Pearl Harbor. The damage to the American psyche as the details and pictures of the devastated Pacific Fleet sunk in could not be overesti-
mated. America was vulnerable. America could lose. Countries
ruled by power-hungry murderers could take over. Hundreds of
thousands of men volunteered or were drafted to put their lives on
the line for democracy. Any able-bodied man who refused to fight
because of some principle was not going to be respected, much
less tolerated. They would be scorned, maybe attacked. Yet Price
chose to stand for his deeply held belief that killing, even in war,
was wrong. At first, he was sent to a Civilian Public Service camp
with other conscientious objectors. There, they would work cleaning up park areas or simply dig holes and refill them. Price found
the situation ridiculous and walked out. His next stop was prison.
The peace-loving Price was now eating and working with men
whose anger and hatred drove them to beat and kill others. Price
did not waver in his beliefs and he made at least one lifelong
friend. Another war resistor shared a cell for awhile with Price.
David Dellinger also was a conscientious objector and would become more famous fighting America's involvement in another war

twenty years later.[9] (Dellinger would be one of the leaders of the anti-Vietnam War demonstrations outside the 1968 Democratic National Convention in Chicago and stand trial as one of the Chicago Seven.) After the war and his release from prison, Price returned to the theater. However, within a few years, Price decided to leave the East Coast and try his luck in Hollywood. He was hired as an acting coach for Warner Brothers Studios and by the late 1950s had a respected stable of young actors and alumni. Three months after Reed signed with Capitol, the record company thought it would be a good idea for him to study at Warner Brothers. He was sent to the studio to meet Price and the teacher took an immediate liking to the young singer. "Here's a raw kid with raw talent and Paton loved him right away," said Marv Davidov, an anti-war activist who became good friends with both men in the 1960s. "He saw something quite unusual in him in terms of energy, talent and a certain naive quality."[10]

Reed's feelings toward Price were just as strong. Price could not have been more unlike Reed's own father. Where Cyril had stressed toughness and keeping a check on your emotions, Price stressed feelings and sensitivity and being true to yourself. While Cyril was a rock-ribbed conservative Republican, Price was not just liberal, but radical. He was, in fact, just the type of man Cyril had feared his son would run into in Hollywood. Reed absorbed it all, both Price's acting lessons and his political views. Reed declared himself a pacifist and started hanging around the meetings of the Society of Friends, more commonly known as the Quakers.

"Although there was a great difference in age, Paton Price became my first true friend; I can also say my second father," Reed recalled. "From the beginning, Paton was a person who told me what I was missing: maturity. Paton taught me a lot about the craft of appearing before the camera, whether as a singer or as an actor. But that was not the most valuable thing he did for my development. First and foremost, he viewed it as his task to convey to his students the humanistic interpretation of the profession of actor. He, who knew the hypocrisy in the U.S. arts business, said again and again 'how do you build a house if the foundation is not shockproof? How do you arouse feelings in the public that you yourself don't have? How do you want to convey the truth when you yourself don't believe in the truth and represent it when you are a liar?' Paton's opinion was unchanged: 'a person cannot create anything worthwhile if he himself is not a worthwhile person.' "[11]

Reed's main focus still was on making it as a singer, but now he added acting to his agenda. He loved the new friends he was making through Price. There was Hope Lange, Robert Conrad (who would become famous in *Wild Wild West*) and Don Murray. Roger Smith, who had starred in several movies including *No Time to be Young* and *The Man with a Thousand Faces*, took a liking to the new student. This also was where Reed met Jean Seberg, who had portrayed Joan of Arc in Otto Preminger's movie *Saint Joan*. Her friendship with Reed would never flag, no matter on which continents the two itinerant actors would find themselves. All were current or former Price students and Paton's place was where they went to hang out. When Price left Warner Brothers to start his own coaching studio, it was his students who wielded the hammers and saws to convert his garage into an acting class-room. "It was fun," Patricia Reed said. "If we were bored, we went to Paton's because that was where the stars were."[12]

Those folks all were great, but for Reed, meeting a couple guys named Phil and Don was the most exciting introduction. Performing as the Everly Brothers, the two young men already had scored numerous Top 10 hits with "Bye, Bye Love," "Wake Up Lit-tle Susie," "Kathy's Clown" and "Dream," among others. In Febru-ary 1960, they signed with the Warner Brothers record company and eleven months later, moved to Hollywood to take acting les-sons from Price. It made no difference to the Everlys, or to Reed, that the brothers were among the top-selling singers in the coun-try and Reed was struggling to make the charts. Nor did it matter that Reed was calling himself a pacifist, while the Everly Brothers would be inducted into the U.S. Marine Corps Reserves in No-vember 1961.

"We've always just chosen our friends, we were all kids," Phil Everly said. "He's the same age as I am. It's not like a hard-core anything. He wasn't political. We just hung out together. It was a great period of life, like college. He liked to laugh. He was good-looking. He could get a girl. It's a good thing when a man doesn't take himself too seriously." Everly saw Price as a friendly man who made all of his students feel at ease and frequently became a life-long confidant. Everly rarely discussed politics with Price but he was aware of the man's background and saw how it affected Reed. "Paton was a conscientious objector in the Second World War," Everly said. "That was a very unpopular thing. He was a man of conviction. What he said, he did. If he believed in something, he stood for it. He just didn't believe in killing. I think a lot of Dean's standing for something was part of that."[13]

While Reed's beliefs were evolving, his main task still was pushing his career. He was recording regularly for Capitol and in 1959 managed a brief appearance on the television series *Bachelor Father*. In the episode, Reed was introduced as a graduate of the local high school, back to perform his latest hit, "Twirly, Twirly," an upbeat number about the baton-twirling girl who owned his heart. He came bounding onto the stage wearing a white shirt, thin tie and a dark sport coat. Four young men sang backup and toward the end of the song, as he sang about the "pretty little ma-jorette," two baton twirling girls strode on-stage. Reed probably spent less than three minutes on the screen, but it was his first national exposure. After months of uncertainty and rejections, it was sheer exhilaration. He was going to make it, he would be famous. Reed once again felt he would be a star. His fledgling career was going well enough that when he returned to Colorado for a short summer vacation that year, it warranted a small mention in a Denver newspaper. Reed was returning to Estes Park, but this time, he would not be cleaning the pools. He would be lying alongside them.

Johnny Rosenburg was twenty years old and he noticed the item in the paper. A spinal operation a year earlier had laid him up for weeks. In order to fight the boredom of his bed and chair-ridden recuperation, Rosenburg taught himself to play the guitar. Once he mastered some of the chords, he started fooling around with original melodies. He discovered he had a knack for writ-ing songs but was unsure what to do next. He had begun playing bars and clubs around town, but he wanted to cut records like the big boys. Rosenburg, full of youthful bravado, decided he needed to meet Reed. He convinced a buddy to drive up to Estes Park with him. Before heading out, Rosenburg grabbed a bulky reel-to-reel tape recorder, loaded it into the car and set out for the Harmony Guest Ranch. He pulled into the gravel parking lot and looked across a grassy plain toward the swimming pool. At first, all he could see were young couples with children, middle-aged guys with potbellies spreading over the top half of their swimming trunks and their wives with their skin beginning to sag. Finally, at the far end of the pool area Rosenbug saw a fit-looking man with a hairy chest lying in a lounge chair. The two pretty young women sitting on the cement on either side of the chair talking to the stranger told Rosenburg he had found his prey. He pulled the heavy tape recorder out of the car and lugged it toward the pool.

"Are you Dean Reed?" Rosenburg asked, casting a shadow over the figure in the chair.

"Yes."

"Well, my name's Johnny Rosengburg and I've got a couple of songs I'd like you to listen to."

Reed stared at the man for a moment, debating whether to tell him to get lost.

"Alright. Honey," Reed said to one of the women, "could you go to the office and ask them for an extension cord. Tell them I need it."

The young woman dutifully fetched the extension cord and Reed plugged in the tape recorder. Rosenburg cued up the tape and from the tinny speaker came the sounds of a man and his guitar recorded in a bedroom. Reed listened, then told Rosenburg to rewind the tape and play them again. Rosenburg like that idea and did as Reed asked.

"I'd like to take those out to my manager," Reed said after the second listen. "How would you like it if I recorded those?"

"It's nice of you, but I really came up here to see if you couldn't get me a recording contract. I don't really want to be a songwriter. I want to sing my own stuff. I want the spotlight."

"Yeah, doesn't everybody. I'll tell you what. You make a demo of these songs. I'll take them back to L.A. and I'll put them on my record. I'll also talk to my manager about getting you a recording contract. If I can do something with these songs, it'll make it easier for you to get a tryout with Capitol. I'm sure you could probably write a couple more songs, if you haven't already. Whatd'ya say?"

"Okay, but only if you get me the tryout as a singer."

"I'll do my best. You want a Coke?"

"Sure. One other question. What's a demo?"[14]

Reed laughed, provided soft drinks all around and explained to Rosenburg that there were little studios in Denver where he could pay to have a record cut of him singing his songs. The two men chatted awhile longer and then Rosenburg and his friend, who had worked hard at making time with the two women, drove home. Rosenburg was not sure he had really accomplished anything, but the next day he headed to the Western Sound studio, made the demos and hustled them up to Dean at the Harmony Ranch. A couple months passed before Reed returned to Estes Park and called the number Rosenburg had given him.

"Johnny, Dean Reed here."

"No kidding. I wasn't sure I'd hear from you again."

"You've gotta have faith, my friend. I've got some good news for you, John, but I would rather tell you in person. Can you come on up?"

"Can a salmon swim upstream? I'll be there within an hour."

Rosenburg broke most of the speed laws as he roared around the curves up the mountain. This time, Reed wasn't by the pool but was waiting for Rosenburg in his room.

"I took your songs into the studio," Reed explained after the men shook hands and exchanged a few pleasantries. "I must have done fifty takes on each of them. No matter what I did, I just couldn't get them to sound as good as you do. I don't know if it was the key, the tempo, or maybe it's just they were your songs and you sing them from your heart. I finally just gave up. But I told my manager what you had said, about how you wanted to be a singer too. He like the sound of your voice on the demos, so he took them to Capitol. They want to sign you, John."

"YEEEEEEEEHHHHHHHAAHHHHH." Rosenburg let out a shout that echoed around the room and bounced off the mountains.

"That's great, Dean. Thank you. Thank you. Man, that's just perfect. I can't tell you how much this means to me."

"Oh, I think I know. This is the easy part, Johnny. The hard work is coming. My manager is Roy Eberhard. He'll be getting in touch with you shortly and he'll tell you what to do. I expect he'll want you to come to Hollywood as soon as possible."

Two weeks later, Eberhard called Rosenburg and told him to head west. When he arrived, he signed his contracts with Capitol and Eberhard and soon was sharing a room with Dean at the Eberhards' Conoga Park home in the San Fernando Valley. Rosenburg recorded under the name Johnny Rose. Unlike Reed, Rosenburg had no interest in acting and soon hit the road doing one-night stands in Salt Lake City, Denver, Kansas City. He scored a regional hit single in the South called "The Last One to Know." Its popularity landed Rosenburg on the New Orleans All-Star Show, a radio program that spotlighted new young singers. Rosenburg would come off the road for a couple of weeks and it would be back to sharing a bedroom with Reed at the Eberhard place. The two would talk or play badminton with their manager's children. "The year out in Canoga Park, I got to know Dean pretty well," Rosenburg said. "He sure the hell wasn't political. We didn't talk politics, that's for sure. He was very self-centered, sold on himself, which is what it took in that business. If you didn't believe in yourself, how the hell could you get anybody else to believe in you. He had that ability more than I did. He was a decent kid."[15]

By late 1960, Dean's career still seemed to be moving forward. Capitol released one of his singles, "Our Summer Romance," and it cracked Billboard's Hot 100 list, although it never made it out of the 90s. To an outsider, it looked like the twenty-two-year-old was on his way. His brother Dale, back from his stint in Antarctica, bought a sporty MG in Florida and drove to Los Angeles for a visit. "He knew the Ricky Nelsons and all that," Dale said, referring to the singing TV star. "He was living pretty good. He invited me to listen to him sing in a nightclub. But I think he was mostly making records. The only thing I remember was going to that lunch. At the lunch, there were always people waving, saying, 'Hi Dean.' He seemed to be getting along fine."[16]

Attending Quaker meetings sharpened Reed's political and spiritual development, but surprisingly, also his musical development. It was through the Quakers that Reed met Marge and John Raitt. John Raitt was enormously popular, having burst on the scene as Billy Bigelow in Rodgers and Hammerstein's musical *Carousel*. He recorded fourteen albums, mostly show tunes, which sold well. He was frequently in demand as a theater actor, which kept him away from the Los Angeles home for weeks and even months at a time. His wife, Marge, was a pianist and often accompanied her husband's singing and took an active role in his career. As Price did, Marge took an instant liking to Reed.

"When I met him, he had recorded one album and he had his glossies and we tried to promote him," Marge Raitt said. "I thought he had a lot of talent. He was very photogenic. His upper body was strong from the rings. I was always surprised by that. It was very impressive. He didn't have a great voice, but it was adequate with the right arrangements. But he was charismatic. He was like James Dean, but better looking. If he had the right breaks, he could have been a teen idol."[17]

Reed and Raitt set to work on their teen idol project. Marge talked to the folks at Decca Records where her husband was under contract. She tried to convince them to sign Reed away from Capitol, but they weren't interested. She tried setting him up with her other contacts in the music industry and with some of the better agents. They were always nice to her because of her status and the star power her husband commanded, but little came of her efforts. It was one of the least successful endeavors to come out of the Raitt household. A dozen years later, Marge and John's daughter, Bonnie, started recording albums in Minneapolis and her efforts culminated in million-selling discs and Grammy awards by the late 1980s.

Marge and Reed spent hours at the Raitt home, with Reed singing into Raitt's reel-to-reel tape recorder. She would point out different phrasings and make him repeat the verses over and over again into the recorder. She gave him vocal instructions, how to project his voice, how to breathe, the subtle techniques that can bump a mediocre singer to the next level. It was the most musical instruction Reed had received since choir practice at Wheat Ridge High School. Raitt also took the sheet music and wrote different arrangements for some of his songs, and in particular, for the other instruments that would accompany Reed's guitar playing. That was a tremendous help because Reed never bothered to organize his own band and had to rely on the studio musicians to back him on his records and occasional television appearances. At the same time, Raitt was becoming entranced with her pupil, even though he was fifteen years her junior. Reed would later tell his first wife that he had a love affair with Raitt, something she adamantly denied. But she acknowledged the pull Reed had on her and other women. "He was very charming," she said. "I'm a very sensitive person. He could be empathetic with people. They felt when they talked to him, he really listened."[18]

His career was not moving fast enough for Reed and his frustration was mounting. Late in 1960, Johnny Rosenburg was sitting in their room at the Eberhards' when Reed stormed in. He slammed the door behind him and began raging and throwing his stuff together in a pile on the bed. "I never knew the reason, but he came back mad," Rosenburg said. "He said, 'I'm getting out of here. You've got talent, I've got talent but neither one of us is going to go anywhere if we keep this guy as the manager. I'm leaving.' I thought he was half-crazy. As it turned out, he was probably a little more mature between the ears than I was. I don't think Roy could have done enough for him. I think Dean was his own manager, period. Nobody believed in Dean Reed more than Dean Reed."[19]

Reed would later explain that his anger was directed at both Eberhard and a talent syndicate. Eberhard saw Reed was struggling and when a syndicate came along that was willing to buy the contract for representing the young singer, Eberhard jumped at the chance to make some quick cash. He sold the contract. "The buyers were part of the organization in Hollywood which concerns itself with everything having to do with show business and is regarded as a type of syndicate," Reed explained. "And so one day two men appeared to me and told me the things, which according to the view of the organization, I was doing wrong.

They told me what kind of shirts I could wear, with which women I could be seen by photographers in teeming restaurants on Sunset Strip and gave me advice to stage a little scandal with Miss So-and-so. I refused. I didn't want to be a slave. I would rather remain without a manager."[20]

Reed packed his stuff and went to live with Price and his wife, Tilly. Other than having a new address and no manager, his routine didn't change much. There was, however, one intriguing development. Both Capitol Records and Reed were receiving reports that something interesting was happening in Chile. "Our Summer Romance," which barely scratched the charts in the United States, apparently was steadily climbing in Chile and other South American countries. By the end of the year, it would become the best-selling English record to that point in Brazil, Argentina, Chile, Uruguay and Peru. "I borrowed $1,200 from a friend and went south to see what it was all about," Reed later told a reporter.[21] The friend undoubtedly was Price. Although Capitol executives knew a personal appearance by the singer might help the company recoup its investment in the Colorado troubadour, they were not willing to put any money into it, or much effort. So with Price cosigning the State Department documents, Reed applied for his first passport. On the application he wrote that he would spend seventeen days in Brazil, Argentina, Chile, Peru and Uruguay.[22] On March 9, 1961, Reed flew out of LaGuardia Airport in New York City, heading south to the tumultuous welcome that would change his life.

Seven

Taking a Bride

*P*atricia Ann Hobbs was gorgeous; there was no arguing that point. At 5-foot-7 and 124 pounds with blonde hair and blue eyes, she won local beauty pageants the way Chris Evert won tennis tournaments. She grew up in the Oceanside area, near San Diego, moving there not long after her April 29, 1939, birth in Alabama. At Oceanside, her life was the stuff of Beach Boys songs. Surfer girl, a true-to-her-school cheerleader and sometime model. She finished third runner-up Miss California for the Miss Universe Contest.

In 1957, Hobbs left California and headed east to Denver to attend Colorado Woman's College where she eventually graduated with a major in liberal arts and drama. Back home in California, she worked for a short time as a weather girl at a San Diego television station. There was no pretension in those early days of local television news. The weather girls were there to put little cutouts of the sun, or rain clouds, on the map and read the weather forecast. Mostly, though, they were to smile sweetly and look alluring in their long blond hair, short skirts and tight tops in hopes of keeping the men glued to the screen until at least the next commercial break. Men, like Reed, studied meteorology. Women, like Patricia Hobbs, studied blouses.

Hobbs spent some of her days in acting classes with Sandy Meisner in Los Angeles and picked up occasional work doing television commercials and small continuing parts on *The Adventures of Ozzie and Harriet, Saint and Sinners* and other shows. After about a year of that, Hobbs headed to New York City and studied at Actor's Studio. She landed a Broadway role, but the fame was fleeting. The show closed after opening night.[1]

In September 1963, Hobbs was back in Hollywood, shooting a commercial. She stopped in at her agent's office to discuss potential roles. One that seemed particularly promising was a new television detective drama called *Checkmate* that was beginning to assemble its cast. They needed someone to play the girlfriend of the show's star, Doug McClure. Hobbs sat in the chair, her legs curled under her, talking intently with the agent and hardly noticed when the office door opened. A young man walked in, stood to the side and told the agent, his agent as it turned out, that he had something to drop off. The agent introduced Dean Reed to Patricia Hobbs and the actress, a little annoyed at the interruption, unfolded her legs to stand up and shake his hand. Reed let his eyes linger over Hobbs' long legs, said how nice it was to meet her, apologized for the intrusion and left. But Reed could not forget those shapely legs. Within the hour he was on the phone to the agent, badgering him relentlessly until he finally gave in and revealed Hobbs' phone number. She was in and out that day and after about twenty tries, Reed finally caught her in her hotel room. He reminded her that they had met earlier that day in the agent's office, but it took some quick talking to keep her on the phone.

"He's not supposed to be giving out his clients' phone numbers," a perturbed Hobbs told Reed. "Listen, I've got to go."

"No, please don't. It wasn't really Schwartz's fault. Besides being my agent, we're good friends. He didn't give it up easily. I had to work him for an hour and promise to raise his fee. You may be the most expensive phone call I've ever made."

Hobbs giggled. "Well, I guess there's no harm done, as long as you don't become the first of fifteen guys from the agency calling me."

"There won't be. That was the other thing I made him promise. Not for you. I just wanted to make sure I didn't have any more competition than all the heads you turn walking down the street.

Did you mean it when you said you had to go, or were you just getting rid of me?"

"Both. I just came back from dinner with Les Brown, Jr. He's performing across the street and I'm supposed to catch his next show. But you've got about a half-hour."

"Alriiiight! A guy can accomplish a lot in a half-hour. Especially on his birthday. You know, I blew out all my candles and wished for you."

"You're full of it. It's not your birthday."

"Yes it is. I was born September 22, 1938. I'm twenty-five today and meeting you makes it the luckiest of all my birthdays. But tell me about yourself. What're you doing in town?"

"At the moment, I'm doing a cigarette commercial. And when you saw me today, I was talking about a role in a new TV show. One of those detective things. It's called *Checkmate* and Schwartz thinks I can get the role of Doug McClure's girl-friend. McClure's the lead on this one, so it could be a good role for me. A real break."

Reed listened intently, prompting her with questions, talking about himself only when she asked and then, always careful not to talk too long before bringing the conversation back to her. He made her laugh. He sang a couple of his songs. The half hour stretched into an hour, then two. Hobbs never went back to hear Les Brown and his band. It was only after Reed finally hung up that she realized she had the telltale warm, round red mark that comes from holding the receiver to her ear too long. The conversation had made time disappear.

"He was charming, a good sense of humor," she remembered. "He was like a country boy. He had traveled all over. He was not your typical Hollywood type. He was not stuck on himself. He invited me to Roger Smith's party. He told me about Paton Price and I thought that might be fun to do. I thought I could meet people through him."[2]

The next night they went to Smith's party and the couple had a great time with the other young and established stars. Reed worked the room, but this time on Patricia's behalf, introducing her to everyone he could, the closing tactic for winning her heart.

She loved meeting the stars, making the connections, and the warm feelings that had been planted in the previous evening's phone call were sprouting nicely. Reed had brought his guitar and was easily persuaded by Smith and others to entertain them with a few songs. He sensed his campaign was working but he didn't rush it. Finally, late in the evening, he noticed Patricia slip away to the bathroom. His heart pounding and his body tingling, he walked down the hall. When she emerged, he was there, slipped his arm around her waist and pulled her to him. His kiss was hard and she gave in willingly. They broke for a second, then kissed again, his hand sliding down past the small of her back to push her pelvis into his. She could feel his intentions and was not surprised when he suggested they return to her hotel room. She agreed without hesitation. They thanked their hosts and quickly headed to the car. When they reached the room, Reed's ardor was palatable. He tried not to rush. He reminded himself that he had been with some beautiful women the past few years. But as Patricia let her dress drop to the floor and unbuckled her bra, Reed quivered as he stared at her full breasts and the long, tapered legs. They fell into bed and he was everywhere on her. They made love and fell exhausted in each other's arms.

The next morning, Patricia's mother knocked on the door. Patricia slowly came out of her deep sleep and remembered she had told her mother to come by about nine so the pair could go apartment hunting. Patricia felt her leg brush against something and turned to see Reed still asleep beside her. Panicked, now, she told her mother she would be right there, put a hand over Reed's mouth and shook him awake. She told him not to make a sound, grab his clothes and hide in her closet. Patricia let her mother in, apologized for oversleeping and asked her to go to the hotel restaurant and bring her a cup of coffee. When she left, Reed finished dressing, kissed her goodbye and left the room. He wasn't gone long, however. He returned bearing doughnuts. Mrs. Hobbs was not fooled. Reed's greased hair had left a spot on his pillow and she had noticed it when she first entered the room. She let it slide, however, and the two women spent the day in a fruitless search for housing. That night, Reed and Patricia went to dinner and then to his apartment, the top half of a duplex whose most distinctive feature was a huge tree growing over the patio. It was in the hills and very cozy. Reed suggested she move in with him. She said no. Reed did not retreat. They spent half the night talking and Reed, by turns charming and practical, threw all his arguments at her. By early morning, a combination of Reed, fatigue and love had worn her down. She changed her mind and agreed to move in with him and at the same time, gave the place a name. Forever more, it would be the Tree House.

"He could talk about anything," she said. "So it wasn't just desire but conversation. We would read to each other. There wasn't a TV in the Tree House. It was reading, music, exploring each other and I did some gourmet cooking. It was a very warm feeling."[3]

The young couple were passionate lovers, always trying to please each other. They would warm baby oil and rub it over each other's bodies. Or they would grab feathers and tickle each other. Their fights were just as passionate. Many of them were over the way Reed wanted Patricia to be, which was friend and lover. But he did not want her involved in his politics or competing with him in show business. What he wanted was what his father had: a woman who would be content to stay home, take care of the house and wait for his return. "But I kept breaking out of that mold and it was the cause of the fights," Patricia said. "He was extremely jealous because he knew I could escape. I broke many, many dishes. I had a physical anger. He wanted to debate. I would not ever throw at him. I never beat him. It was such anger and passion. I had to break something. I broke the closet doors and I would rebuild them the next day."[4]

Once again, Reed was having trouble getting regular work around Hollywood. But he did get an engagement in San Francisco at a coffeehouse where Joan Baez also was playing. The couple drove there together and spent a romantic weekend wandering around the city with Reed performing at night. Still, as quickly as they fell in love, it began to unravel almost as fast. Marge Raitt and Paton Price separately were telling their pupil the same thing: this was the wrong time in his career to be getting serious about a woman. He needed to be free so that he could go where the career might take him. Besides, the teenaged girls who might be the fuel to push his career down the track would be more interested in him as a single guy than a married man. High school and junior high girls were less likely to write their first name and his last name in their notebooks if there already was a Mrs. Dean Reed. In mid-October, Reed returned from a week in Mexico City where he had been singing in the clubs, his popularity undiminished south of California. He confronted his girlfriend in their apartment and told her they couldn't live together anymore, repeating Raitt's and Price's arguments almost verbatim. He wasn't ready to get serious, it would be bad for his career, Reed told her. Patricia had news of her own. She was pregnant. Suddenly, Reed's restraint disappeared and the apartment erupted into a terrific squabble. It ended with Patricia storming out and spending the night in a motel. Even the news that she was carrying his baby was not enough to sway Reed, and the relationship appeared over. However, an accident a couple days later provided Patricia with one more chance. Reed was thrown from the horse he was riding and broke his collarbone. He had it taped in order to do a scheduled television interview at Price's house. But the pain was searing and constant. It also made driving a car nearly impossible, so the next day he called Patricia and asked her to drive him to Mexico. She agreed without hesitation. "I thought I could worm my way back in," she said.[5]

On the way, they stopped in Phoenix to visit Reed's parents. It was a strange introduction to the family for the California girl. As they drove up to the trailer house, she noticed a big blackboard out front on which Cyril had written his views, in large block letters, about an upcoming election. Cyril's conservative stance, and his brazen way of making it known, was startling for the young, liberal woman. No one was home, so they let themselves in and Reed decided to take a bath to ease the pain. Patricia was washing him down, an intimate task for an unmarried couple in the early 1960s. At that moment, Ruth Anna walked in and "that was my introduction to her. She was very good about it," Patricia recalled. After a couple days visiting with his mom and dad, Reed and his girlfriend crammed the car full of their stuff and resumed their journey south. The road trip seemed to rekindle the love that was dying a week earlier.

"It was a beautiful trip, a wonderful time," Patricia said. "It was October and candles were lit in the villages for the Day of Death (similar to Halloween). It was very romantic. We would chase after wild donkeys. He romped around with the wild donkeys in his sombrero. It was one of those innocent trips. We would drive with the top down and look at the stars. Then we got down there and he changed and decided he didn't want to get serious again."[6] The trip to Mexico City took most of five days and it seemed as though her plan was working. She was sure they were becoming a couple again, especially after they secured an apartment together. But Reed had a different idea and insisted Patricia get an abortion, something that was illegal in the United States. She resisted and countered that they should get married. Reed stood firm and his pregnant lover eventually caved.

"He dropped me off at a sleazy little neighborhood, a sleazy medical clinic," Patricia said. "The doctor had blood all over him and Dean dropped me off, said bye and left. I started to cry. They gave me something to make me happy. It was just a board for the table and the sheet, which was patched. When Dean came to pick me up, I was really mad. I was furious. I thought he used me to drive down. I had lots of cramps and got an infection."[7]

Reed had driven to Mexico, in part, because he had landed a role in Columbia Pictures' *Love Has Many Faces*, which starred Lana Turner, Hugh O'Brien, Cliff Robertson and Stephanie Powers. The movie was filmed in Acapulco and Reed left Patricia in Mexico City to recuperate while he was on location. Before he left for the filming, he told Patricia they were not going to be together anymore. He told her he had a lot of things to do and she would just be in the way. She cried for an hour, but Reed would not be moved. He told Patricia to get dressed for a scheduled dinner with his local agent, Lonka Becker. She went reluctantly, put on her party face and hoped things would be better in the morning. They weren't. Reed was over her and as coldly as he had forced the abortion, he now just as cruelly dumped the woman he had wooed so hard just a few months earlier. It was a coldness at odds with his growing concern and work on behalf of the poor in South America and blacks in the United States. Johnny Rosenburg had witnessed it earlier. Reed's first priority still was to his career and he was fully capable of doing whatever was necessary to keep it moving.[8] When his part in the movie was completed, Reed did not return to his Mexico City home, but headed back to Hollywood. But Patricia did not sit around pining for Reed's return. Becker, who also represented Anthony Quinn, was impressed by the young starlet and landed her a role in the same movie as Reed. It was not a large part, Patricia played another beach girl, but she viewed it as a way to propel her career. She jumped on an old bus, filled with chickens and poor peasants, and rode it to Acapulco, where the film company put her up in a nice hotel and told her where to report for the next day's shooting.

O'Brien, who had gained fame playing Wyatt Earp from 1955 to 1961 on ABC's weekly television series *Life and Legend of Wyatt Earp* wasted little time finding out the name of the new bit player in his movie. He introduced himself and asked Patricia out on a date. Despite being fourteen years older than the twenty-four-year-old actress, O'Brien had no trouble persuading her to accompany him. Soon they were going diving together. When O'Brien did publicity interviews and appearances for the movie, he would bring along Patricia and never fail to mention her as a budding young star who also appeared in the film. She moved into his luxurious villa and they were seen together everywhere around the resort town.

The publicity shots were transmitted north and it wasn't long before Reed saw the picture of his old lover and read the accounts of Hugh O'Brien and his new flame. A newspaper photo from February 13, 1964, for instance, headlined, "The News in Acapulco," showed a stylish Patricia Hobbs and O'Brien side-by-side with Mexican actress Dolores del Rio "at the Acapulco Hilton cocktail party" given in del Rio's honor.[9] The photo provoked in Reed an intense jealousy and longing that surprised him. He threw some clothes together in a suitcase and instead of firing up his car, booked a flight to Mexico City and called Patricia from their old apartment. But the conversation was short and terse. "I don't want to have anything to do with you," she told him and hung up.[10]

Reed was flabbergasted, but not for long. The next day he hatched a plan, a crazy macho scheme. He and two of his friends drove from Mexico City to Acapulco. Reed was going to find O'Brien and with the help of his two friends, beat him up. How, exactly, that was going to woo Patricia back into Reed's arms was never really clear, but the idea made him feel better. The plan had one other major flaw. Reed failed to do reconnaissance on his enemy. When he arrived, he discovered that O'Brien and Patricia had flown back to Mexico City the same day. Reed and his buddies, much less excited now, dragged themselves back home. But in the perfect ending to his bad day, Reed opened the door to his apartment to find his girlfriend there. Whatever feeling of triumph he might have felt was quickly extinguished. Patricia told him to get out, that he wasn't welcome in their apartment. Reed could not muster his usual energy and overwhelm her arguments. He was dogged tired and emotionally spent. He resorted to begging, telling her how sorry he was for all the wrongs he had done her, asking her to have pity on a tired man, pleading with her to let him stay the night. Patricia was unmoved. He spent the night in a hotel. "I was doing other films in Mexico and I really was getting a life started and I was enjoying it," she explained.[11]

In a letter home, she described the torment she was causing the two men and her own uncertainty. "What a triangle I'm creating between Hugh & Deano," Patricia wrote her mother. "They're both serious—Deano more so since he has proposed a dozen times. Hugh is also serious—but our relationship is much too new for a marriage proposal—but it could lead up to something like that. One is more successful than the other at this time—they're both jealous and don't want to share me. Each has asked me to make up my mind. And each as [sic] a lot to love, each as great and good points and I'm so mixed up now I don't know whose children I want, when or where! Wish you were here to referee."[12]

Reed never saw that letter, but he knew he was not in a good negotiating position. He had, after all, forced her to have an abortion she didn't want, walked out on her in Mexico and now was trying to strong-arm her out of the arms of a well-known, well-connected Hollywood star. Reed decided to fall back on his charm and his guitar, a combination that had worked for him since high school.

Patricia was in the apartment, doing her hair, pulling on outfits, looking for the right one for another evening with O'Brien. The look had to be perfect, because although O'Brien had not said a lot about the upcoming evening, he had intimated that it would be a memorable one for the both of them. Just loudly enough to be heard over the usual din of the city, she began to discern the strumming of a guitar from below her window. At the same moment, there was a knock on the door and when she opened it, three of the neighborhood children were standing there, each holding a large bouquet of roses. The guitar strumming continued, but now it was accompanying a love song and the voice was unmistakable. Patricia picked up the youngest of the children and they all walked to the balcony and listened to the serenade. After several songs, which by now had drawn a small audience of neighbors, Reed got down on his knees and called out his marriage proposal to Patricia. The crowd chanted, "Si, Si," and after a few moments, she took one of the roses, tossed it down to Reed and said simply, "Si, señor." The crowd applauded and a celebration broke out. Reed's charm and zest trumped O'Brien's Hollywood stature. "Dean would steal roses for women from yards and that was very exciting," she explained. "He would stop the car in the middle of the road and dance with you; all the things you thought James Dean would do."

Patricia reluctantly told Reed she had to keep her date with O'Brien. Photographers were everywhere this night. O'Brien and his girlfriend went to a bullfight with other movie stars, then to dinner. When they returned to O'Brien's villa, Patricia finally told him she had agreed to marry Reed. O'Brien was outraged. He smashed furniture, he slapped Patricia once and threw her on the bed until her pleadings finally made him stop. The anger was fueled by many things, not the least of which was that he had told his press agent that he would propose to Patricia that evening and he was confident the agent could announce their wedding plans to the press the next day.[13] The next night, Reed and Patricia went to the movies and watched *El Cid*. Charleton Heston is El Cid, a pure Spanish knight in the eleventh century. Sophia Loren is Chimene, a woman who at first loves El Cid, then hates him and eventually marries him and falls in love with him again. "Can a man live without honor?" El Cid asks rhetorically. "No." Patricia cried through much of the movie because she saw Reed as that pure knight. The evening and the movie made a lasting impression on the couple and in the years to come they would refer often to the lead characters. It was a good choice for them. Reed was every bit as handsome as Heston and Patricia was one of the few women anywhere who could have stood in the same room as Loren and not suffered in the comparison. El Cid's questions about an honorable life were the ones Reed was wrestling with and the "now-I-love him, now-I-don't" sequence had begun in the couple's life. Later that evening, Reed proposed again to her. They made small cuts on their wrists and commingled their blood. Patricia fell asleep happy that night beside her fiancé, but awoke frightened and crying. It was a terrible nightmare, one that would visit her again and again. In the dream, Reed was in trouble and people, speaking a language she could not understand, were after him. She tried to hide Reed, but they found him and carried him away. When Reed reappeared, he was underwater, reaching for her. The wind blew and Patricia saw herself as an old woman and Reed's ghost appeared, telling her to meet him under the apple tree. The scene shifted again and Patricia was on a grassy hill, flowers everywhere and at the bottom of the hill grew a huge apple tree. Standing there was Reed, very much alive, motioning her to run to him. Between sobs, Patricia recounted the dream to Reed. He held her and stroked her hair, whispered to her that everything was all right. From the dream sprang a ritual. Whenever the couple parted, or even just went to sleep, they would tell each other, "I'll see you under the apple tree."[14]

They did not believe in long engagements and on March 23, 1964, Dean Reed wed Patricia Hobbs. The day before, as part of a prewedding celebration, Reed rode a wild bronco at a Mexico City rodeo, in part to impress his mother-in-law.[15] The wedding ceremony was performed by a Mexican minister on a Sunday afternoon in the couple's apartment, just off a park. No one from Reed's family made it there, but Patricia's mother attended and helped her daughter with the dress the bride had specially made for the ceremony. The wedding party consisted of an old Mexican general, Miguel Aleman, as well as Reed's friend Arturo, who had driven with Reed to beat up Hugh O'Brien in Acapulco. Arturo's wife and Arturo's brother's girlfriend served as bridesmaids. Reed and his bride argued before the ceremony because Patricia wanted say, "I do," while Dean insisted on "Si." Patricia lost the argument but whatever resentment she may have had disappeared when Red surprised her by singing a new song he had composed for her, "With You by My Side."

> I've traveled around this world once or twice
> to find me a woman to find me a wife.
> Then one day on the day of my birth
> I found you my woman, my woman of worth
>
> With you by my side, the world is at my feet.
> I can tell you my love, there is nothing as sweet
> As you by my side and the world at my feet.
> We'll go through life as one
>
> As I caress you at night
> I can swear I lose, I lose all my fright.
> And until the day, the day that I die
> I'll thank the stars and wonder why.[16]

Afterward, they spent the night in the honeymoon suite in a downtown hotel. "It was very romantic," Patricia said. "The next day, Dean left for the other side of Mexico, Cancun, for ten days. He had a gig."[17]

Reed and Patricia had the kind of star power in Mexico that Humphrey Bogart and Lauren Bacall had generated in Hollywood. They were in demand separately and as a couple. Their faces, and Reed's voice, were everywhere and they did all they could to cultivate their stardom. Reed would mount letter-writing campaigns, sending off ten letters himself, and then getting Patricia and the maids to write phony fan letters under aliases to the same stations, pleading with them to play the new Spanish record by that American singer. Reed and his wife were good, too, with the press and knew the way to keep the publicity coming was to feed them stories, fine meals and wine. The song Reed wrote for their wedding, "With You by My Side," became a big hit for him in Mexico.[18]

The couple also starred in comic books, which were very different in Latin America than the DC and Marvel Comics American boys were buying. Rather than the bold and colorful drawings of superheroes saving the world, or at least Gotham City, the comic books of Mexico and South American countries tended to be soap operas. Instead of drawings, the comic books were photos of the characters in various poses with the dialog balloons superimposed. Reed and Patricia would often pose as the comic book characters and the sales put money in their pockets and put their faces constantly before the public. "We couldn't go anyplace in Mexico City without being recognized," she said. "I had my own maid, dressmaker and hairdresser. We went to some very top, top parties. Homes with pools and waterfalls inside. That was who we hung out with: the rich and politicians. This was before his revolutionary days."[19]

Outwardly, at least, Reed was philosophical about his popularity in Mexico and South America, and his relative obscurity in the United States. He had given it some thought and had formulated his own theory for the different reactions. "Down there, I'm different," he said in an interview." And they seem to like a Norte Americano who knows how to say 'gracias' in their own language."[20]

The Reeds were signed to star in a movie, *Guadalajara in the Autumn*. As filming began, Patricia was once again pregnant with Reed's child. This time, there was no talk of abortions. Reed was ready to be a father. The film was nearly finished, there was one more scene to shoot, a crowd scene with Reed singing to Patricia. In the middle of filming, however, she doubled over with pain. Reed grabbed her around the waist and the movie crew hustled her to a nearby farm house. They put her in a room and Patricia remembers people worriedly looking at her. But as her gaze moved beyond the gathered knot of people, she could see through the open doorway chickens, ducks, a dog, pig and donkey in the house and yard. A doctor was rushed to the house and gave her a shot to ease the pain, but it made her goofy and Patricia began laughing hysterically at the scene. The situation wasn't funny. She was suffering a miscarriage, and within a few minutes, the doctor told the couple they had lost a son.[21]

It was the saddest day of Patricia's young life. Reed, too, took the miscarriage hard. He had been ecstatic when his wife told him of the pregnancy and early on, Reed sat down and composed a song for their baby called, "I Want You to Know."

I want you to know that clouds don't cry.
I want you to know that rivers sometimes run dry.
I want you to always question why.
I want you to know.

I want you to know that the color of a man's skin
Has nothing to do with the love that is within.
I want you to know that there is good in all men.
I want you to know.

I want you to know that all Gods are the same
That people only call him by different names.
I want you to know that they all teach the same.
I want you to know.

I want you to know that wars bring only pain
That all mothers cry when their sons die the same.
I want you to know that life is more than just a game.
I want you to know.

I want you to know when you are old and gray
That Patti and Dino tried in their very best way
To show you the truth each day and every day.
I want you to know.[22]

The mourning period lasted longer for Patricia. When filming on the movie finally wrapped, she gave in to Reed's arguments that she quit the business, that she stay home and be a housewife. "Dean didn't want me to work," she said. "He would say, 'I don't want to compete with my wife.' He didn't want men looking at me and he wanted me to dress conservatively. He wanted me to stay home and wash his socks."[23] In the early years of his career, Reed made a point of sitting down on his birthday and typing a review of his previous year. Because of the crush of his nearly constant work, he postponed reviewing his twenty-sixth year until November 7. It found him in a reflective mood about his lack of emotional, spiritual and intellectual growth, but taking a wife and losing a child consumed him.

"The biggest event of my life during the past year was the finding of the woman whom I want to be at my side for the rest of my life," he wrote. "I am more deeply in love than I ever thought existed. But our first year of marriage has not been the type of marriage which I wanted and will want in the future. Neither she nor I will settle for the type of life which we have led the past year. We have hurt each other very deeply at times during this period but after many hours of contemplation, I am sure that the problem was not with who she was, but what has been our situation of life. I believe that we have both learned a great deal about marriage by trial and error and if we never forget, and put to use what we have learned, we will be a very lucky couple and will be much ahead of the majority of married people. With her at my side, in the way which I now know she can be at my side, there is nothing which I cannot attain in life. During the year, I probably felt the most pain I have ever felt when we lost our first child—although we actually didn't lose a child—only an image of a child that was to be. I am beginning to trust more and more in life and now I feel it was for the better. We shall have time in the future to have these children which we both want so badly. During this period, I wrote a song which I feel is one of the deepest songs that I have ever written—it is a song which a father sings to his son and which says—'I want you to know.'"[24]

But Reed was getting restless again and there seemed to be more opportunities in one of the countries that had first embraced him. Toward the end of 1964, Reed left Mexico and went house hunting in Buenos Aires. The Reeds were moving to Argentina.

Eight

Adventures in Argentina

It had been a hot day in Buenos Aires and a long one for Reed. As he drove out of the city and toward the tony suburb where he and Patricia lived, Reed inhaled deeply the balmy night air roaring through his open window. He was surprised to see his wife still up and waiting for him. She handed him a glass of wine and they sat down in the living room, in front of the great stone fireplace. They talked for awhile and Patricia rested sideways against her husband. Reed slid his hand down her blouse and felt her warm, firm breast and gently massaged it as he spoke. The woman responded, reaching back over her head and pulling his lips down to hers. They kissed, long and full. Reed was now fully inflamed. He pivoted so swiftly and cleanly that he was on his feet leaning over his bride and still supporting her head. He reached under her legs and arms, lifted her gently and headed up the stairs to their bedroom. Patricia had anticipated his every move and whispered for him to open the door to the guest room. Inside, Reed found the room several degrees cooler than the others and that his darling had created a love nest. Incense was burning, red satin sheets covered the bed and candles, dozens of them, flickered throughout the room. She had designed the room to arouse his passion, although with the beauty he carried in his arms, the work was unnecessary. Reed lowered his lover onto the satin sheets. He pulled off his clothes and stood for a moment in his tight briefs so his wife could admire his strong, hard body. He leaped for the bed and nearly slid off the side, crippling the sensuous moment as they both laughed at his exuberance. To recover the moment, Reed slid his hand under Patricia's hair and pulled her face toward his mouth.

CRACK. CRACK. CRACK.

The house exploded with noise, the sharp pop of gunfire and the distinctive sound of shattering window glass. The couple rolled off the bed and onto the floor. Reed crawled to the telephone and called police.

"This is Dean Reed. Somebody's shooting at my house. Get someone here quickly," he said, repeating the address twice.

"Are these rifle or pistol shots?" the officer asked.

"How the hell should I know? It's gunshots. They could be breaking into the house to kill me. Hurry."

"Certainly, sir. Now, are they rapid fire, or is it more like a pop, silence, another pop?"

"What the fuck difference does it make?" Reed screamed into the phone. "Somebody is shooting at the back of my house. Get your asses over here before they kill me and my wife."

He slammed down the phone and tried to figure out what to do if the gunmen stormed the house. He had no weapon of his own except for kitchen knives. He couldn't remember if they had locked the doors. He was sweating and his mind was seizing up from the fear.

The Reeds caught a break. After about thirty seconds, the gunfire stopped and the couple heard several men yelling from the street: "Go home, Yankee, or you will die." Two cars roared off into the night and the attack was over. Dean and Patricia found each other's arms and held on tight. Reed didn't try to soothe his wife's frayed nerves by telling her it was all right. He couldn't. All he could think about was that if those men had come into the house, he and Patricia would have slaughtered. Neither his fame nor his usual daring-do would have been worth a damn.

"Señor Reed, Señor Reed?" It was the housekeeper and her husband calling to them from the living room. He called down to tell them he and Patricia were fine and asked them to wait. The

Reeds slowly let go of each other and with hands still shaking, pulled on their clothes. The police hadn't arrived, so Reed called his agent and the manager of the television station that broadcast Reed's weekly variety show. The agent never showed, but the television manger arrived within a half-hour and together with the couple and the housekeeper, he surveyed the damage. The attackers had concentrated most of their firepower on the master bedroom, assuming the Reeds would already be asleep. Bullets had shattered the windows and balcony doors. Glass shards were everywhere and bullet holes pocked the far wall like acne. A couple of slugs had stuck the headboard. Shooting from below, the angle was too great to hit someone lying in a bed. But had the Reeds been sleeping there and sprung up at the first sounds, a bullet might well have found its mark. The disinterest of the police in the whole affair, which Reed now realized began with the silly questions the desk officer asked him, continued. No squads arrived that night. It wasn't until well past daylight when an officer from the day shift rode his bicycle up the Reeds' driveway, knocked on the door and took a report.

The nighttime attack was the culmination of several months of increasing terror directed at the Reeds since they moved to Buenos Aires in late 1964. Arsonists had set a fire in the back fields of their villa near the housekeeper's cottage. Poisoned meat had been fed to their German shepherd, killing him. Vandals had spray-painted Nazi swastikas on the garage and the front and side gates after Reed had sung, "My Yiddish Mama" on his television show. Those attacks were annoying and in the case of their dog's murder, heart-wrenching. But Reed and his wife still were in their twenties, adored by millions and still possessed the feeling of immortality that is the special gift of the young. Bullets fired at the house, however, were something all together different. "Before we got shot at, we thought it was a game," Patricia said. "We weren't hurt. We were not physically harmed."[1]

When Reed arrived home the next evening, he found two things he had not noticed when he left for work. A red hammer and sickle were painted on his garage door. And four young men, armed with guns, had arrived to volunteer their services. They identified themselves as Peronists, the followers of charismatic former president Juan Peron and his wife Evita. The men expressed admiration for Reed's work with the poor. They told Reed that paid killers were at his house the night before, probably sent by the political police. They offered to guard the house, an offer Reed accepted. For two months they kept watch and occasional shots were fired, although no more bullets struck the house. The Reeds slept only in the guest room, where they felt more secure. The couple also bought handguns.[2] Reed was not going to find himself in the situation where his only weapons were kitchen cutlery. "He took real risks, always," said Reed's friend Marv Davidov. "He took it to the limit."[3]

In a letter to Patricia's mother, Reed tried to describe some of what had transpired, leaving out some incidents so she would not worry about their safety. "Have had 2 exciting weeks—Last week was made Honorary Fireman for saving man's life—Also last week my name came out on a list like the black lists before the French Revolution calling me a Communist. My name was with the top writers and educators so it didn't bother me to [sic] much. But then the night afterwards a bunch of guys came out to our house while we were sleeping and painting the hammer and sickle in red paint all over the house. The newspapers got the story from the police and it hit the front pages saying that some right fanatics had attacked my house. Well, since then men have been coming out each day with guns offering to fight for me—We have police stationed in the house each night and when I go to work one goes with me. It is all very silly, but it puts Patti's mind more at ease."[4]

The hatred directed at the Reeds couldn't have been more foreign to the couple. They had been popular in Mexico. Reed had been beloved in Chile, Argentina and the other countries of South America where he had performed regularly the past three years. They had expected more of the same when they arrived in Buenos Aires in the waning months of 1964. Reed purchased the two-story, four-bedroom house with white stucco and tile roof. The back yard was a couple of acres deep and included a swimming pool and pine trees. The master bedroom was upstairs with windows and a balcony facing a side street lined with large, leafy oak trees that provided welcome shade in the hot summer. It was luxurious and staffed by two servants.[5] Reed had no trouble making the payments. He was traveling the circuit, playing sold-out shows in Argentina and Chile. He had a weekly television show in Buenos Aires and he made a movie with his friend and popular singer Palito Ortega called *Mi Primera Novia* which did great business at the box office.

His wealth, instead of insulating him from the desperate poverty around him, seemed to propel Reed toward it. When Martin Luther King was awarded the Nobel Peace Prize, it confirmed for Reed much of what he had come to believe. "As each year goes by, I am surer that Pacifism must become a way of life for the subjected peoples and countries to gain their rights and liberties," he wrote. "He (King) has shown that it does not mean sitting on one's ass and letting the other person or country take advantage of you. He has shown that not sissies and cowards are pacifists but that only the most courageous of men can be pacifists. May the Latin American Peoples study our 'negro revolution' and may they use it as a guide line for their revolutions before bloody revolutions take place by the subjected peoples against their military dictatorships."[6] To encourage that kind of peaceful revolt, Reed was performing at gatherings for labor unions and at protest rallies. As Reed, himself, would later write, "In South America, there are only three categories of people: the privileged class, the blind people and the revolutionaries. I became a revolutionary."[7] In another interview, Reed elaborated on what was happening to him. "South America changed my life because there the difference of justice and injustice, poverty and wealth are so clear. So you have to take a stand. I became a revolutionary. You were either for the status quo which means for the twenty percent who have all the wealth and all the power or you will stand with the eighty percent who were illiterate, who were hungry who somehow wanted a better future. I felt this fame, that by destiny I had in South America, had to be dedicated to this eighty percent."[8]

One of the guides on his revolutionary journey was the Argentine writer, Alfredo Varela. Reed met Varela through the author's thirteen-year-old daughter. Reed was performing for free at a labor union rally when he noticed a shy girl who wasn't quite into the music the way the rest of the crowd was. Reed now expected the entire audience to thrill at his performances and if he

noticed even one person out of a thousand not enjoying themselves, it bothered him. Reed sought out the girl to find out why
the music had not moved her. The girl told Reed she liked the
music, but she enjoyed his political stance even more and invited
him to lunch with her family so he could meet her father. Reed
agreed and when he arrived the next day, he was surprised to dis-
cover her father was the well-known writer.[9] Varela was aware of
Reed's outspoken support for the poor and groups like labor organizations who were trying to improve the people's lot. Varela was
a strong proponent for a leftist government that would redistribute
the wealth. It was an introduction both men wanted to make and
they soon were fast friends, talking to each other frequently and
eating meals together.

Varela was an active member of the Communist Party in Argentina. In 1951, he wrote a book about his travels to the Soviet
Union and called its government the hope for all humanity. In
1960, he wrote enthusiastically about socialism coming to America
in the form of Fidel Castro's revolutionary government in Cuba.
Varela realized that in Reed he had discovered a kindred spirit, if
not a potential party member. He suggested that Reed accompany
him and other members of the Argentine delegation to the Congress of World Peace and Disarmament in Helsinki, Finland, in
July 1965. "I've known you now long enough to know that we
have made a good choice," Varela told Reed. "You are a citizen of
the USA but you are living in Argentina, our people like you, and
besides, peace knows no borders."[10]

While the congress was dominated by the Soviet Union and
other communist regimes, it was open to all nations and it attracted at least two major antiwar writers from the west, Bertrand
Russell and Jean-Paul Satre. Reed, the reader, was impressed by the
two men and was thrilled to meet them.[11] Reed spent the week at
the congress sitting in on sessions, listening to speakers and giving
at least one speech criticizing the growing U.S. involvement in
Vietnam. He also spent time meeting with Soviet officials, mostly
seeking help in setting up an interview with Lt. Valentina Tereshkova, a Soviet cosmonaut and the first woman in space. Reed was
a bit of a curiosity, one of the few Americans attending the peace
conference. The official line from Washington was that the Con-

gress for World Peace was a Communist platform for its anti–U.S. propaganda and as such, should be ignored. Reed was an acknowledged star among the Latin American delegates at the conference, but the overwhelming majority of the people there had never heard of him.

Nonetheless, toward the end of the congress, a dispute broke out between the Soviet delegates and their allies and the Chinese delegates and their supporters. For more than ten years after Mao Tse-tung led his revolutionary band and established China as the world's most populous Communist country, the Soviet Union and China had been allies. But that friendship began disintegrating in the early 1960s. In July 1963, reports were coming out of Moscow that Mao's government had sent a letter to the Soviet Central Committee severely criticizing the leadership and policies of Premier Nikita Khrushchev. The Chinese accused the Soviets of being soft on capitalism. The Russians were publicly stating they wanted to avert a world war and peacefully coexist with the United States and other western Democracies. This was ridiculous policy, Mao informed Moscow. Instead, a communist civilization could be built from the ruins of a world destroyed by nuclear war and they should embrace the Conflagration, not shy away from it. This spat by turns amused and concerned Americans. Khrushchev was viewed in America as the man who had brought the world to the brink of nuclear war less than a year earlier when he began shipping missiles to Cuba. President John Kennedy had placed a naval quarantine around the island and for several tense days in October, as Soviet ships steamed toward the nation ninety miles from Florida, it looked like there would be war. Americans were hardly ready to accept the Soviet leader as the voice of peace. And yet, here was a nation talking even more belligerently than Russia. Of course, if those two countries were carping at each other, it would make it harder for them to make common cause against the United States and its allies, as they had during the Korean War. Indeed, the Soviet Union and China had beefed up their common borders with additional troops and now eyed each other with deep suspicion.

The 1965 peace conference played out against this backdrop. With both the Soviet Union and China well-represented at the

World Peace Congress, the jockeying for leadership between them had gone on almost from the opening gavel. Now, that barely controlled struggle had broken free and the delegates were shouting at each other and shoving one another. Bertrand Russell, seeing the conference degenerating into the hooliganism of a European soccer match, pulled Reed toward him and suggested he go to the speaker's podium and begin singing. Reed did as requested. The guitar slung over his shoulder, Reed told the delegates that back in the United States, civil rights demonstrators frequently held each other's hands to weave themselves into a strong web to repel the attacks they knew would come. So please, he urged them, take the hand of your neighbor. When the group was slow to follow his commands, Reed told them to do it or he would come down into the audience and force them to hold hands. Some of the delegates chuckled and slowly, the men and women were clasping hands. Reed then told them that the civil rights demonstrators would sing as they stood shoulder to shoulder. Strumming his guitar, Reed began to sing, "We Shall Overcome," with its simple words repeated again and again. It worked. Soon nearly everyone was holding hands and singing. Only the Chinese declined to participate, but at least they were no longer actively trying to break up the session.[12]

The Soviets were pleased with Reed, not only because he brought peace back to the conference, but because of his pronouncements against American foreign policy. The chief delegate there cleared the way for Reed and his camera crew from *Welcome Saturday*, his Argentina television show, to travel to Moscow July 22 to interview Tereshkova. Back home in Buenos Aires, the U.S. Embassy was keeping an eye on Reed's movements. A memo to FBI Director J. Edgar Hoover outlined how the regional security officer at the embassy had pointed out two stories in the local paper, *El Mundo* (*The World*) in mid-July and again July 23. The articles detailed Reed's attendance at the congress and his travel plans to Russia and his expected return to Argentina July 28.[13]

Saturday nights belonged to Reed. Argentineans gathered around their television sets to watch his show. The program was nearly indistinguishable from the variety shows beamed out of Hollywood and New York back in the United States. Reed would come out, sing a few songs, introduce his guests and let them perform, if they were entertainers. If they were newsmakers and not entertainers, Reed would interview them, as Steve Allen or Johnny Carson had been doing. A couple weeks after his return from Finland and the Soviet Union, Reed rolled the tape of his interview of cosmonaut Valentina Tereshkova. It was a huge ratings success. The interview itself was fairly innocuous, with Tereshkova talking about what it was like in space and Reed's invitation to come visit Argentina and his wish that all people could live in peace. Yet the tenor of the interview was wrong for the times.

Argentina had lived under military rule from 1955 to 1958. That government had closely aligned itself with the United States. The Soviet Union and Communism were the enemy in this cold war and all things Russian were therefore evil and all things Western, inherently good. A civilian government was reinstalled in 1958, but just four years later, the military overthrew that president as well. For less than two years, Arturo Illia of the People's Radical Party had been ruling the country after the military again allowed free elections. He was a reformer who had terminated contracts of the larger U.S. petroleum companies drilling and refining oil in the country. He liberalized politics, lifting bans the military had placed on come political parties, including the Communist Party. He even went so far as trying to normalize relations with the Soviet Union, Cuba and other socialist countries. Reed had met the president a couple of times and considered him a friend. Illia's attempts to moderate the politics of his nation made life easier for Reed. "Considering the free atmosphere under the presidency of Arturo Illia, I had never had any serious difficulties," Reed said. "I could sing my songs, I made records, my name was on the hit lists, I played the male leading roles in films and I could still say what I thought about the political and social problems of the world."[14]

Illia did not have enough time to change everyone's thinking about the world, or to completely remake the government. So when Dean Reed, an idol to hundreds of thousands of Argentine youths, had a perfectly reasonable and pleasant conversation with a Soviet space hero, it was too much for the more conservative and reactionary members of Argentina's leadership. While there is no indication that the U.S. Embassy paid any attention to the interview, the still-functioning secret police needed no prompting. After the show, the political police arrived at the studio.

"Señor Reed, would you come with us please?"

"I don't think so. I'm tired and I want to go home," Reed replied.

"Señor Reed, as you can see, there are three of us and only one of you. And I can tell you that no one here at the station has the guts to take us on. Really, we have no qualms of beating your head in to gain your cooperation. But I would think those types of injuries would be very bad for your career."

Reed looked around and saw that the reputation of the secret police had done its job. The station manager, crew members, everyone had scattered to the far corners of the studio. They at least knew who had confronted him and could tell his wife if she inquired, so Reed followed the officers to the waiting car. They drove in silence and pulled up to an old building near the harbor.

The men escorted him into a room that had the spartan look of interrogation rooms the world over. Straight-backed chairs, a table and bright lights greeted the American. He was told to sit in one of the chairs and two of his captors came in the room with him and shut the door.

"Do you know why we've brought you here?"

"I really don't," Reed responded. "I've committed no crime. I've said nothing against the government. Hell, President Illia is a friend of mine. I think you guys have made a mistake."

"Did Moscow pay you for this broadcast?"

"No."

"Come now, Señor Reed. How much did they pay you?"

"Nothing. You are obviously talking about my interview with Valentina Tereshkova. The interview was my idea. She is the only woman to fly into outer space. I figured that would be interesting to my audience. It was nothing more than putting on a good television show."

"Don't play us for fools, Señor Reed. You went to Helsinki for a communist gathering. You traveled with our communists. You must be a communist and your communist bosses wanted you to put the space bitch on television."

"That's crap. I'm not a communist. I was lucky to have a chance to interview her."

"Did Moscow pay you for the broadcast?"

"No," Reed said, his voice rising.

"How much did they pay you?"

"Nothing," he shouted back.

His interrogator gave Reed a quick, hard slap.

"Do not raise your voice to me, Yankee communist. Let me explain to you what I think you are up to. You say Illia is your friend. But in truth, your real friends are Varela and the other communists trying to destroy Argentina. None of you think our president is doing enough of your bidding. Nor do your masters in Moscow. So they arrange for you to interview this space whore. In fact, they pay you because you are, after all, a greedy American. It's good propaganda for them. Maybe the stupid Argentine people will see the communists as fine, friendly people instead of the evil, conniving bastards that they are."

"A communist has never kidnapped me from my work, driven me to a secret hideout and slapped me," Reed replied.

"So, you do think that communists are better people than right-thinking capitalists here in Argentina, eh Señor Reed?"

"I think they are better than you. But I don't think they are any better, or worse, than President Illia."

"Again. Did Moscow pay you for the broadcast?"

"No."

"How much did they pay you?"

"Nothing."

"Why are you doing this Soviet propaganda?"

"I'm not doing Soviet propaganda. I believe art and sports and science are international. And especially scientists, athletes and artists must believe in peace. The politicians always trail behind. We are in the vanguard."

"So, you would be happy with peace at any price, even if it meant a communist takeover of Argentina? That is the thinking of a coward. But it confirms my suspicions. Moscow did pay you for your broadcast, didn't they?"

"No."

"How much did they pay you?"

"Nothing."

"Come clean with us, Señor Reed. We can keep this up all night. When I get tired, I can just turn it over to the next shift. And you know, some of them are not nearly as agreeable as I am."[15]

Reed's new friend wasn't bluffing. They questioned the singer for five hours. They offered him nothing to drink. They prevented him from using the toilet. In his writings, Reed revealed little about his emotions that night. He seemed intent on portraying his intelligence, the way he sized up the political situation. He was confident that the time, with Illia in power, was not right for them to persecute Reed or launch an anti-communist witch hunt. Reed's assessment of his predicament proved to be true, but as the third hour flipped into the fourth, he must have had doubts. After all, this was Reed's first arrest anywhere. Always before, he could take out ads or make inflammatory statements in interviews and the worse that happened was that the U.S. ambassador wanted to chat with him. This was different. He was being hustled away, under cover of darkness, to a secret place where no one need know where he was for hours or even days. His wife could call every police station in Argentina and never find out where he was. There was no tradition of charging or releasing someone within thirty-six hours or allowing the arrested man a lawyer or even a phone call. Eventually, hoping they shook up the cocky American, they sent him home, tired but unharmed. The arrest had the opposite, but not quite equal, effect on Reed. When he opened the door to his house, he was sapped and nearly lifeless. Patricia put him to bed. After a long sleep, Reed awoke to his wife telling him that the couple were now in serious trouble and they needed to rely more on their friends. He took that advice and began making regular phone calls to Paton Price, other friends and sympathetic newspaper reporters. The arrest caused another reaction in Reed, a more powerful one than the transitory fear and fatigue. He now saw himself as immune to the arrows of the powerful. He could challenge the government, any government, and nothing would happen to him. "Dean made light of it a lot of times," Patricia said.

"He would say, 'there is no way a bullet could get us.' So he would get the energy and push more."[16]

Patricia, too, was infected by Reed's radical fever, although she tried to apply the cold compress of reality. They had lived well in Mexico, had a grand villa in Buenos Aires and Reed could salve his conscience by giving concerts to the poor and the union organizers. That was not enough for Reed and after his return from Helsinki he started telling Patricia that they had to change their lifestyle. "That was a blow to me," she said. "I believe in charity work. I promised I would tone it down a little bit."[17] The legions of poor who were kept sealed off from the wealthy of Buenos Aires by the walls of the barrio were suddenly as visible to her as they were to her husband. Frequently, she would walk from her villa and enter the barrio carrying food and blankets. On one of the visits, Patricia entered a hovel and saw a child lying on an old blanket on the dirt floor. The child was running a high fever. Patricia helped the child's mother and after a few hours left for home. She stopped first at the clinic and beseeched doctors there to return with her, but they refused. When Patricia went back the following day, she tried to convince the mother to let the wealthy American take the child to the hospital, but the mother was afraid to let her daughter leave. She refused Patricia's offer. On the third night, as Patricia held her, the child died.[18] Reed was away on a concert tour, but when he returned, his grief-stricken wife poured out the details of what she had witnessed in the barrio. Reed had witnessed similar scenes, but the raw emotion Patricia brought to the death of a child moved him to write a song, "The Things I Have Seen."

> So many times in my life, I look at my people and say,
> that I must be from another earth, or at least from another day.
>
> I've seen a man because he is black, not be allowed to sleep,
> I've seen this man when he is hungry, not be allowed to eat.
>
> I've seen a man because he was poor, bow to another man. I've
> seen a man kill another, because he was from another land.
>
> I've watched men who thought their God was better than all
> the rest

kill a man to save his soul. I doubt in peace they rest.

I've seen many people with disease, and many times death did come
Just because the man was poor and the doctor he wouldn't come.
When will they learn before they do harm, to look for the truth throughout.
And only through searching this whole world will they find what the world's all about.

I hope that before I leave this earth, I'll be able to find, a place where the people love instead of hate, a land that I can call mine."[19]

Most people go through an entire lifetime with only one or two moments of heroics or terror. The young American couple packed in several in a matter of weeks. One evening, the Reeds were returning home from the city when Dean spotted a house fire. He slammed on the brakes and leaped from the car, with Patricia close behind. Neighbors had formed a ragtag bucket brigade, passing buckets of water from person to person with the last one flinging it on the flames. The Reeds took a spot in the line of volunteers even though the smoke pouring out of the windows, doors and cracks made it clear they were losing the fight. Reed asked the man next to him if everyone was out of the house and was told that they thought so. But a man's screams from inside proved them wrong.

"Patti, I'm going in to get him," Reed said.

"I'll go with you," she replied.

"No, you stay out here. I'll handle this," he said and started heading into the smoke.

"Okay, but wait, Dean. I've got blankets in the car. Soak 'em in water and wrap them around your mouth and head to protect you from the smoke."

Reed agreed and they sprinted to the car, grabbed several blankets and shoved them into the water buckets. Reed grabbed one, held it over his mouth and nose and headed in. Patricia was right behind him, but now there was no time to argue. They made it to the middle of the house without seeing anyone. The smoke was getting thicker and the visibility was down to an arm's length. They heard another scream from farther inside.

"Stay here this time," Reed commanded sharply. "The smoke's getting worse, I'll need to follow your voice to find my way out."

"Yes. Hurry."

Reed picked his way along, bent over, trying to stay beneath the rising smoke. The blanket was working as a filter, but wisps of smoke were beginning to find the openings into Reed's airways. He found an older man huddled in the corner of a back room, coughing and terrified. Reed grabbed the man's hand and shouted to him in Spanish to follow him out.

"Patti, where are you?"

"This way, Dean. You can make it. Keep coming. I can't see you yet. Keep following my voice. Come on, baby, back out the way you came."

Reed homed in on his wife's voice. He was hacking and coughing now, just like the man clinging to his hand. Reed's eyes stung and watered from the smoke, making it impossible to see. He was moving blindly. He knew if a hole opened up in front of him, he would fall in. He had to trust and hope now, and he moved quickly to the voice. No holes opened up, Reed didn't run into any walls and within seconds, Patricia had his hand. She threw the last blanket around the old man and they retreated out the front door.

As they stumbled out into the air and collapsed in the yard, all three of them coughing and gasping for pure air, a shout and then applause went up from the crowd. They dropped their buckets and gathered around the trio. When the man finally could see through his watering eyes, he was startled again when he recognized his rescuer as the famous singer and actor. He thanked the Reeds profusely. And then he asked for an autograph.[20]

Reed's friend Varela was not done working on the singer's social conscience. One afternoon, not long after returning from Helsinki but before the attack on the Reed house, Varela called and asked if he could have dinner at Reed's house and bring a guest. Reed enjoyed having company and agreed immediately. An hour later, the doorbell rang and there was Varela. Next to him, the Reeds' surprise, was not another well-dressed intellectual, but somebody who appeared to be an older peasant. His face was partially hidden by his well-worn coat collar and a hat pulled low. What was impossible to hide was that the man was in poor health. He wheezed loudly with every breath and he hunched over, as though there might be more air for his weak lungs closer to the floor. Patricia recognized the wheezing and the struggle for air as asthma, an affliction she shared. Patricia ushered him into the bathroom and handed him the medicine she had brought from the United States. She showed him how to use the inhaler and then left. But now she had seen his face and she knew he was no peasant, although she was having a hard time putting a name to him. As she walked back toward the kitchen, names flitted through her head until one stopped her in her tracks. CHE GUEVARA.[21]

Ernesto "Che" Guevara, one of the most famous visages of the 1960s, was born and raised in Argentina, the son of a fallen aristocratic family. He was afflicted by severe asthma, which sometimes confined him to bed for days at a time. But he fought the restrictions the condition imposed and eventually became a physician. In 1952, at the age of twenty-three, he jumped on his motorcycle in Buenos Aires and headed out on a ten-thousand-mile journey that took him through Chile, Peru and Bolivia and cemented his feeling that the people of South America were badly treated. In 1955, a CIA-backed overthrow of the Guatemala government sent him packing to Mexico, convinced now that Marxism was the answer and the United States was the problem. In Mexico City, Guevara met Fidel Castro and they became fast friends. By 1957, the two men and a small band of followers were living in the Sierra Maestra mountains of Cuba. Just two years later, they routed the army of dictator Fulgencio Batista and instituted a Communist government on the island, with Guevara as Castro's right-hand man. In 1965, Guevara and Castro had a falling out, perhaps staged, and Guevara disappeared. Much of the Western world wondered where he had gone or even if he was still alive. Eventually, he resurfaced in Africa, leading another rebel band. It went badly and then he tried again in Bolivia, only to be killed by government troops in 1967.

But now, here he was back in Buenos Aires, his home turf. He had been sleeping by the river, in the barrio, and it was easy for Patricia to put the name to him because "I was in love with him." Guevara joined her in the kitchen and prepared sauce for the spaghetti the four would eat. After dinner, the men smoked cigars and drank coffee and brandy while Reed played his guitar. Eventually, the men got down to the business of the world. They spoke about nuclear testing, socialism versus religion, teaching the peasants before giving them weapons, the defeat of the CIA-backed Batista supporters at the Bay of Pigs and assassination attempts on Castro and Guevara by the CIA. And always, woven throughout the discussion, were the peasants of South America. They spoke of their hunger, their unemployment and their brutalization by a system that cared nothing for the poor while bestowing more riches upon the wealthy. It was not until four in the morning that Varela and Guevara, under cover of darkness, took their leave. The meeting left Reed with much to think about and it changed him.[22]

"Dean was very serious. He wasn't playing games anymore," Patricia said. "He did a lot of thinking after Helsinki. We had been the cute couple. He said, 'I have something to tell you, Patti. I think I am going to be a communist.' I cried. I said, 'No, you can't be a card-carrying communist. They are the enemy. Che did it because he was born in South America. You were born in America, where they have food and good schools. Be a socialist, be a pacifist, that's okay.' We didn't talk for a few days. Then he said, 'I will go without you.' When he turned into a revolutionary and socialist, the bitterness started in on him. After he met Che, he decided he wanted to be a revolutionary and a socialist."[23]

Later that year, Patricia had to deal with another tragedy. Again she suffered a miscarriage and it was beginning to look as though the couple would never have children. But this time, a doctor examined her and discovered that her miscarriages had nothing to do with the abortion she had in Mexico, as she feared. Instead, he found that she had two uteruses and a septum dividing them. The doctor operated, removed the septum and united the uteruses into one.[24]

It was becoming increasingly evident to Dean and Patricia that they would have to leave Argentina. Besides being targeted in their own home, they could see that Illia's hold on power was weakening. Some members of the government were now openly accusing Reed of being a Communist Party member and therefore a threat to Argentina, charges Reed denied. On March 25, 1966, Reed traveled to San Martin, Argentina, to participate in International Days of Protest. The event was designed to lend support to the North Vietnamese who were fighting the South Vietnamese and American troops in a war to unify the country under a communist regime. Reed sang and spoke against U.S. involvement in Southeast Asia.[25] It was Reed's last appearance in Argentina that year. On March 28, the newspaper *La Razon* (*Reason*) carried a paid advertisement signed by Reed in which he told his fans that the time had come for him and Patricia to leave their country. Reed wrote that they were departing with tears because of the happiness and goodness they received during their year there. "We are part of you and I hope that all of my acts and statements have been well understood since their only purpose was to manifest my desires for peace and the well-being of all of the peoples of the world," Reed wrote.[26]

As it happened, their timing was exquisite. Three months later, the army moved against Illia and his People's Radical Party. They installed one of their own, Gen. Juan Carlos Ongani, as president and Argentina's policies returned to protecting the rich and arresting anyone who suggested dividing the wealth more fairly. Patricia remembered that they left Argentina at the urging of their friends, including Varela, who could see the coming coup. People lined the roads to the airport, waving at the couple and throwing flowers. Thousands more were at the airport to see them off and their old friends, the Argentine political police, kept a close eye on the proceedings. As the plane took off, Dean and Patricia held each other and Patricia sobbed into her husband's chest.[27]

Conquering the Soviet Union

*E*ven revolutionaries need a vacation. When their plane touched down in Paris, Reed bought a Peugot automobile and the couple hit the road. For the next two months, they roared along the roadways of France, Austria and Germany and then passed through Checkpoint Charlie in West Berlin and toured the Communist countries of East Germany, Czechoslovakia and Hungary. Their first stop back in the Democratic West was Italy and then over to Spain.

The West was fun and for the girl from Southern California, it was a romantic way to forget the stress of the final months in Argentina. But Patricia's mood soured as they entered the Eastern Bloc. Just twenty years removed from the atrocities of World War II and the Nazis, Patricia saw too many reminders of the terror Adolf Hitler unleashed in those countries. When the Communist regimes wrested control from Germany, they removed freedom. In Hungary, she could still see bullet holes in the buildings where Soviet troops quashed the rebellion in 1956 as the Hungarian government tried to move away from the Soviet sphere and toward a more capitalistic and free state. "I thought it was terrible," she said of the trip through Eastern Europe. "People were scared, they wouldn't smile, wouldn't talk to me and I'm used to being talked to. I was scared at all times."

Reed was not scared. He was taking it all in and enjoying being places most Americans were no longer visiting. He couldn't understand his wife's trepidation and crying jags and became annoyed with her as she spent more time in the hotel and less out strolling the sidewalks. In Prague, the strain became so great that Reed threatened to leave his wife once and for all. Something was happening to him. When Patricia would point out the fear in the eyes of the locals, Reed would shrug it off and point out that nobody was going hungry as were the children in the barrios of Argentina, no one was denied medical attention because they were poor.[1]

After the road trip, Dean and Patricia picked an unlikely spot to settle down. They rented an apartment outside of Madrid, Spain. It had all the amenities, including a swimming pool and tennis courts, but the government could not have been more antithetical to Reed, what with Fascist dictator Francisco Franco entering his third decade of absolute power. Still, Reed was planning to make two movies, including one that would be a joint venture between Spanish and Argentine film companies and directed by Enrique Carreras of Argentina.[2] Spain also had a strong Argentine expatriate community that included former president Juan Peron.

Reed grasped the strangeness of a leftist in a right-wing country. He and Patricia thumbed their noses at some of Franco's petty laws. They necked in the back of a cab in violation of laws against kissing in public. Still, Patricia was nervous during their stay. Reed shrugged it off and turned his attention to the films and playing a few club dates. He also banged away on his portable typewriter, writing about the trip through Europe. He sent the pages off to Paton Price, who sold the stories to newspapers and magazines in the United States and sent the money back to the young couple. Even as he wrote, Reed's next trip was taking shape. His performance during the raucous Helsinki conference the previous summer, and more important, his anti-American statements, had caught the eye of one of the Soviet delegates. The official stance of the Soviet government was that rock 'n' roll was more capitalist decadence and not allowed in the USSR. But the Soviet Peace Committee, backed by the government, made an offer that Reed could not resist. They invited him to tour the Soviet Union and perform in eleven cities across that vast empire. Reed was thrilled by the offer and accepted immediately. Even

more than he had in South America, Dean Reed would be breaking new ground. It would provide an opportunity to spread his
message of peace between people of the world, and it would re-
verberate with the audience because here was an American, their
enemy, bringing the message.

Reed saw another big opportunity in the invitation, this one
not nearly as altruistic as world peace. Whenever the occasional
American entertainer did perform in Russia, usually a folk singer,
or maybe some choral group or orchestra, it warranted at least small
media attention in the States. But Reed was going to the Soviet
Union as the very first rock singer. Not Elvis, not the Beatles, not
Diana Ross and the Supremes, not even his old friends the Everly
Brothers could claim that honor. No, when the Communist regime
finally decided to loosen its tight cultural control, they turned to
DEAN REED to bring them rock music. Surely, this would gen-
erate huge publicity back in the States. Even the stupidest record
company guys (and Reed knew there were plenty of those) had to
realize that kind of publicity was worth a recording contract and a
quick tour of the United States to cash in on the novelty of the
man who rocked the USSR. Reed was going to give the Soviets
everything he had ever learned about putting on a show.

As usual, Reed's appearances were not cleared with the United
States government and embassy officials in Moscow were surprised to see posters of an American and a review of his October
4 performance in the Communist paper, *Pravda*.[3] The embassy had
no idea who Reed was and were intrigued by *Pravda*'s statements
that he had a "remarkable biography," and "left his country as a
sign of protest against the unjust war in Vietnam." J. C. Guthrie of
the American Embassy wrote a three-page report on Reed's visit.
Admitting that Reed never came to the embassy and embassy staff
could not get tickets to his shows in Moscow or any of the other
cities he toured, they had to rely on information from others.

As a performer, he has been a smashing success," Guthrie
wrote. "Tickets to his Moscow performances were virtually impossible to obtain, even for Soviet theater people,
wise in the ways of ticket procurement. The fight for tickets apparently threatened to become disorderly at times
and the crowd reaction was almost a Soviet equivalent of

the screaming reception accorded the Beatles in the Western countries.

An American reporter who managed to talk with Reid [*sic*] and attend a Moscow performance reports the following. His program covered a wide range of songs: rock and roll, calypso, Negro spirituals and songs from Broadway hits. He sang one of his own songs of protest over Vietnam. Reid has a good voice and very effective stage presence and contact with the audience. He induced audience participation, dancing the twist with girls from the crowd in the aisles and literally forcing the audience members to join in some songs, in spite of the unfamiliarity with this practice. The audience response was electric and apparently not confined to the jet set of the younger generation."

A Canadian diplomat saw Reed perform before a nearly sold-out audience of twenty thousand people at a Moscow stadium on November 26 and agreed he had a good voice but mediocre guitar skills.[4]

The American embassy was aware of Reed's professionalism. As usual, Reed had no band of his own, but put together a combo of Soviet musicians to tour with him and back him on his songs. After a couple weeks of rehearsals and now several shows, Reed and the band had become a tight unit. The drummer, bass player and other musicians were getting a feel for this strange syncopation, and more important, they were becoming very familiar with their American leader and what he would do onstage. A half-hour before one of his shows, Reed was getting worried. Vladimir, his drummer, had not arrived. The theater manager scurried up to Reed and whispered something to his translator.

"Vladimir just called. He's sick and can't perform tonight," the translator told Reed.

"Really. Well, I guess I can't perform tonight either," Reed responded.

The stage manager blanched.

"He says the rest of the band is here. The audience is here. They came to hear you. They won't even know your drummer is missing," the translator said for the manager.

"You're right. They came to hear Dean Reed. But without a drummer, it is not the full Dean Reed experience. I'm not going on until you get Vladimir over here."

"But he is sick. Surely, you can understand and just go out there and sing and play your guitar."

Reed fixed the theater manager with a hard stare and spoke slowly and tersely to his interpreter.

"Tell him I'm a professional. I work hard at this and I expect everybody else to work just as hard. I'm not going to put on some fucking half-assed show and embarrass myself. Understand?"

"He says you have a contract to perform tonight. If you don't perform, you don't get paid. And he'll tell party officials and they will cancel the rest of your tour and ship you out of here. You'll never perform in the USSR again."

Reed gave a caustic little laugh.

"Tell the little shit not to try negotiating with a capitalist. It's him who needs me. The party officials are right over there. Go ahead and tell them. In fact, I think I'll tell them myself that my fucking drummer is not here and he's screwing up the whole deal."

The manager told Reed not to approach the party officials and the two men went around and around, but Reed refused to budge. The show's start time came and went. Half an hour went by and the crowd, not used to shows starting late, was confused. Forty years of Communist rule had cowed large groups so there were not the chants or catcalls American audiences employ when bands are slow to take the stage. Instead, there was a quiet murmuring. Finally, Reed agreed to a compromise. The theater manager found a substitute drummer to start the show and promised to get Vladimir to the theater. After the long delay, Reed bounded onstage and the crowd roared. Halfway through his show, the manager dragged a badly hung-over Vladimir into the building and he slipped in behind the drum set between numbers.[5]

The embassy monitored Reed's interviews with the papers. In one of them, Reed said his favorite saying from Latin America was "If a young person is not a Communist, he is a coward." He added that although he is unfortunately not related to John Reed (the American author who lived in Russia and wrote about its Communist Revolution) he always tried to be like him. He concluded by saying that Soviet young people are the happiest of any he has met in the world.

"It is the Embassy's conclusion that Reid [*sic*] has let himself be used by the Soviets, especially through their publications, to serve the Soviet anti-United States campaign related to Vietnam. His public appearances, however, have had the primary effect of exposing a large and delighted Soviet audience to some of the types of popular music currently in vogue among the young in the West."[6]

For Reed, it was like Chile 1961. Huge crowds, sold-out shows and an adoring public, who, although they didn't know what to do, were soon following Reed's every lead. Soviet teenagers were used to performers who stood stock-still at the microphone and sang their ballads and folk songs. Reed was like nothing they had seen or heard. Sometimes he wore tight pants, a white shirt and a formal vest but no tie. Other times, he would don a mod outfit of striped bell-bottoms and paisley shirt. The music had an infectious beat and the performer was everywhere, moving across the stage, jumping down into aisles, pulling the girls out of their chairs to dance with him as he sang. He used his other old trick and learned the Russian words for "You are very beautiful," and would say it to the young girl he had just danced with, the girl's mother, or an old lady sitting in the audience. The ploy never failed. The women always smiled and melted before him. The guys were enjoying the shows just as much and the audiences couldn't get enough of him. "I remember a concert in Russia," said Patricia, who accompanied her husband on that first tour. "I'm walking with the music and clapping and the audience didn't know what to do. But he (their government escort) was flirting with me and he started doing what I was doing and then the audience did."[7]

Before the first performance, Reed was unsure of himself and his set list. All he knew about the Soviet people was what he read in U.S. newspapers and magazines. The combination of Soviet control over its people and visiting reporters and the journalists' own bias toward the world's other nuclear superpower had resulted in a stereotyped sameness. The reports consistently told of a repressed society where the people stood in line for scarce goods. But they also stood in formation as part of the largest army in the world, ready to swarm across Western Europe as soon as their power-crazed leaders gave the word.

"It was still very difficult for me in Moscow at that time," Reed recalled of his first concert at the Estraden Theater, directly across from the Kremlin. "About the Soviet people—what they thought, what they felt, what they loved—I knew, of course, even less. Much of my repertoire at that time must have appeared strange to this audience. 'Besame Mucho,' for example, this sentimental love song from Latin America, the rock songs and cowboy songs and even hit tunes like 'I Did It My Way,' which at that time had been around the world for a long time, but I thought that the hit tunes had not gone behind the 'Iron Curtain' which at that time I still believed existed. But when I sang, what became immediately apparent to me was that the Soviet people have a refined feeling for the simple things of life. The public in the Estraden Theater heard from the cowboy song that it is about people who want to have their fun after hard work, whether they ride noisily through the streets of a small city in Texas, sit by the campfire in the prairie or court a girl. Somehow, there was a sense that such a song was expressing the same feelings as a Russian farm boy when he played his harmonica in the evening on the village street, danced the Gopak or climbed up after the neighbor's daughter. It only took about fifteen minutes and I didn't feel like a stranger anymore. I was thousands of kilometers from my home but the people in front of me were suddenly as close to me as one human being can be."[8]

Back in his early days in Chile, Reed had met Lew Jaschin, a famous Soviet soccer player who was in South America to play in the 1962 World Cup matches. The meeting prompted a small incident when the soccer player invited Reed to be his guest at the match and Reed reciprocated with an invitation to one of his shows. Chilean political and opinion leaders suggested that Reed was cozying up with the Soviets because he was a closet communist. Reed denied it, but as a compromise, he had a Santiago radio station make the arrangements for the team to see Reed perform. The soccer players never made it to the show, but the two men became friends, and here in the Soviet Union, Jaschin attended one of Reed's shows and joined him backstage afterward. Reed was happy to see his old friend amidst all the Russians who were eager to become his new pal. The tour was becoming a big party for Reed. Everywhere, people wanted to shake his hand. Champagne and vodka flowed freely. Reed tried to refrain because he wanted to be sharp for his shows and because he had never developed much of a taste for alcohol. For the first week of this tour, Reed and Patricia found themselves in bear hugs that would soon give way to vodka and round after round of toasts. They toasted friendship, they toasted peace, they toasted Reed, they toasted Patricia and the couple in turn toasted their hosts and new friends. Soon everyone was drunk and the next morning, Reed and Patricia would be hung over. They slogged through their days until the oxygen and exercise forced out the booze. It only took a few days of repeating that scene before the young couple decided that youthful vigor could not defeat practiced drinkers. But trickery might, and they could still maintain the good relations they had forged. Nearby plants started absorbing spirits through their roots and the Americans made more frequent bathroom trips, returning with considerably less in their glasses. Patricia even carried an empty bottle in her purse and would surreptitiously fill the bottle with her drinks. Whether the Russian hosts noticed, they never said anything and the parties continued. Reed and Patricia managed to hang onto their sobriety.[9]

The American was being paid half in Soviet rubles and half in U.S. dollars. The rubles were worthless on the world market but they could buy merchandise in Russia. While Reed rehearsed, Patricia would visit museums and theaters for the history and culture before turning her attention to shopping. She bought big Russian hats and warm fur coats, dishes and real silverware. She bought a movie camera so she could record much of what they saw.[10] Patricia was enjoying the tour. Reed was pleased with his reception and he was happy to show off his wife to the band, the Russian officials and music stars he met backstage. Patricia, as she often did since early in their life together, carried a 35 mm camera with her and took photos to document the shows and life on the road. Patricia had a good eye for shots that could also be used as publicity shots later to boost her husband's career. In letters home to her mom, she described the eighteen-piece orchestra Reed had traveling with him, the selection of songs from rock 'n' roll to folk to his own compositions and some Harry Belafonte calypso tunes. He always included Chubby Checker's 1961 hit, "The Twist," because it was an easy dance. Reed's little professional secret was that he couldn't really dance to his own music, didn't have the rhythm to let his hips and legs go where the beat might take them. The twist was his camouflage and it never failed to leave the girls thinking he was the dancing king.

It all worked beautifully. In one of his first concerts, Reed returned for six encores before finally retiring to his dressing room. But twenty minutes later, the officials handling the concert pleaded with him to go back out because the crowd would not leave. When he did, a small riot broke out as the fans stormed the stage to get to the singer. The next morning, the phone began ringing at eight o'clock. Russian reporters wanted to interview him and the calls lasted most of the day. The tour took them to Leningrad where it was cold and snowy and then south to Georgia and Armenia and cities along the Black Sea where it was warm and reminded Patricia of California. Eventually, they headed back to Moscow for more shows in the capital.[11] But as Reed pushed on to another Soviet republic at the end of the tour, Patricia stayed behind in Moscow with one of the officials who helped organize Reed's tour. Patricia was pregnant again and while Reed was away, the familiar trauma of a miscarriage visited her. She was rushed to a Moscow hospital and a telegram was dispatched to Reed, seeking his permission to complete the abortion. Reed wired his permission, then sent another telegram, saying "Patti, be brave for I love you." He followed that with another wire that read, "Our love is tall as mountains, our love is deep as sea, our love is as warm summer day, our love will always be a French kiss.—Deano[12]

While in the Kremlin hospital, Patricia met wives of revolutionary leaders from Mozambique. The Soviet Union was backing their attempt to overthrow the government and Patricia was impressed by the stories the wives told. When the couple finally reunited, Patricia related to Reed all she had heard. Reed turned her stories into a song, "Freedom is the Word of Today."

People down in Africa
Mozambique to Angola
Rhodesia and South Africa
They want their freedom today.

The brave ones of Viet Cong
Know from where the bombs they come
And they turn their guns to the sun
For they want their freedom today.

The working class of Italy
A future of justice they see
And they march so as to be free
For they want their freedom today

From Brazil to the Gaucho land
The people are beginning to stand
Liberty they will demand
For they want their freedom today

And right here in the USA
The people are beginning to say
That injustice has had its day
For we want our freedom today![13]

His two-month tour of the Soviet Union was a huge success by any measure. The crowds were large and enthusiastic. They liked the music and they liked the American. But somehow, the Iron Curtain blocked the news. If record executives heard about the excitement Reed created in Russia, they didn't give any indication. The weeks turned to months and Reed heard nothing from back home. Following the tour, Reed headed back to the couple's apartment in Spain, but with plans to find a new home in Italy. On the way, he stopped in Prague, Czechoslovakia, where he performed several songs on state television and did radio interviews. As he had with some of the rubles in the Soviet Union, Reed donated his performance fee to Aid to Vietnam. Technically, Reed was now supporting the North Vietnamese, the same fighters who were not only killing their South Vietnamese brothers, but also in increasing numbers, American troops. The donation was spurred by practical considerations. The Soviet Union and its satellites used currency that could not be easily converted to dollars or other western currency. While there were ways around the problem, they were complicated and Reed realized it would be easier for him, and gain him greater standing with his hosts, by making it a donation. Reed had given the issue some thought and developed a justification for sending money to his country's enemy. "The people in Vietnam, and in all the countries of the world, have the right to arrange their affairs as they like, to settle their internal problems if need be by revolution. Our soldiers have no business in Vietnam, it is an aggression."[14]

Dean Reed was no longer the pacifist his friend Paton Price had made him. It would take a few more months to finish the intellectual journey, but Reed was beginning to view armed conflict as legitimate if used in the service of revolution. If the revolution was on behalf of people trying to install a government that would serve all the citizens, Reed was fine with armed insurrection. When that conversion was complete, he tried to explain it to his father. "You mention that you 'hate' Paton Price because of the bad influence that he has had on me," Reed wrote to Cyril. "I think that I must tell you that Paton hasn't written to me in over 5 months, because HE DOES NOT AGREE WITH ME POLITICALLY EITHER! For you see, Paton is a pacifist—in the true sense of the word—he does not believe that one man has the right to take another man's life. I don't believe that anymore. I believe that every Vietnamese has the right and duty to shoot any North American soldier that sets his foot upon Vietnamese soil. He has the right and duty to shoot down any foreign plane that is flying over his country burning and maiming his women and children. So you see, Paton and I now differ, for he believes that even they are wrong to kill. I believe that all killing is a wrong, but that everything is relative. Obviously, the man who is defending his land and country and home has a right to kill an intruder who is invading his home and land. That is only just."[15]

Reed had no luck changing his father's view and never expected he would. But he spent no time dwelling on it. He had larger audiences to convert. Reed's changed thinking came just as he embarked on his most productive years as an actor and as a radical.

"Lights, Camera, Deportation"

9 n the late 1960s, Italy was a second Hollywood for American actors. Clint Eastwood, Yul Brynner and others traveled to southern Europe to make films. While Hollywood had been cold to Reed, Italy's welcome was as warm as the breeze off the Mediterranean. Reed was pursed by directors and starred in movies as fast as they could make them. The Italian directors cast him opposite such well-known performers as Anita Ekberg and Nadja Tiller. In 1967, it was *Buckaroo*. In 1968, it was *Twenty Steps to Death*, and *The Three Flowers*, a joint Italian and Spanish production. And in 1969, he made *Death Knocks Twice, Machine Gun Baby Face, The Cousins of Zorro*, and *The Pirates of the Green Island*. In all, he made eight films after moving to Italy.

But it was 1968's *Adios Sabata*, that brought Reed tantalizingly close to the American fame that had eluded him for nearly ten years. The movie was one of the Spaghetti Westerns made in Italy but with American audiences in mind. The leading role went to one of the top actors of the time, Yul Brynner. Idolized for his role in *The King and I*, and the lead in the 1960 classic, *The Magnificent Seven*, Brynner was still a marquee name, even if his films had lately fallen short of box office expectations. Reed had second billing behind Brynner and his role kept him on the screen right up to the closing credits. United Artists released the film in the States in 1971, but even as it was being made, Reed convinced himself that at last American audiences, and more important, American directors, would see his work and approach him to star in their movies. While the film still turns up occasionally on cable channels, the calls from Hollywood never came. Reed's behavior on the movie sets was changing, too. He would often get up and make a speech in the morning to the rest of the cast, telling them how he felt about the problems of the world. He would make speeches about helping the poor, liberating black people in America, getting U.S. troops out of Vietnam. "These are shallow people and they didn't tolerate it," Patricia said. "I said, 'Dean, get all the money you can so you can fight money with money.' The rich were saying, 'to hell with Dean Reed.' He pissed off Yul Brynner. When Dean walked by, Yul would say, 'that's the communist bastard.' "[1]

In August 1967, during a break from filming, Reed and Patricia drove into the mountains outside Rome to a resort that was well-known for its downhill skiing. In the summertime, the resort was nearly as popular for its scenery. The couple hiked into the woods and Patricia constructed a lean-to out of branches. The couple had nearly broken up before Christmas 1966, not long after the Russian tour. Patricia, in fact, had flown back to California to stay with her mother for a couple of months and for a few weeks took up with an American Football League player. Reed eventually flew to California and they reconciled. Now they were going to try again to have a baby, and they wanted to conceive it in the high country under the stars. That night, they cooked their dinner over an open fire. As the summer sun dipped behind the mountains and dusk turned to dark, Reed and Patricia sat before the fire, sipping wine and talking. Reed stroked his wife's long hair, kissed and began unbuttoning her blouse. They slowly removed each other's clothes and made love while the cool mountain air caressed their naked bodies.[2]

Not long afterward, doctors confirmed that Patricia was pregnant. Reed headed to Mongolia, a trip the Italian press likened to the journeys of their own Marco Polo centuries earlier. It was hardly on the same scale, but singing rock 'n' roll in another Communist-controlled country was blazing new trails. He traveled around the region, sent pictures and stories back for publication in the Italian newspapers and met with the Dali Lama. After a month, he returned to his wife and brought her gifts of the finest silks.[3] Patricia's pregnancy was difficult and for several weeks she was confined to bed. Both mother and father worried. They had been through this so many times now, in so many countries: the joy of the doctor's pronouncement that Patricia was with child, the anticipation and then the devastating gloom when something would go wrong and Patricia's body rejected the fetus. When Patricia delivered a healthy baby girl in a Rome hospital on May 2, 1968, it seemed a miracle to the couple. After seven miscarriages, to finally hold the product of their love deeply moved both parents. Reed smothered his wife in dozens of roses that he piled on top of her in the hospital room, overpowering the usual hospital smells of disinfectant. He held Ramona, cooed to her and then went back to their home and did what he so often did at special moments. He wrote. This time, it was a letter to his daughter, who was given the names Ramona Chimene Guevara Price Reed. In many ways, the letter bore a striking resemblance to the old yearly letters Reed used to write himself on his birthday. This letter to his daughter summed up what he had learned on his own journey, and from whom he had learned it.

Dear Ramona,

This is my first letter to you, my daughter, born into this world so unexpectedly quick on May 2nd. Patricia and I chose your names today, and I am sure you will do justice to each of the five very different names ... It's quite a handful, I know, but there are reasons for each one.

Ramona ... will remind you that your ancestors on your mother's side were Indians. It will remind you of the brave and courageous battle that your people fought when they defended their land. But the most important thing is that it will remind you of the important role that nature played in the life of your people, and in the lives of your mother and father. Because you were conceived on a bed of grass, and only the leaves on the trees hid the love of two people from the eyes of the stars. You, and your mother and father were, at that moment, one with nature, and I hope that it will make you as free and independent as the animals in the forest, and the birds in the sky. You will be united with nature because you will understand that you are a living being like all others, that are evolution's children as you are yourself.

Chimene … will remind you of that night that I, your father, finally had the sense and the courage to ask your mother to be my wife. It will remind you of your mother and of her womanliness. Your mother and I saw a film, *El Cid*, for me that was a very memorable day. The hero was a very brave man who rode a white charger, who had dedicated his life to this people. And his wife, the beautiful Doña Chimene, devoted her life to him. Patricia became my wife because she believed I was such a man in shining armor on a white horse. Life showed that the armor lost its shine and that the white horse turned gray, but her romantic womanliness was unchanged. So your mother wished you to carry this name Chimene, so you will become such a woman.

The name Guevara … will remind you of the qualities that every man and woman should make their own. The man who carried this name did not live his life to fulfill his own wishes, but rather to serve all mankind. You, my daughter, will one day be able to judge whether your father always behaved correctly or not. And I will always do my best to honor this name. Because a man's life only has value if he dedicated it to his neighbor, to the search and the battle for a more just and human world.

Price … will remind you that you must find your own truth, and that you must defend this truth without fearing the consequences. Because the man who bore this name devoted his life to the search for truth, and when he believed that he had found it, he was brave enough to defend it against the world. He never turned away from what he felt in his conscience to be right, even if he had to go to jail for it. This man became my best friend. Your opinions may change several times throughout your life, because knowledge only comes to us drop by drop, slowly and sometimes against our will, but only in this way you will find your own truth.

Reed ... will remind you of your grandmother and your grandfather, who brought up your father with many self-sacrifices. You are also part of them. The name Reed will also remind you of honesty and integrity with which your grandfather lived his life, and of the love that your grand-mother gave to me, your father. Both these things contrib-uted to make me what I am, and both of them will love you the way I do. But the name Reed will always remind you of the most important person in my life. The one who did not bear the name of Reed from birth, but took it on, knowing that it would bring her joy and happiness in the future, as well as tears and sorrow. This person is Pa-tricia, who had to suffer so much to bring you into the world. Remember the one who had to spend so many painful hours in hospitals before she could, full of hope, face the hour in which you were born. She has already wept so many tears for you, and will surely weep often again before you have grown up. She has given me the strength to fight. I have learned from her what love is, and what mutual respect and patience mean. She understands that when I stand up for a better life for mankind I AM ALSO FULFILLING A RESPONSIBILITY Toward HER AND YOU, RAMONA, BECAUSE YOU ARE BOTH PART OF MANKIND.

These are your names, my child. Bear them with pride. Your mother and I love you, and will do everything we can so that you and your life will do these names justice. SLEEP WELL, MY CHILD.

Your father."[4]

While Reed was making movies and becoming a father, he didn't neglect his duties as a raconteur. By now, he had turned much of his attention to the Vietnam War and the United States government's increasingly bloody efforts to prop up the South Vietnamese government and its army, which had proven itself inca-pable of fending off the troops from North Vietnam. In this regard,

Reed was no different than hundreds of thousands of young men and women back in the States who were mounting huge demonstrations on college campuses, selective service offices and federal buildings throughout the country, demanding an end to the war. Reed's good friend Marv Davidov, for instance, was leading regular protests against Honeywell's corporate headquarters and production plants in Minneapolis and its suburbs because Honeywell was one of the chief manufacturers of bombs and other instruments of war used in Vietnam. But unlike many of his ideological cousins in the United States, Reed seemed as concerned with the success of the North Vietnamese, and the death of its fighting men, as he was with the bloody toll exacted on his own countrymen. "He thought the U.S. government was killing our boys," Patricia explained. "He thought if we pulled out, there would be no more war. He didn't think of it as killing Americans. He would tell the Vietnamese, we need to pull out, but you need to let the prisoners out. He was like Jane Fonda. He thought it was a political war."[5]

On May 25, 1967, Reed spoke at a well-attended antiwar rally in Rome at the Piazza Navena. The nighttime rally was a star-studded affair. A report by the U.S. State Department to the FBI stated that Reed was joined at the microphones by an unidentified Italian movie actor and a Greek movie actress. The report quoted another American, Harold Humes, but did not report what Reed said, other than to note it was "Anti-American."[6] During the summer of 1967, the South Vietnamese government of Lt. General Nguen Van Thieu and Vice President Nguen Cao Ky were up for reelection. In early September, the duo received only 27 percent of the vote, but it was double that of their nearest competitor. Reed couldn't resist the opportunity to comment on the campaign and wrote a letter to the editor of the *International Herald Tribune*, the respected newspaper spun off from the *New York Herald Tribune*. The *Herald Tribune* was published in Paris and functioned as the paper for Americans living or traveling in Europe. In another memo from the U.S. Embassy in Bern, Switzerland, to the director of the FBI, Reed's letter was clipped and sent with the message that "this may indicate that Reed is at present in Rome." It's written in the Dean Reed style, with the usual praise for the American people, but disdain for its allies in South Vietnam and his frequent use of the exclamation point.

"Finally, my belief in the ultimate intelligence of the American people has been restored, for I read that in the latest poll, the majority of American citizens have doubts that the Vietnam elections were completely honest," Reed's letter read in part. "Of course, that is the understatement of the year!

"After the candidates were thoroughly screened, then the process of screening the voters took place. Only those areas that were under the control of the U.S. forces were allowed to vote—which means that between two-thirds and three-fourths of Vietnam were not allowed to vote!—which is like allowing only the conservative and racist South of the United States to take part in the elections of the President.

Free elections indeed! The only thing free about the elections was the free manner in which they were rigged and stage-managed from the first to the very last day."[7]

All the years of living and working abroad had taught Reed ways to take advantage of his U.S. citizenship. In spring 1969, demonstrations against the Vietnam War were at their height in the United States and in other countries, including Italy. Italian police were cracking down, trying to prevent the mass protests that embarrassed Italy's powerful and wealthy ally. One Sunday, Reed's activist friends called the American actor to tell him of another peace rally in Rome. Reed agreed to join them and discovered they were heading toward the U.S. Embassy. It was a large horde that descended, but the police were out in force, lined up three deep, and they stood immobile between the demonstrators and the embassy. Reed, for reasons he couldn't recall, was wearing a tie that day and as he muscled his way to the front of the crowd, his friends were telling everyone to let him through, that this was an embassy employee. Reed had his U.S. passport out and was flashing it at the police. In his halting Italian, he told the officers what his friends had said, that he was an American employee and needed to get to work in the embassy. The police, more intent on keeping the thousands of demonstrators at bay, gave Reed a cursory check and let him pass through the barricades. He walked through and over to an area near where the U.S. ambassador and the Rome police chief were watching the confrontation. Reed turned to the crowd and raised his voice to be heard.

"Long live Ho Chi Minh," he chanted, referring to the North Vietnamese leader. "Long live Ho Chi Minh. Stop the bombing terror. Stop the bombing terror. All the aggressors out of Vietnam. Long live the other America."

With the first chant, the ambassador and police chief snapped their heads around, saw who was leading the chants from inside the embassy grounds and ordered Reed's arrest. Police officers quickly closed on him, handcuffed him and led him away from the embassy. Reed, pleased with the clever way he slipped past the cops, smiled all the way to the station. After a couple hours, he was released.[8]

While publicly relishing his anti–establishment stance, privately, the American was expressing serious doubts about Communism and the Soviet Union. In the mid–1960s, under the leadership of Alexander Dubcek, Czechoslovakia flirted with a more open society. Tight censorship of artists, the media and government critics was loosened. The government experimented with some free markets, rather than the tightly controlled and centrally planned economy of most Eastern European countries. Criticism of the Soviet Union to the east was tolerated and there was talk of loosening the Russian reins around the Czech nation and perhaps establishing closer relationships with Western Europe and even the United States. Naturally, Western officials applauded the moves, hoping that if they could entice one nation out of the Soviet orbit, other countries would eventually come careening out of the inner space of the Iron Curtain. In August 1968, that dream was crushed. Soviet Premier Leonid Brezhnev ordered the Red Army to cross the border, oust Dubcek and restore a hard-line Communist government in Prague. The sight of Soviet tanks patrolling the streets of the Czech capital surprised and concerned people throughout Europe and the United States. One of those was Dean Reed.

After spending weeks agonizing over what he had seen, Reed went to his typewriter and on September 29, 1968, banged out a three-page, single-spaced letter to Yurii, a Soviet author Reed met in his first tour of Russia two years earlier. Yurii had written a book that argued that each country had to remake Communism in its own way so it would fit with the culture and traditions of each nation. It could not be imposed from without. "Yurii, for many weeks now I have been debating with myself whether I should make my feelings heard by my dear friends in the Soviet Union," Reed wrote. "I have finally decided that since my entire mature life has been dedicated to the truth and to the following of my conscience it would be the first dishonest and immoral act on my part to refrain at this time from speaking out against an act which I feel is anti-Marxist and an act which has done immeasurable harm to the progressive forces throughout the world and subsequently also an act that truly was not even in the interests of the Soviet Peoples. It is a form of hypocrisy for the Soviet Government to invade another socialist fraternal country because of the fact that the form of socialism which that country wanted to build was decided by some of the leaders of the Soviet Party not to be compatible to the interests of the Soviet Union." He went on to say that millions of people in the Third World were now convinced that they had to worry about both American and Soviet imperialism. The invasion would produce two other repercussions, Reed told his friend. First, it would strengthen the hand of conservative forces in the United States who would use the incident to rally around Richard Nixon in his campaign against liberals and specifically Hubert Humphrey in the November elections. Second, it would make it harder for young people in capitalist countries to embrace Communism, which was already a courageous and difficult act, he wrote. "You must realize that I am a very dedicated communist now and the slow and painful path from which I have arrived took the last ten years of my life," Reed concluded. "By following my conscience, I have suffered many times, but not half as badly as many of my comrades in S.A. [South America] and other comrades throughout the world, including the Soviet Union."[9]

Even though he was making movies and living well in Italy and traveling throughout Europe and the Soviet Union, Reed had not forgotten the people of South America who had first made him a star. Not much had changed in Argentina since he and Patricia fled in March 1966, but Reed decided to take a shot at returning there in August 1969. A Buenos Aires newspaper *La Razon* reported that Reed was scheduled to arrive August 14 and appear in a series of television shows on Channel 9.[10] Apparently, Argentine officials were reading the papers, too, for they were waiting for him when he finally flew into Buenos Aires airport on August 16. He was denied entry into the country, so Reed called the U.S. Embassy from the airport and spoke to the duty officer, Louis Villalovos. Reed told Villalovos he had no idea why they wouldn't let him into the country, although it was his guess that it was because Reed was "a Kennedy man, a progressive and a pacifist." Reed further explained that he had a contract to appear on shows for Channel 9. Villalovos spoke with the Argentine Immigration officials at the airport, but they were not helpful. All they would say was they had orders not to let him into the country.[11]

The Argentine government held fast and Reed was put on the next flight to Chile. Plunging straight ahead had failed, so Reed decided to try an end sweep. Chile and Argentina share a huge border that extends for thousands of miles. Not all of it can be guarded and Reed's friends knew how to slip him through to the other side. They drove him across and landed him onstage in time for his first scheduled performance. During his August 20 appearance he went through his repertoire of songs, many of them newer ones he had written. One of them hit the mark and the police grabbed him after the show. Reed sent a telegram to Patricia, telling her he was once again under arrest by Argentine authorities. Patricia fired off a quick letter. "I have just received a telegram from Buenos Aires telling me that my husband was arrested for singing a song which he wrote. The dictatorship declared the song 'subversive' because it talked of peace, liberty and democracy!"[12] The police kept him locked up for a couple of days and then expelled him from the country. This time they made sure the flight was leaving the continent so there would be no way for him to sneak back in. Patricia was glad to have him safely back in Rome with her and baby Ramona, but she also was becoming more perturbed by Reed's disregard for his own safety. She could understand protesting in the United States or even the democracies of Western Europe, because they understood civil rights and followed the rules. But taking on the dictatorships of South America made no sense at all. "That was scary," Patricia said of Reed's Argentina arrest. "That was when I accused him of having a death wish."[13]

The surprise for Patricia could not have been in Reed's thoughts but that he followed through. For several years now, Reed had been talking about his willingness to put his life on the line for his beliefs. If anything, he was becoming more adamant about it. "Do you realize that for millions of people in South America who make up the oppressed majority, and for millions of Soviet citizens, that I am the MOST HONEST AND MORAL AMERICAN to come out of America in the last years??!!!!!! Why you say? Because a man is judged on the motives of his actions as well as his actions. That will be the way that I will judge my sons and daughters. My motives are the cleanest. I am ready to suffer imprisonment and death—NOT FOR PERSONAL PROFIT BUT IN ORDER TO HELP TO MAKE THE REST OF HUMANITY LIVE WITH JUST A LITTLE LESS PAIN AND HUNGER AND INJUSTICE!!![14]

Eleven

Trouble at Home, Victory Abroad

When Reed first landed in Hollywood after leaving college, Ozzie Nelson and Jim Anderson were the archetype for loving, if somewhat befuddled, husbands and fathers on *The Adventures of Ozzie and Harriet* and *Father Knows Best*. Reed must not have watched too many episodes, because his marriage to Patricia was crumbling. With his fame came women from every nation, all of them gorgeous and all of them happy to give themselves completely to the American singer, for a night if he wished, longer if they could. Reed did not always resist and Patricia was well aware of it, although she professed to be unconcerned with his philandering, which continued even after the birth of their daughter.

"When he had these other affairs, I wasn't really jealous," she said. "Our fights were passionate, as was our love-making. Paton taught me his affairs were just a form of masturbation, as long as it wasn't a love affair. Most were like prostitutes or people who showed up."[1] Patricia also described her husband as "not good material for the domestic type of life. He could not deal with everyday responsibilities. He was a risk when it came to being a husband or father."[2]

Reed tried to be a good husband. He showered Patricia with letters whenever he traveled away from her on business, and his most frequent complaint was that she rarely wrote back. "Anyway, thank you. Since you refuse to write to me because you can't find five minutes in a 24 hour day just to write the husband that you say you love, I guess a cable is better than nothing. I wonder if you have ever thought exactly how much time it would take just to write the same thing and send it once every couple days—I know that you are now a very busy business woman, but I would think you could dedicate five minutes a day to me—even if you didn't feel like it—just to make your husband happy." He concluded by saying, 'even if I don't understand your love and am hurt by it, I do love you very much and can't wait to be with you. Your husband, Deano."[3]

If Patricia was lackadaisical about her letter writing, Reed wrote more epistles than the Apostle Paul. Sometimes they were packed full of news, sometimes they were philosophical about their marriage, but frequently they were just love letters. Reed longed for his wife, whom he called Kitten or Legs and frequently, Mrs. Reed. Sometimes he wrote two a day and often he wrote several a week. Writing seemed to ease the aching in his heart, although the letters never made it disappear. "I go to sleep with you in my mind and heart and wake up with you there—I walk through my days and nights hearing your voice and remembering our day together in the country—Those will be the type of days we will have from now on. I wish I could fly to your side—I love you so much my wife."[4]

From the beginning, the relationship between the two had been like NASA shuttle missions. Their passion would ignite and they would soar into orbit, as they did after their first meetings, the Mexican romance and during the Soviet tour. After a few weeks or months, there would be a fight, a coldness and they would suddenly be touching down on a dusty runway and as often as not, Patricia would be returning to her mother. Indeed, after spending Christmas 1966 together in Spain, the couple was fighting again. Patricia split for California and while Reed was in Spain and Italy, she was dating another man. Reed eventually flew to Los Angeles to discuss whether they should continue the marriage or break it off. Patricia and her mother went to great lengths to make sure he did not find out about her other suitor. Although they agreed to give it another go, the letters from 1967 reflected Reed's turmoil. And it gave some hints as to what he saw as the problems in the union.

> Hi Kitten!
>
> Surprised to get two letters in two days! But of course, as always, I still haven't received even one letter.
>
> You know, I keep coming back to the same one truth— whether or not the exciting love that we're told exists or if it does not exist except for very short periods of time. For I come back to the point that what a terrible error we would regret for all our lives if we got a divorce and both of us remarried—I'm sure for the first months and even years we would be happier than before for we would have that new feeling of excitement that can only come from something New. But then what if after three years of marriage, we both felt the same disalusionment [*sic*] again and would think—shit—it just doesn't exist—so why did I part with Patti—For I guess we were pretty compatible— as much as any woman I will find I'm sure. Why did we hurt each other so much? I'm sure my first feelings of disalusionment came for reasons of your constant sicknesses which of course you hated as much as I, but it was still their [*sic*]—the fact that I'm sure the biggest attraction I had for you when I married you was a physical attraction, and that that is what came to almost nothing throughout the marriage—that we have never been able to make love physically like we did before we got married, for it hurts you—It is even worse than before marriage—Now I must withdraw each time, or put in diaphragms and then feel nothing.... And one reason for marriage is so that a man won't have to have those worries that he used to have with single women. I wanted so many times to make love, just when I felt like it, when I loved you and saw your eyes and body, and wanted to feel it, but you have grown so conservative with me—You never wanted to do it outside or wherever it might have been. I ache for your body, but the body that I remember in the tree house—the body that seemed at that time to really want mine—the woman

that would scream and scratch and give me hickies—the one that would be rammed across the floor and still want more....that love I have had none since we got married ... and that my body is aching for—with or without you—I would much rather have it with my wife.....but since I could not get it from you for the first two years, and just secretly resented it and remained true to you in thoughts and body. But this past year my mind has been wandering, and I can't control it for I have such a hunger—Physically I still remained true—which made me resent you at times even more—Obviously, I now deeply admire you, respect you and love you more than at the time we got marriage [*sic*]—Then it was purely physical—I have grown very near you with three years of pain, tears and some laughter... there is no woman that I admire more than my mother and you. You are truly an exceptional woman. I really felt like calling you tonight and saying, "We'll both try harder—try to make me lose some of my seriousness— I would like to laugh and have more fun in my life—I just need someone to help drag me along at times and make fun of me without getting mad at me."

He signed it, "Love, your searching husband—Dean," and in the margin wrote, "I miss you!![5]

There were other letters like that one. They revealed that Dean Reed, the romantic from the Old West, was struggling with his beliefs. He entered the marriage idealistically, and he was sure Patricia did too, firm in the belief that the thrill of the early months would stay with them forever. It was the excitement of new love, where being away from Patricia, even for just a few hours, would make him absentminded as he daydreamed about her. And when he first caught sight of her again his body would tingle and he would lightly catch his breath. Her every word was golden, her laughter a delight. That radiant love had not lasted. But Reed now was trying to replace it with something else. He told Patricia that he now accepted that ideal marriages did not exist outside of fairy tales. Still, he was now willing to dedicate himself to a lasting relationship with her. But the romantic died hard. Even in the midst of letters trying to logically analyze love, Reed would still pen a letter that smoldered with passion.

My Dearest Wife,

Well, I will start this off with something that I haven't said at the start of a letter for a long time—One gets into the habit of saying it at the end, but if one takes the care to write it at the first, then it means he truly and deeply feels it—You know something, I love you Mrs. Reed....I miss you so terribly and think of you throughout my days. How I long to touch you and watch your hair blow in the wind, or run along the beach with you—or just eat dinner with you by candlelight, a meal that was made just for me by the one who loves me—that I all miss—and then to sit in bed and watch television and then slowly, piece by piece, to take off your clothes for you—and as the breathing gets heavier and heavier, my lips become moistened and our temperatures go up—then I kiss your body, slowly with love as well as passion—Then I enter, and your ass in my hands and it moves while I enter and withdraw slowly and almost bringing you to the brink, but never letting you go over—Until we both cannot stand it much longer—and we scream into the night our love. O my darling, how I need you!!!

Please have patience with me, and our love will grow and grow, for I will try to be a better husband—for I don't want to leave you—now or never. I'm sorry I hurt you there for awhile—Please forgive me—I will try better—I have met so many people—married women, and single girls—And I see that only you are the woman that I want in my life—you are so above all others in my eyes—I'm tired and should go to bed, but I don't want to stop writing, for it makes me feel that I'm nearer to you right at this moment. All my love to you, Your Husband, Deano.[6]

The wooing and the letters had the desired effect and as the months moved ahead, so did their marriage. Patricia apparently took to heart some of what Reed had written and was willing to make love outdoors when they conceived Ramona. Reed kept his part of the written bargain and tried to make his wife happy and for most of the rest of the year, there was only peace and love in the household. When the news came that his wife was pregnant, Reed doted even more, hoping that this time she could take the baby to term. He was a wonderful, caring father after the difficult delivery and for much of the rest of the year. But it was not long before the couple fell into their old patterns and the problems resurfaced. Reed was shoving Patricia out of his revolutionary work and she hated having a large part of him cut off from her. It was the same arguments they had in Mexico and in Argentina, but this time Reed had an easier time winning the debate. After all, there was baby Ramona and someone had to be with her when Reed took to the streets or the stage to sing another protest song.

In March 1970, Patricia was left behind to care for the baby while Reed flew to Sweden for the Stockholm Conference on Vietnam, another international gathering called to discuss the war in that Southeast Asian country and the United State's enormous involvement in it. At the conference was his old friend Marv Davidov, who was living in Minneapolis and leading antiwar demonstrations against Honeywell Corporation which made the cluster bombs Davidov and his allies said were killing thousands of innocent civilians in Vietnam.

"We hung out the whole week," Davidov said. "By the end of the conference, the people were shouting for him to sing. The Russians, the Yugoslav partisans and he got up and sang partisan songs from the Second World War. Everybody was cheering, it was wonderful. He said to me, 'I'm giving a concert in Moscow. Stay in Moscow on your way back and I'll introduce you to people you could never meet by yourself—Soviet ballerinas, (Premier Leonid) Brezhnev, whoever.' But I had to come back."[7]

Reed composed a new song for the conference called "Peace," which he performed in the main hall. He gave a five-minute speech to the gathering before strapping on his guitar. He no longer harbored any doubts about his position. In Reed's mind, his homeland was completely wrong and the North Vietnamese were blameless in every way. The speech also introduced the idea he had been toying with, of testing himself in battle, even if it was as a traitor against the United States.

"Dear fellow peace workers, peace fighters and peace cru-
saders—if there are any of you left," Dean addressed the
audience. "Once again we all meet together under the
same roof—people of many different nations and organizations who feel the need to dedicate part of their lives and
talents in the urgent search for genuine peace in Vietnam.

We who have known you—the representatives of the Vietnamese peoples, are always happy to see you again. But it is
tragic that our love and friendships bring us together always in times of crisis and new criminal acts by the US
Aggressor upon your peoples. I, as an American, feel like
embracing you and saying, "I'm sorry."

But then when the conference has ended and I am with
my wife and child in Rome my conscience tells me that I
have not done enough myself for you are not only fighting
for your liberation, but also for mine. You are not only giving your blood for your own freedom, but you are sacrific-
ing yourselves for the freedom of all mankind.

And again, when I am taking quiet walks by myself my
conscience again tells me that I have not done enough for
while I am singing, you may be crying. While I write po-
etry, you are writing history. I would feel honored to stand
side by side with you, not only spiritually and emotionally,
but also physically in the just battle which you are fighting
for us. My life as well as my talents shall always be at your
service. I love you."[8]

After the conference and the quick stop in Moscow, Reed returned to Rome where he passed a restless spring and early summer. The world's attention, and Reed's, was turning toward his second home, Chile. Since 1960, the governments of first Jorge
Alessandri and then Christian Democrat President Eduardo Frei
had undertaken land reforms. The huge holdings by a small per-
centage of the country's wealthiest families were slowly being
turned over to the peasants. Stranger still, Salvador Allende, a socialist, was touting something other than the usual anticommunist,
friend of America, friend of the wealthy Chilean pledges voters in
that country had come to expect. Instead, Allende was talking

about attacking the huge disparity in wealth between the rich and poor, nationalizing industries if necessary, and pushing education and health care for everyone. He had failed with that message in three previous runs for the presidency, but this time, his campaign was catching fire.

For Reed, this was the kind of revolutionary talk he had been waiting for. It was the sort of message he had espoused himself while living and working in Chile. It bothered him to be across the Atlantic from all the action. Plus, Reed was all too aware that the prospect of an Allende victory was bothering President Richard Nixon and his advisers in the White House. Reed loathed Nixon. He was surprised and saddened when Nixon eked out a victory over Hubert Humphrey in the 1968 elections and it had prompted him to write a song lamenting the election and the turn his country was taking. Now, at last, everything was coming together. A man of his own political persuasion was running for president in Chile. Reed's popularity and his status as an American in Chile could be used to denounce the United States' foreign policy and boost the candidacy of Allende. "In Santiago, Chile, I sang at the voting rallies of the people's front," Reed wrote. "Nevertheless, at this time I was much less a singer than an agitator. I considered myself to be an Internationalist; at the same time I was a patriot as I had never been before. For the Unidad Popular (Allende's political party) was for me a power that could put those people in the USA in their place, those who oppressed not only in Chile, but also in their own country. It was not coincidence that I had just decided at that time to demonstrate against the claims of world domination by the government of my country. The Chileans and all of the people in the world should see that the United States consists not only of Wall Street and the Pentagon, but also that it has citizens who take a stand for freedom and justice."[9]

On August 31, 1970, just days before the Chilean elections, Dean Reed appeared at the U.S. Embassy in Santiago. As usual, he had alerted his friends in the press and reporters and photographers were on hand to witness whatever the singing star might have in mind. Reed walked up to the main gate of the embassy and produced a bucket of water and an American flag. As the photographers clicked away, Reed repeatedly dipped the stars and stripes into the bucket.

"To the peoples of the World," Reed began. "This North American flag is dirty with the blood of thousands of Vietnamese women and children, who have been burned alive by bombs of napalm which are dropped from U.S. planes of aggression, for the sole reason that the Vietnamese Peoples want to live in peace and liberty with independence and self-determination. This North American flag is dirty with the blood of the Negro Race of the United States who are assassinated in their beds while they sleep by the U.S. Police forces as a policy of genocide for the sole reason that the Negro Race wants to live with dignity and with full civil rights as United States Citizens. This North American flag is dirty with the blood and pain of the American Indians who are forced to live in semi-concentration camps. This North American flag is dirty with the blood and tears of the millions of people of the majority of the countries of South America, Africa and Asia who are forced to live in misery and injustice because the U.S. Government supports the dictatorships which keep these people in bondage. This North American flag is dirty because the great principles of democracy and liberty on which it was founded have been betrayed by the United States Government. As a good United States citizen who loves his country enough to fight to correct its errors and injustices and to try to make it a great country not only materially and militarily, but morally and spiritually, here today in Santiago de Chile, I do symbolically wash the flag of my country—the United States of America."[10]

As Reed expected, he was arrested and the flag was snatched from him. "He was briefly detained for causing a disturbance, not for any offense against the U.S. flag," according to a State Department report on the incident.[11] Regardless of the reasons, the protest and Reed's arrest made a big splash in the local media.

"He was in Chile to help Allende, who he knew, and Pablo Naruda," Marv Davidov said, referring to the Chilean poet and another friend of Reed's. "The Frei government took the flag and Naruda got it back and as the plane was getting ready to leave, he gave Dean the flag. People thought it helped Allende."[12] That flag tapped the sentimentality in the American. He never let go of it and nearly fifteen years later, he proudly displayed it in his East German home. "For me, it is a piece of my homeland," he explained. "Even as much as I like living in the GDR and as much as I am grateful to this country, I am an American."[13]

Whether Reed's little escapade helped or not, less than a week later Chilean voters went to the polls and elected Allende their president. The election results were news around the world and front page headlines in major American newspapers. Allende's election was a historic shift, and while it was not a Communist government, it was no longer the safe ally American presidents had come to expect from South America since the end of World War II.

Reed returned to Rome before election day and had his passport and 3,000 lire stolen from the glove compartment of his convertible sports car on September 12. Reed quickly applied for a new passport from the U.S. Embassy in Rome, because he was planning several trips, most important, a return to Chile for Allende's inauguration. The president-elect requested Reed perform at one of the major inauguration events in November. The United States government of Richard Nixon was outspoken in its unhappiness over Allende's election. The CIA and others backed dissidents, hoping they could block Allende's victory from being made official. Embassy officials closely monitored the new regime, including the inaugural festivities. One official watched Reed's performance and wrote that he was "booed off the stage by the assembled populace for his obvious lack of singing talent."[14] Maybe—although given the nasty tone of the memo from beginning to end, it may also be that the embassy's hostility toward the socialist Allende was easily transferred to Reed, who after all, had been an annoyance for years with his anti-American stances. In any case, the photos from that night present a different picture. Reed looks confident, dressed in a tuxedo, beaming and shaking hands with the new president.

While sitting in his Santiago hotel, Reed was moved to write a letter to his two-year-old daughter. Reed knew his frequent travels and his hot and cold relationship with Patricia were hardly the stable influence Ramona needed. Rather than lamely explaining it to her years later, Reed decided to lay it out for her at the moment it was all fresh and let her absorb it when she was older. For a man who was no longer attending church or professing a faith of any sort, the letter is almost biblical in content, echoing refrains from the New Testament. It also is inexplicably sad, in parts sounding as though he never expected to see Ramona again and concluding with "I would have been proud to have been able to have you by my side as my comrade," even though he would return to her within days.

> There may be people who will say that I was a poor father for I should have dedicated my life only to you and your mother. But the battle in which I am participating is a battle for a world where you Ramona and your sons and daughters shall be able to enjoy this world where a new man shall be born—one who shall not be selfish and who shall feel that all children are his children and that all human beings are his brothers. A world where you Ramona shall be able to live without the constant fear of tomorrow—for the basic necessities of life shall be assured to you and your children by law for the sole reason that you were born. Only true freedom and liberty can arrive after these steps are taken for it is absurd to talk of the ritual and cultural life of one if his entire life is dedicated in the constant battle just to survive. You Ramona shall continue my battle for the destiny of the world is in the hands of your generation.
>
> I shall remember our 2 ½ years together until my last gasp for life but you shall not remember a moment together. So shall it be. But you shall know me. For you shall see my face in all mankind who are struggling to break chains. You shall see my face in the old sailor with wrinkles in his face from the message that the winds have sent. You shall see my eyes in the youth who with defiance and courage withstand the assault of the charges of the police who with their heavy batons try to break the heads of the students hoping in doing so that the principals [sic] of justice and equality shall come spilling out with the blood. You shall

feel my tears when you hear a choir in Chile singing "We Shall Overcome" or upon hearing the clear and pure voices of children singing in the Amazon jungles to the steppes of Mongolia.[15]

Two months after penning that note to his daughter, Reed was again touring Russia and found himself on the wrong side of American public opinion. American television often is criticized for being violent and lowbrow, but Soviet television tended to be downright boring. Reed was interviewed on a Moscow television program and the Soviet version of TV Guide listed the topic as "Youth in the Struggle against Imperialism." Still, more than a few young Russians probably tuned in, lured by the chance to see their singing idol. Reed talked about the blood on the American flag and about his arrest in Chile for his symbolic washing of Old Glory. He told the interviewer that his arrest showed that the old Chilean government took its orders from the United States. He concluded that one day a "clean American flag will fly over socialist America." The U.S. Embassy in Moscow apparently had forgotten about his earlier appearance in the country and called him a "particularly obnoxious character." Nonetheless, they respected his abilities. "Reed gave evidence on TV at having a fine speaking and singing voice and the impression he conveyed was one of sincerity and idealism. While the more sophisticated members of the Soviet audience will probably question Reed's facts and perhaps his integrity, his manner and nationality may lend some credence to his hysterical charges against the U.S. among the less literate. The Embassy would appreciate any information which is available which would be useful in discrediting this individual, including facts about his citizenship and passport status."[16]

Even more combative was Reed's published skirmish with a fellow artist, Aleksandr Solzhenitsyn. Solzhenitsyn had done the one thing Reed desired. He had suffered mightily for his art. Solzhenitsyn wrote long, complex novels that questioned and denounced the totalitarian regime of the Soviet Union. His most scathing book, *The Gulag Archipelago*, earned him the Nobel Prize for literature in 1970 and it was based, in part, on his years in Soviet prisons where he was sent for crimes against the state. His high international profile, and the Nobel Prize, made it difficult for the Soviet government to continue its attempts to muzzle the author, so they expelled him from the country. Solzhenitsyn eventually landed in the United States, where he lived on an isolated estate in the mountains of Vermont. From there, he would occasionally lob wordy criticisms at Leonid Brezhenv and his ruling party, and with the practiced aim of the social essayist, his critiques usually managed to hit their target and sting the ruling elite. His writing conjured up a mystical Russian nationalism based on a return to simple rural values he associated with nineteenth century Russia. While he hated the totalitarian Communist regime, Solzhenitsyn seemed comfortable with a czar-run government and he was openly distrustful of democracy. Americans, most of whom had never read his books, initially cheered him, even though he was a prickly man who demanded privacy and did little to ingratiate himself with his new neighbors. Solzhenitsyn eventually criticized his new country, its materialism and what he perceived as its moral weakness. But for now, he was taking shots at the great Russian bear and his new countrymen rooted for him as though it were some kind of international boxing match.

Reed took it upon himself to set Solzhenitsyn straight. In an "Open letter to A. Solzhenitsyn," published in *Literaturnaya Gazeta*, Jan. 27, 1971, Reed tried to make the Russian author see the error of his ways.

"As an American artist I have a duty to respond to some of your accusations which have been published in capitalistic publications throughout the world," Reed wrote.

In my opinion, these accusations are wrong and the peoples of the world have to know why they are wrong.

You stamped the Soviet Union as a 'deeply ill society gripped by revenge and injustice.' You say that the Soviet government 'could not exist without enemies and that its whole atmosphere is saturated with only one thing—hate that reaches racism.' It seems that you are actually speaking of my home country, not yours! Not the Soviet Union but America has wars and creates tension-filled situations conducive to wars in order to provide a working base for its economy and an opportunity for our dictator, the war industry, for greater wealth and for the opportunity to ac-

quire the power over the Vietnamese people. This at the
expense of all freedom loving peoples of the world and
with the blood of our own American soldiers."

Reed was just getting warmed up. He went on to say America
was violent, with more people murdered since 1900 than the total
number of American soldiers killed in World Wars I, and II, Korea
and Vietnam. He said the mafia had more power than corporations. Racism in America allowed slavery and now allowed police
to beat up "every Negro who dares to stand up for his rights."
Then he launched what would become Reed's justification for
the lack of human rights in the Eastern European socialist regimes.
It was an argument he would use for the next fifteen years when
people pointed out that as an American he was free to slam his
homeland, but the people of the Soviet Union, Poland or Hungary had to keep quiet.

> After that you say that the "first condition of every healthy
> society, even our society, is the freedom of speech, honest
> and complete freedom of speech." Try and spread these
> thoughts among the suffering nations who have to fight
> for their existence and who have to live against their will
> under the pressure of a dictatorial regime which stays in
> power only because of United States military help. Speak
> of your ideas to people whose "health" consists of suffer-
> ing all their lives from lack of medical attention and half of
> whose children die at birth because there is no money for
> doctors. Speak about it to the peoples of the capitalistic
> world whose "health" consists of constant fear of unem-
> ployment. Tell the American Negroes how much "health"
> and "freedom of speech" have actually helped them in
> their justified struggle toward equality with whites when
> freedom of speech in many parts of America means that
> the murder of Negroes is comparable to a bear hunt.
> No, Mr. Solzhenitsyn, your claim that freedom of speech
> is the first requirement for health is wrong. The first re-
> quirement consists of changing the world morally, spiri-
> tually, intellectually and physically enough so that its peo-
> ple are able to read, write, work and live in peace with
> each other.

Reed wrapped up the lengthy letter by lauding the steps the Soviet Union had taken to shape a better world and returned to the points he made to his father about the relativity of every situation.

> The Soviet Union is at all times half a step ahead of the rest of the world. Do you really wish that your nation abandon the role of the most progressive leader in the world and return to the inhuman and cruel conditions which rule the majority of the world where the nearly feudal atmosphere of many states is full of injustices in the direct sense of the word?
>
> It is true that even in the Soviet Union there are injustices and things lacking but everything in the world is relative. In principle and in deed your union is trying to create a healthy and just society. Apparently mistakes do appear in life and some injustice occurs but a union based on just principles has undoubtedly more chance to arrive at justice than a union which is based on injustice and on exploitation of people by the people. My country's union and government are behind the times because their purpose consists of trying to salvage the world's status quo. It's your country which is trying to take progressive steps in the name of the people. And if it is incomplete, in some respects and stumbles because of that, we cannot condemn the whole system because of these inadequacies. We have to salute it because of its courage and because of its desire to establish new paths.[17]

As Dean became more committed to a socialist, or even Marxist, outlook on the world he was still able to see the flaws in the Communist system but just barely. He was more dedicated to finding fault with the capitalist economies of the West and justifying the shortcomings of the Eastern Bloc. His eyes still worked, so when he visited Moscow's GUM department store, the Nieman-Marcus of the Soviet Union, he saw long lines of people waiting to buy the limited supply of imported shirts and other clothing. It was an indignity foreign to American shoppers, he knew, but he had an explanation. It had cost the Soviets millions of rubles to rebuild their cities after the devastating battles against the Nazis in World War II, and they did it without assistance from other countries. And it was still costing the Soviets to blunt the "imperialistic aggressions" of the West, and particularly the United States. In order to stop NATO countries, the Soviets had to provide oil for Cuba, weapons for Angola and Nicaragua, factories for Vietnam, tractors for East Germany and all the nuclear missiles and conventional weapons to keep the peace, Reed reasoned. By the late 1970s, Reed would even be arguing with his old friend and mentor Paton Price. Where in the 1960s, Reed had nothing but admiration for Price's conscientious objector stand during the Second World War, fifteen years later Reed was calling it a mistake.

"Paton Price and I had different world views during the last years of his life," Reed said. "He was bourgeois Democrat. I feel myself to be a Marxist. When we met in the fall of 1978, we frequently argued. But it was an argument among people who respected each other. Paton said at the time, 'I am to blame that we argue. I have always said and say it still today that each human being must find his own truth, which he then must defend with all the consequences. You have found another truth than the one that I have found. But you must always stand for it like you do today. Only when you do that in the future will you remain my friend.'"[18]

If Solzhenitsyn ever saw Reed's letter, there is no evidence he wrote any type of response. Not that Reed expected one. He made his point, continued to play full houses in Russia, and then headed home to Italy to see his daughter before heading off to South America. It was to be the most dramatic turn of his life since his tumultuous welcome in Chile a decade earlier.

Twelve

Busted

"Señor Reed, you are under arrest. Please come with me."

For Dean Reed in 1971, this was a tired old phrase, especially from his friends in the Argentine secret police. It was not entirely unexpected, although Reed was a little surprised that they accosted him on the streets in broad daylight, just two hours after his press conference. It was the usual assortment of four or five agents who confronted him on the sidewalk. Still, he was not particularly concerned. He had been arrested many times and most of the detentions resulted in a few hours of questioning and then his release, usually to a waiting plane out of the country.

Reed quickly realized this would be different. Instead of a trip to the local police station, Reed was driven to Vila Devoto prison. He was met by members of the secret police who fingerprinted him, took his picture, forced him to don prison garb and then locked him in a cell. There was no public record of the arrest, nor were any formal charges brought. Dean Reed had disappeared.

Vila Devoto prison had a few political prisoners behind its bars, but mostly it was filled with murders, rapists, thieves and other common criminals who preyed on the good people of Argentina. Apparently, General Juan Carlos Ongania, Argentina's dictator, was hoping the criminals would assault Reed and make his life miserable. A colonel led Reed down the prison cellblock.

"Now we have to cut your hair," the colonel said. "We have the other prisoners do it in the prison barbershop."

However, as they passed the cells, a roar went up.

"Dean Reed, Dean Reed. Give him to us."

Homosexuality was a crime in Argentina and they were passing the cellblock where about forty gay men were being held. They recognized the singing star and were eager to have the handsome American in their area. The outcry startled Reed and frightened him.

"You go in there if you are not good," the colonel told Reed.[1]

The singer might have done better in that cellblock than he did in the barbershop. The prisoner wielding the clippers did a horrid job. Reed had always had luxuriant and well-coifed hair, neatly combed over. This prisoner had a careless hand, cutting great tufts in some areas, little in others and not caring what it would look like combed. When he was done, the hair was nearly military short, but uneven and ragged. When the American got a look in the mirror, he gasped. Reed was something like Samson. Much of his strength came from his hair. He was a vain man, and he knew that a his success was closely tied to his good looks, not the least of which were the locks that accentuated the handsome face. It brought men over to his side and it led women to his bed. Now that was a mess. Reed's strength and confidence was too.

The other prisoners treated Reed well. Most just wanted to meet the superstar and chat with him. So the government, and its prison officials, had to resort to the other measures at their disposal to chip away at the American. Reed's meals were meager, nothing more than tea and some bread for lunch and bean soup for supper. The kitchen was not concerned about sanitation and bugs often found their way into the soup. The meals provided few calories and left him with frequent diarrhea. Other times he vomited and the toilets were not fine porcelain potties with running water. They were not much more than a chamber pot. No one was in a hurry to clean those toilets and the smell only aggravated Reed's weak stomach.[2] The late autumn evenings were cold and the missing windowpanes brought the chill in on the breezes that easily penetrated his thin blanket. Reed was suffering now at the hands of others. The only time someone had tormented him like this was when he was ten years old and enrolled in the Colorado Military Academy. Shivering in his cell, Reed thought back to that time.

The military uniforms the boys wore did not automatically drape them in the discipline their parents had hoped for. The men who stood in the front of the classrooms were strong enough to command the cadets' attention through threats and an occasional slap or punch. Women teachers aroused no such fear and on this day, several of the boys started talking in the back of the room. When the teacher, a woman who had taught with Reed's father, tried to get them to quiet down, another group of boys started talking. One of them threw a spitball at her. His classmates' behavior disgusted Reed. He got up from his chair, moved toward the front of the room and turned toward the boys.

"Hey, shut up and let her teach," Reed shouted.

"Shut up yourself, Reed. What a teacher's pet."

"You're a bunch of real tough guys, picking on a woman. You don't pull this stuff with the men."

"We're tough enough to take care of you, Reed."

"Boys, that's enough now," their teacher said, finally regaining control. "Dean, please take your seat. The rest of you, let's turn our attention back to the blackboard."

Reed's feistiness had caught the other boys off-guard and it was enough to swing the power back to the teacher. The boys already hated Reed and his brother Dale for being "day boys," kids whose parents let them come home every night, while the majority of the boys had to remain behind in the barracks, seemingly abandoned by their moms and dads. Now they harbored one more grudge against the day boy. He had broken ranks with them and sided with authority. It was a crime they would not let go unpunished. The cadets gathered in their barracks and schemed. A few days later they made good on their threat to take care of Reed. They lured the boy into their dorm, pulled off his pants and poured a caustic liquid on his butt. It burned the skin, raising painful blisters. Reed was unable to walk normally or sit down for several days.[3] Reed winced at the memory. He had handled that, he would handle this. But his strength and his confidence were flagging.

Things had started out well for him when he first touched down in Santiago, Chile, back in February after the long flight from Rome. The Allende government was in its first year. Chile was now Reed's model, a Marxist president trying to bring reforms to the government and to society, changes that Reed was sure would benefit the poor and trim the power and wealth of the upper class. Reed wanted to be part of it, so he stayed through May, traveling the country and performing on behalf of Unidad Popular, Allende's political party. In many ways Reed was performing the way Woody Guthrie did in 1930s America. With his guitar under his arm, Reed would travel with representatives of Unidad Popular from town to town, helping them organize workers. Reed's repertoire for this tour contained few of his love songs and rock numbers. Instead, he loaded up on folk songs and revolutionary songs, all designed to move the people into the unions and the political party, not the dance floor. In the larger cities, he played fine halls. But in the smaller towns, the stage was often hastily erected and automobile headlights were employed as a spotlight. Reed was not living the life of a superstar. He was not spending the days in the mountains and retreating to a plush hotel room in Santiago for the night. He was hitting the small towns and the farming villages. He lived and worked side-by-side with the people he encountered. It was Reed at his best. He was not worried about his career back in the United States, or even expanding his popularity in Chile. He was spending his time talking to everyday people and listening to their dreams and the realities of their often hardscrabble lives. In a letter to his mother-in-law, Reed described his thoughts and feelings.

"As you know, for years I have had many doubts about the present political systems throughout the world which allow the majority of the peoples to live with hunger and poverty while a small minority live with immense wealth and privileges. Knowledge which has come drop by drop throughout the last years has made me define my personal philosophy toward these injustices and the part that my life should play in the battle to correct these evils and injustices. My position has become more revolutionary year after year for I see how the people who have the immense wealth will never give it up to the peoples by their own will and that in order to survive, the peoples of the world will have to battle for their own survival. Here in South America, the majority of the peoples have never seen a school or a hospital."[4] The Chileans touched his heart, but in a different way than when they had worshipped him as the conquering rock star in the early 1960s. Now they were sharing their homes and their thoughts with him. Out in the countryside, he didn't need to be separated from the people by a phalanx of police officers but could talk to them one-on-one or in small groups. Reed poured out his feeling before his departure in large ads in three of the largest newspapers in that country.

"The hour has come which must come, the hour of my departure," Reed wrote in the ads.

> I have lived for four months at your side, in hours which were so meaningful and stirring, for both the Chilean people and also for me ... I came to Chile in order to live at your side in order to help you and in order to prove my solidarity for our great plans to finally live in freedom and justice. I came in order to learn and to teach; for if there is between two partners love like between you and me, then there isn't only student and only teacher, but both partners are students and teachers at the same time. I will never forget the past four months which I have lived at your side. How could I forget the hours with mountain people of El Teniente and Chuquicamat, the conversations with farmers at Concepcion, the meetings with the workers of Santiago, Arica and Valparaiso, the moments with artists before their entrances, the visits with the people who sat in prison. All of these Chileans have various outlooks on life, each has a different past, but all have a future which will unite them. All look today with hope and trust to the future—to a new Chile. These words should be more of a reunion greeting than a greeting of departure. For we shall always be close, where there are injustices to fight. We shall be close to each place where there are workers, farmers, intellectuals and students who are fighting for a world where justice and peace rule. We shall be close to each place where there are people who have become aware for their fundamental rights and we

shall fight together with these people. We shall also be near to each place where a flower blooms, where the sun rises, where a child laughs because our future will be a world where the purest and highest human values are in effect. In this world, the children will be the only privileged class and the men and women will not only dedicate their lives to each other, but also all of humanity and will be solidarity behind each one who needs it. That will be a world where people live in peace and in dignity. Chileans, I wish you luck for your path. You have taken up the historic duty and I know that you justly want this task. Never give up. Always follow the truth. I am always ready to help you. I embrace you. Dean Reed.[5]

Reed was not just singing during this time. As is the case with many actors, Reed had become intrigued with the notion of directing, of having control over the film. So, as he traveled, he interviewed workers and peasants on film and listened to their stories of life in Chile and the changes they were expecting under Allende. But by the end of May, Reed decided it was time to move on to a place that was not the political paradise the American saw in Chile.

In Argentina, General Juan Carlos Ongania was still in power, five years after the overthrow of the civilian government of Arturo Illia. It was a typical military government. Opposition parties, especially left-leaning ones, had been outlawed and their leaders were in prison or silenced by threats. Workers had used massive strikes to protest government policies in the past, so Ongania outlawed work stoppages. When workers in Cordoba launched a major strike and rally in May 1969, police brutally suppressed it. Reed had made several attempts to enter Argentina, but was always quickly stopped, usually at the airport, and put on the next plane leaving the country. In June 1971, Reed made another attempt to get into the country to show his solidarity with the Argentinean Democrats, who still were resisting the one-man rule of Ongania. In a letter to his wife a couple weeks earlier, Reed outlined his plan and why he thought he would be successful. "There are many political interests involved and this time I think that shall be forced [*sic*] to allow me to enter or arrest me on false charges. I don't think personally they want a political scandal at this time but one never knows. Enclosed is my last farewell in Spanish to the Chilean people. If something happens I would like Ramona to have it."[6]

Instead of flying in, Reed traveled overland from Uruguay and successfully slipped by the border guards. Still a popular figure, despite his five-year absence from the country, Reed called a press conference in the office of a lawyer friend. Despite the potential dangers to the reporters and their organizations of disseminating views critical of the regime, the television and radio stations and newspapers showed up. The atmosphere in the lawyer's office mixed tension and excitement. Reporters may feign aloofness and cynicism toward public figures, but they are as happy to bask in the smile or familiar word of a superstar as any teenaged girl. But banter with a singing star pales against the possibility of government agents storming into the newsroom and hauling away the reporter or photographer because they reported critical comments. It wasn't a game. Everyone there knew of at least one person who had been held for at least a few hours. Reed greeted the gathered scribes and photographers, made some small talk with the ones he knew from his stay in Argentina, then launched into his written statement.

"I have always believed that every person not only has the right, but also the duty to personally take part in the battle against injustice," Reed told the reporters as the tapes rolled and cameras clicked.

> As an artist, above all, someone who has had the luck to be
> successful has a special duty to use his influence for free-
> dom and social progress in the world. There are types of
> weapons which a person can use in the righteous battle for
> social progress. A writer can use his pen in the battle
> against the enemy, an actor can use the film, a singer can
> use his guitar for it and a revolutionary in the jungles of
> South America, whether it be in the jungles of the cities or
> the jungles in the country, can be made to use a weapon in
> order to defend, by the means of force, the rights of the
> people against the aggressors who are taking action against

the people in the majority of the countries in South America, which are ruled by military dictators. Such an uprising is only a reaction to the years of hidden dictators. It usually doesn't make the headline when thousands of children die due to lack of medical help. It is the result of terror against the Argentinean people when millions of people must live in constant fear of not being able to bring up their families with the most primitive means of survival, when children must go to sleep hungry every night. These are kinds of terror which are public, for example, when the Argentinean police and army are employed against peaceful demonstrators or against workers who strike for better standards of living and when hundreds of Argentineans are thrown into prison and tortured. The people of Argentina have a hundred more times the right to rise up against its dictators as did my ancestors, the American settlers, when they rose up against Britain in 1776.

Argentina has been ruled for years by General Ongania who has forbidden all political parties and under whose dictatorship all honest citizens must live in constant fear, as so-called subversive persons are jailed. Progressive Christian Democrats, Socialists, Communists and followers of Peron are all today in prison for the same reasons because they speak up for the true freedom of the Argentinean people. Just recently, Signor Vandor, who was the president of the largest union, was murdered because he took a stand against the working class being enslaved. Likewise, the former president of the journalist union has been murdered by the police. After a long absence from Argentina, I feel obligated to a modest and personal act of solidarity with the people of Argentina whom I so love. I must tell these people that we, who live in Europe, have not forgotten their difficulties and their righteous battle. They should know that we view the military dictatorship in Argentina as cruel as the military dictatorship which presently rules in Greece. I must say that. Because if a dictator is allowed today to go unpunished when he treads on the rights of the Argentineans, the same thing could happen tomorrow in Italy or in the USA. I believe that progress will triumph in the world, with or without my help, but I have the opinion that my life only has meaning if progress wins with my help.[7]

The general was outraged by Reed's comments. This damn singer had accused him of all sorts of atrocities against his people, including murder. He had called for an uprising against him, using force if necessary. Well, screw Dean Reed. General Ongania had ruled his country for five years. Nobody, not even the U.S. government, had interfered with his rule or his methods and he was sure they wouldn't start now. He had gone easy on Reed before, detaining him briefly and then flying him out of the country. But the annoying American hadn't learned his lesson. It was time to make this Reed bend. Ongania gave the order. Two hours after the press conference, Dean Reed was arrested while walking down the street.

Reed's spirits and confidence were flagging. The isolation and boredom of prison life were wearing him down. Here was a man who had always been active and for the better part of the past ten years, had performed before thousands and met hundreds of people. Now, confined to his single cell, Reed was reduced to doing his exercises and sitting, sitting, pacing and waiting. He had nothing to read, no writing pad and very little human contact. Time passed with excruciating slowness. Prison officials loaded something else on Reed's tottering psyche—psychological torture. A handful of other political prisoners were locked up in prison with Reed. Their only crimes were speaking out and demonstrating against the dictatorship. A couple of those prisoners were the friends who had helped Reed sneak into Argentina. The torture chamber was just down from Reed's cell and he could see the guards drag his friends down the hallway into the chamber. He could hear them crying out in pain, begging the interrogators not to hurt them anymore, that they were sorry for ever speaking ill of the general and his associates. The anguish of his friends nearly broke Reed. On the most basic level, it was horrible to hear his comrades suffering. Worse, it reached deep into Reed's mind and worked on the part of him that felt it was his fault that they were arrested and now faced sadistic tormentors. On the other level, the anticipation and fear of believing that he would be next nicked his defenses. "He said the only thing he thought of was coming back to us," Patricia said. "He had dreams of us."[8] Tucked in his cell with nothing to do all day and all night, Reed replayed in his mind the sounds of those torture sessions. It was an enormous relief when his frequent complaints finally got him a job cleaning the prison walkways.

Back in Rome, Patricia knew something was wrong. Despite their strained marriage, Reed had been good about regularly writing and calling. She knew her husband was planning to breach the Argentine border and she was well aware of the potential dangers if he did. When a week went by with no word from him Patricia began writing and calling the couple's friends in Argentina. Meanwhile, in Los Angeles, Paton Price also was becoming alarmed about the whereabouts of his friend. He organized other friends and they began a writing campaign to the Argentine government demanding to know what had become of Dean Reed.

Finally, sixteen days after he was plucked from the street, Reed was able to get a letter smuggled out of the prison. One of the larger Buenos Aires newspapers took a chance and ran the letter, which also mentioned that he was being held for alleged subversive activities against the government. Now people knew where to concentrate their efforts. Patricia asked her friends, including Reed's old movie costar Palito Ortega, to visit him at the prison and bring him fresh food. At some risk to their own freedom, they did as they were asked. One couple brought him coconuts and papaya. Most of the visitors were turned away and none of Patricia's letters got through. However, a sympathetic guard made sure the food found its way to Reed's cell and he relayed the gist of the messages that were piling up for his American prisoner. In addition, the weakened opposition parties and labor unions, including the actors union, stepped up their demands for Reed's release. "I embrace you sincerely and you should know that this embrace is a symbol that the entire Argentinean people would like to embrace you," wrote Jose Rucci a union general secretary. Those letters, coupled with the pressure from Price's U.S. writing campaign, led to Reed's release after twenty-one days in prison.[9]

Patricia wired money to Reed and he used it to immediately buy an airline ticket to Rome. When he got off the plane, his wife was shocked at what she saw. "I'm sure they thought they had broken him," she said. "When he got off the plane, he stumbled. He was like a dead man. He came out nervous, with a bad haircut. He picked his nails more than ever. He couldn't smile for a long time. He had sores on his body. He was so skinny and he had a flu-like thing he caught there. He smelled bad. His only enjoyment was his daughter. He was tortured in some way, but he wouldn't talk about it. He would just clench his jaw. He started having bad dreams and he always slept well before that. He cried."[10] General Ongania had not broken Reed but he had mangled him badly. Any feelings of invincibility Reed had retained from his earlier brushes with political arrests or shots fired at his house had vanished.

Reed slowly recuperated in Rome, but not even the joy of playing with his three-year-old daughter, nor the harshness of his confinement, could rejuvenate the acting couple's marriage. When Reed had left for Chile and Argentina, he considered it the first step in ending the marriage. In a letter to his mother-in-law, he admitted he had not been a dedicated husband and father, in large measure because he thought it was more important to fight injustice around the world. "For some time now, Patti and I have lost the communication that is important in a marriage and I feel that it was better to separate before we began hating one another. I respect Patti so much. She is a good woman and human being and has tried to be a good wife to me. If the marriage has failed, it is probably due more to me—or anyway to the situation in which I must live. I am sorry for the pain that I have caused Patti—and I have caused much—but I cannot change myself, and I would just cause her more pain in the future as she would case [sic] me pain also."[11] Patricia understood what was happening and while Reed was gone, she landed a role in an Italian movie. Their lives were playing out as they had when Reed dumped her in Mexico eight years earlier and she landed a movie role there. That time, her independence and the love affair with Hugh O'Brien brought Reed back to her. But like most sequels, this one could not live up to the original. One night, after his return from South America,

Reed drove down to a town just outside Naples where Patricia's movie was filming. They ate dinner at a romantic seafood restaurant, but Reed soon killed the mood. He told his wife to quit the film and come back to him or they would get a divorce. It was the same old fight the pair had waged since before their wedding. Reed was the breadwinner. Patricia was supposed to stay home.

"I said, 'I can't, we are in the middle of filming and I'm the star,'" Patricia said. "He said, 'you either quit the film and come back to me or we are getting a divorce.' I said, 'get the divorce.' He didn't expect that. But I said 'this is stupid. You go off on all these trips...' and he would bring gifts back and tell me these fascinating stories and I was jealous because I was not there. When we broke up, I was thirty, very attractive, feeling good about myself. Men were attracted to me. Men with money and fame and they took me to incredible places. Dean wanted me in the house. His dad was very conservative and wanted women in the house and Dean was the same way."[12]

The couple made a pact. The first one to meet someone else they wanted to marry would tell the other and they would quickly obtain a divorce. In the meantime, they lived separately, with Reed dropping by to play with his daughter whenever he was in Italy. But Reed would soon leave the Western world behind. He was about to become Comrade Reed.

Early Dean Reed publicity shots, including a Capitol Records brochure for his single, "Our Summer Romance." The song barely cracked the Top 100 in the United States, but was a top seller in Chile and Argentina.

Rock 'n' Roll Radical

(Top) Reed's Soviet Union shows sold out and young fans besieged him for his autograph.

(Bottom) Reed practices his bow hunting with a native tribesman in the Amazon jungle of Brazil in 1962. When he missed a performance, newspapers in Chile and Argentina reported he was missing in the jungle and feared dead.

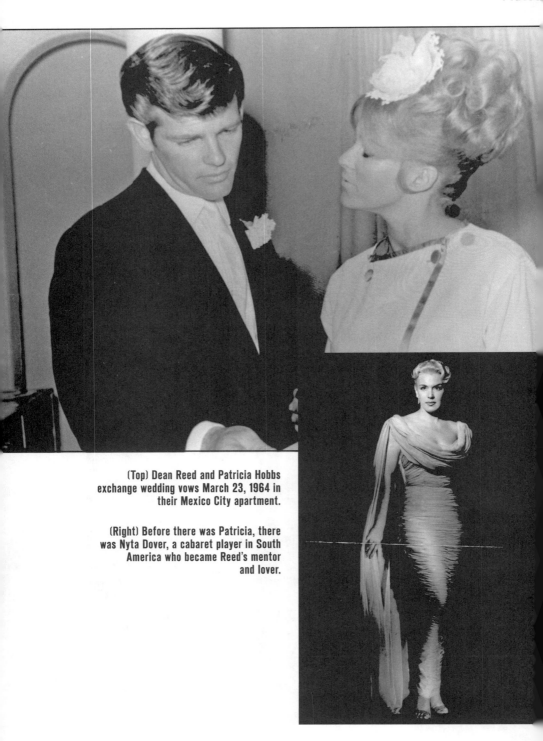

(Top) Dean Reed and Patricia Hobbs exchange wedding vows March 23, 1964 in their Mexico City apartment.

(Right) Before there was Patricia, there was Nyta Dover, a cabaret player in South America who became Reed's mentor and lover.

Publicity shot for Reed's first East German starring role in *Life of a Good-for-Nothing*.

Dean Reed shakes hands with his friend, Salvador Allende, the socialist president of Chile at his 1970 inaugural party. Reed was one of the performers that night.

(Top) In the late 1960s, Patricia Reed, shown in one of her publicity photos, successfully broke into the European movie scene.

(Right) Dean, Patricia and baby Ramona in Rome in 1969.

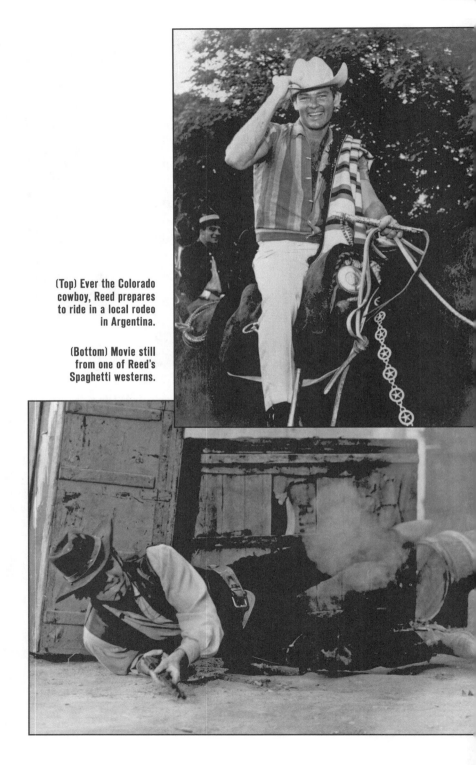

(Top) Ever the Colorado cowboy, Reed prepares to ride in a local rodeo in Argentina.

(Bottom) Movie still from one of Reed's Spaghetti westerns.

The mod Dean Reed performs in Moscow. In the autumn of 1966, he became the first American rock star to perform in the Soviet Union.

Thirteen

Taking a Bride (Part II)

Reed spent much of the summer of 1971 editing his film on the Chilean workers. Word of the movie was relayed to the organizers of the Leipzig Documentary and Short Film Festival in East Germany. The chief organizer, who was well aware of Reed's singing career in the Eastern Bloc, extended an invitation to show his film at the week-long festival in November. Reed readily accepted.[1]

The invitation came against the backdrop of President Richard Nixon's pursuit of a diplomatic thaw with the Soviet Union that he called détente. It was inspired in part by West German Chancellor Willy Brandt, who was negotiating with his East German counterpart, Erich Honecker, to ease travel restrictions between their two nations so families could see each other for the first time in ten years. A key part of détente was cultural exchanges, and with or without the thaw, American leftists such as singer Harry Belafonte and activist Angela Davis, were pleased to accept the invitation to Leipzig. Like all good organizers, the Ministry for Culture, Department of Film, hedged its bet. They showed Reed's film, but also asked him to sing. Reed was happy to oblige and gave a large official concert during the festival and a more impromptu performance at his hotel.[2] While Nixon and Brandt viewed détente as a way to thaw the Cold War, they hoped that easier access to the styles and glamour of the West might dent the rigid control the communist governments exerted over their citizens. The East Germans had a different view.

They saw détente as a weakening by the West, one to be exploited. They used it to flood Bonn and other West German cities with spies. They assumed the Western powers would attempt to do the same and the sudden appearance of the American played into the secret police's paranoia. "The question here concerns what Dean Reed was doing at the documentary film festival. He doesn't make documentary films. Not only was he at the festival, but as an honored guest! Officially, the invitation is from the Ministry, but who is behind him? The question is how did he come to the DDR at all?"[3]

Living in Leipzig was the recently separated Wiebke Dorndeck. Born during the early years of World War II, the thirty-year-old Dorndeck was a sometimes fashion model. She also was socially ambitious. Her family had been reduced to living in a tree house in the latter days of the war and the struggles continued in postwar East Germany under the Communist regime. "She's a real survivor," Patricia Reed said. "For her to get the prize was everything to her. She was a lousy loser. I liked her. She had to survive, wanted a better part of life and did everything she could to get it."[4]

When Wiebke learned that superstar Dean Reed would be coming to Leipzig, she plotted her approach. She was dating a photographer at the time and she knew that he would be shooting the concert. She convinced him to let her help him carry his equipment, hold the flash. The night of the concert, Wiebke arrived wearing a low-cut blouse and a tight skirt. It wasn't until Reed hit the stage that the photographer's assistant made it clear the provocative outfit was for the star, not the shooter. Wiebke worked the stage like a model's runway, pivoting, moving, always making sure Reed could see her as he performed. She flirted outrageously, winking at him, smiling, bending so he got an eyeful of cleavage. Reed never needed much encouragement while on the road and he wasn't going to let such an open invitation from a fashion model go unanswered. After the show Reed invited Wiebke backstage then back to his hotel room where they made love into the early morning.

A few days later, Reed was invited to Potsdam, just outside East Berlin. Wiebke moved into phase two of her campaign. She arranged to be one of the models working there and even though she was wearing a dark wig, Reed recognized her as she pranced down the runway. As she hoped, Reed asked her out that night and it culminated the way their first meeting had with sex until dawn. "Wiebke was a Doris Day-type, " Patricia Reed said. "She had freckles. She was good at enticing men. She was terrific in making love."[5]

Reed was hooked. The East German film company, DEFA, signed him to a major role the next year in the first joint East–West German film, *Life of a Good-for-Nothing*. In the late winter of 1972, he made another Russian tour. As with the others, scalpers raked in a hefty forty rubles ($48) for his tickets and teenaged girls ripped his yellow velvet bell-bottoms and rocked his car as he tried to leave after the show. An American magazine correspondent caught up with him in Moscow and described his voice as weak and watery but "he startles, disarms and enchants his audience by descending among them, embracing all the girls he can get arms around, reciting in phonetic Russian, 'Vy ochen krasivaya' (You are very beautiful)." He told the audience that even his protest songs were love songs because, "If you love mankind, you must protest injustice." Still, he admitted that he gets homesick for the United States and cries when he listens to Frank Sinatra or Bing Crosby records. "If Nixon is welcome in Peking, I should be welcome in Hollywood," Reed said. "After all, I'm not a Maoist."[6] For the moment, Hollywood was out of the question, so Reed found himself traveling to East Germany and slipping over to Leipzig to stay with his new lover. The fact that Reed spoke little German and Wiebke no English did not bother either of them.[7] Wiebke was an intoxicating woman. Like all of Reed's women, she was beautiful. She was a sexual woman. But there was one other attribute Wiebke possessed that intrigued Reed. She was a communist.

"Wiebke was a masturbation for him," Patricia Reed said. "It's a terrible thing to say, but she was his first communist wife. It was just his wanting to marry a communist. To actually live the life, not just to talk about it. He was a man without a country."[8]

Reed was open about the fact that it was the love of a woman that brought him to East Germany. He told people that if it had been a Russian woman, a Pole or Hungarian, he would have settled in those countries. But they all had something in common. They were citizens of a Communist nation. "I was very happy to come to a socialistic country," Reed said. "I was very curious to see how people live in Socialism. It is true that I had often been to the Soviet Union and to other socialistic countries, but only as a guest. I lived in hotels, ate in inns, in spite of all the hospitality, I remained a foreigner. I was curious abut the socialistic daily routine. Today, I can say that I know it and love it with all of its joys and all of its problems."[9]

Reed approached Patricia in spring 1973 and said he wanted to get a divorce so he could marry Wiebke. True to their pact, that they would quickly divorce when one or the other wanted to remarry, the couple flew to Santo Domingo in the Dominican Republic. They plunked down $400 for the quickie divorce and then had one last romantic weekend together. Reed caught a plane to New York, and while waiting for his flight to Germany, he penned a quick note to his now ex-wife. Reed had picked up some powerful enemies over the years but they were politicians and others in authority. In many respects, they weren't real people to him. But the romantic could not bear to have acquaintances, and especially lovers, thinking poorly of him. "Well, we both begin new chapters in our lives," Reed concluded the brief note. "I hope you know that if you are ever in need and I can help—I surely will. Give my love to Ramona. Take Care. Love, Dean."[10]

On June 30, 1973 Reed made Wiebke the second Mrs. Reed. "They were married in a little village and all their film friends were there," Patricia said. "All the villagers threw flowers as they walked through the town. She had a wreath of flowers in her hair and he had a Nehru jacket on. It was like going back a hundred years. They lived in a tiny cottage."[11] But they were not long for the small house. Soon, Reed was applying to the East German authorities for permission to live indefinitely in their country and to move to East Berlin, where he would be closer to the DEFA studios and the television station where he would occasionally sing and produce variety shows. Reed did not have to work hard to convince them.

"The approval of his application lies in the state's interest," according to the Stasi records. "It would, therefore, be recommended that Dean Reed's stay in East Germany be granted for an undetermined amount of time."[12] Soon, the newlyweds were living in a comfortable two-story house overlooking Zeuthener Lake in suburban East Berlin. Indeed, 1186 Berlin, Schmockwitzer Damm 6, would be the last address for the peripatetic American.

Fourteen

Spy

hey called themselves the Ministry for State Security, but they were more commonly known, and feared, by the East German people as the Stasi. They were ruthless and they were efficient. They had the dual mission of infiltrating the West and keeping tabs on the people at home. In both cases, the Stasi was a stellar organization. West German governments, especially Willy Brandt's, were repeatedly shaken by the discovery of Stasi spies in the highest offices, stealing state secrets and planting false information with Brandt's advisors. At home, any attempt at dissension was quickly quashed. The Stasi had an extensive network of informants, which at times seemed to include just about every citizen in East Germany telling stories about their friends and neighbors to the Stasi agents. That kind of information and control produced a cowed and suspicious populace.

"There was a lot of fear there," said Phil Everly, who visited and performed with Reed twice in the late 1970s and early 1980s. "I saw a drunk in Berlin and his girlfriend was trying to calm him down. He was shouting and I asked my interpreter what he was saying. She said he was saying the Soviet Union was wonderful in a sarcastic manner. When we were doing the show, a couple of the musicians had been to San Francisco and one of them got real excited talking about it and his friends were shussing him. It's crazy."[1]

The four volumes of Stasi documents obtained after the fall of the East German government show that they began spying on

Reed almost from the moment he arrived in East Germany. They knew his movements, they opened and copied his mail, and at least part of the time, they tapped his telephone. One of the Stasi's reliable collaborators over the years had been a young Leipzig woman born Wiebke Schmidt, who took her husband's name, Dorndeck, during her first marriage. While she did not provide volumes of information about her American lover to the agents, she did answer their questions about him in at least one report. Nor did the agents push her for much, at least not right away.

Those first years in East Germany were good ones for Reed. Following on the heels of *Aus dem Leben eines Taugenicht, (Life of a Good-for-Nothing)* he made *Kit und Co* in 1974 and *Blutsbruder (Blood Brothers)* in 1975, the latter movie set in the old American West. He was meeting people who would become his good friends, if not immediately, then in later years. Gerrit List, a producer at DEFA, worked with Reed in *Life of a Good-for-Nothing*. Renate Blume, one of East Germany's leading actresses, co-starred with Reed in *Kit und Co* and would later play a larger role in his life. Besides the movies, Reed was performing throughout the Eastern Bloc and Russia and was regularly staging huge variety shows on East Berlin television.

Despite the fact that the money he made in East Germany, Russia and elsewhere in the Soviet sphere could not be converted to dollars, Reed managed to scrape up $300 every month and send it on to Patricia as child support for Ramona. Patricia, as was her habit, was slow about writing him and Reed sent her more letters, telling her to at least once a month acknowledge she had received the child support payment. When Patricia eventually moved back to California with Ramona, Reed simplified his life by setting up an account in Los Angeles and giving Paton Price access to it. Price would make the monthly child support payment from the account. Patricia and Reed parted amicably and he was in regular contact with her and their child, letting them know what he was doing and how his career was progressing. "For the first years, the government gave him a lot of freedom," Patricia said. "He didn't live the life—he didn't have to live with ten people or not have meat on the table. He could have lived in Russia, but he wanted to be close to West Berlin."[2]

Reed would deny that he was living differently than other people in the Communist country, telling anyone who asked that his salary was meager and the rent on his house was very cheap, just like other folks. But the fact was that his house was nicer and he obtained a car immediately, rather than enduring the usual five-year wait. Indeed, there was rarely a need for Reed or Wiebke to wait in line for anything, something the common East German citizen could only dream about. Part of the reason was Reed's American citizenship, which allowed him to travel to West Berlin, South America or the United States to earn hard currency or purchase luxuries. But the East German government also was looking out for Reed. Here was an American who was willing to spout the party line, defend socialism to the West and condemn American foreign policy. It would not do the regime any good to alienate Reed, nor would his defense of socialism ring true if U.S. audiences saw him living in a hovel. And there was one other reason. The Stasi wanted Reed to spy for them.

The Stasi watched Reed for years. They read his mail and followed his comings and goings, both to the East and the West. What intrigued them were his regular trips to the U.S. Embassy in East Berlin. This, Stasi officials figured, could be very useful. In April 1976, they drew up an elaborate plan involving Reed.

"Plan for the follow-through for the acceptance of 'Contact.' To be contacted: Reed, Dean. Goals of the acceptance of 'contact.' Get to know Reed personally; What is his reaction to our appearance and how he feels about the Ministry of State Security (MfS). Is he ready to stay in contact with the MfS and to solve assignments. Does he talk about contacts in the US Embassy in the DDR."

The memo suggested conducting the first meeting at Reed's home and with the help of Wiebke, who was an informant during her first marriage. The approach would be innocuous, almost peaceful in its intent. It concluded by noting that Reed "could bring about qualitative information for the MfS about the activity of the USA Embassy against the DDR."[3]

The famed German bureaucracy moved slowly on the suggestion and it wasn't until a year later, in June 1977, that approval was received to contact Reed about cooperating with the Stasi.

The meeting finally took place at the Reeds' house at 5 p.m. August 17, 1977. The conversation went almost exactly as scripted by the Stasi agents after the initial chitchat.

"Now, Herr Reed…"

"Please call me Dean. As we say in America, Herr Reed is my dad."

The two Stasi agents smiled and Capt. Hauptmann Sattler, continued.

"Certainly, Dean. It's just as minor government officials, it seemed rather pretentious to be calling such a big star by his first name."

"Yes, well, as you can see, I'm not big star here. Wiebke takes center stage in the house, which I expect is the same in your homes, eh? Anyway, you know I'm an admirer of East Germany and the way its government provides for the basic needs of its citizens, so I'm flattered that government officials would come to visit. Although, I have to admit, I'm a little surprised that it's agents of the Stasi."

"We thought you might be," Sattler responded. "But I'm afraid our role in the DDR has been misunderstood. You see, since the breakthrough in the diplomatic blockade, what is often referred to as détente, contacts between the DDR and the West have grown dramatically. We embrace this. Dialogue between all people of goodwill can only bring about a more peaceful world.

"Yes, yes, I have always believed that," Reed said.

"But with those contacts, there comes some danger," Sattler said. "When people have viewed each other with suspicion for a long time, the first contacts can be tricky. And we would not want the process derailed because of a misunderstanding or a misstep."

"Of course not," Reed agreed. "I think the leadership of Erich Honecker and Brandt in this situation is brilliant and represents the best hope we have of not only a peaceful world, but showing the West a different way to live, something different than their greedy capitalism and the foreign policy aggressions it requires to sustain it."

"Exactly, Herr Re…, er, Dean. What we need is to know as much beforehand, so we can determine which contacts are honest and sincere and which ones are meant to hurt our country. After all, there are plenty of people who would love to see this initiative fail. And you possess many abilities which uniquely qualify you to help in this peaceful mission."

The agents had done their research well. This type of flattery always slipped past Reed's defenses. They were telling him he had unique abilities, but more important, that his abilities had to do with making the world a better, more peaceful place. The talents had little to do with his singing or acting. He asked them to elaborate.

"Well, sir, you are a U.S. citizen, an actor and a singer," Sattler said. "Because of that, you might very well come into contact with various diplomatic agencies. All we want is a chance to talk to you about those contacts, should they occur. And again, we only ask because we need to protect the U.S. Embassy as well as expose any subversive plans and intentions against the DDR."

"I don't have a problem with that," Reed responded.

Like all good interrogators, the two agents had to make sure Reed was sincere and not just setting them up. So now they asked him a question, knowing from their surveillance, what Reed's answer should be.

"Do you know of any possible contacts? It could be anything—meetings, invitations, visits to foreign government offices, really anything at all."

"Sure," Reed said. "From time to time, I stop in at the U.S. Embassy. And I've gotten to know the vice-counsel there quite well, a fellow by the name of Jacques Klein. He's a good man and we have nice chats about all kinds of things. You know, sometimes it's just fun to talk about basketball or the latest Hollywood movies. As a matter of fact, Klein called me not long before you guys arrived. He invited me to an embassy party at the end of the month. I told him I would let him know."

Reed had just aced the Stasi test. They knew most of this and were pleased with how candid he had been.

"If it's not too inconvenient for you, we would appreciate it if you would attend that party and then let us talk to you about it the next day," Sattler said.

Reed agreed without hesitation. The agents thanked him and Wiebke for their time and the drinks they had been sipping and departed. Sattler returned to his office and wrote his report on the meeting. "He was very consistent in his appearance and is also eager to support the MfS," the Stasi agent wrote. "There was no negative demeanor. He seems calm and balanced. His manner is modest. He seems to be first and foremost an artist, without the exaggerated manners of a star. To this point he has shown interest. This must be put to use by the MfS."[4]

Even though Sattler couched his presentation as a defensive measure, a way to protect the peace process from sabotage, Reed was well aware of the Stasi's reputation. He had to know he was treading into the deep end, very close to treason. What exactly he was thinking, whether he actually believed Sattler, or thought he could control the Stasi and use them for his own purposes, is unknown. For once, Reed did not share his visit from the agents with any of his usual American friends. When Marv Davidov learned about Reed's Stasi relationship ten years after his friend's death, he said it was news to him, but not necessarily a surprise. "What could he learn at a U.S. embassy?" Davidov asked. "I wouldn't trust any police agency at any place in the world. I have no doubt they were attempting to use him. I think he would work against American imperialism according to his moral and political code."[5]

Reed and his wife attended the embassy party on August 31 and he enjoyed the surprise his appearance caused the Americans. Reed had been noncommittal about coming and never called back to confirm. It was a typical cocktail party, with chitchat among the guests. Many of them knew Reed and his work and wanted to talk to him about his movies and records. A woman maneuvered him away from Wiebke and boldly asked to sleep with him. One of the diplomats tried to bait Reed and show him up by discussing the issues of the day, particularly the neutron bomb, a new weapon developed by the United States that destroyed people but left the buildings standing. The United States caused a furor in Europe by saying it was considering deploying the weapon in Germany to use as a deterrent if the Warsaw Pact armies of the East thought of invading the undermanned NATO troops. The only real development during the evening was an invitation from the U.S. officials to show his movies in the private embassy theater. Reed told them he would be happy to and the Stasi agents were pleased with the offer. Reed freely related all this information, as well as who attended the party, to Capt. Sattler the next day. Before leaving, Sattler gave Reed two telephone numbers he could use to contact the Stasi. And he asked Reed what code name he would like to use. Without hesitation, Reed replied with Victor, a reference to his Chilean friend Victor Jara, a singer, who was killed while in captivity after the overthrow of Allende's government in 1973.[6]

Reed turned out to be a prickly spy. Just a month later, on October 28, the Stasi agents again visited Reed at his apartment. This time, they wanted him to spy on the Palestine Liberation Organization, the sworn enemy of Israel. Just five years earlier, an offshoot of the organization called Black September grabbed the world's attention by bursting into the dormitory of the Israeli athletes at the Olympic games in Munich, West Germany. They held the athletes hostage for two days and killed two of them, while demanding the release of two hundred Palestinians from Israeli jails. A botched rescue attempt resulted in the death of nine other athletes, five terrorists and a German police officer. In an ominous foreshadowing of suspicions about Reed's own death, a Moroccan waiter was murdered in Norway the following year, apparently by the Israeli secret police who mistook the waiter for the mastermind of the Olympic plot. The televised horror of the Olympic takeover soured much of the world opinion toward the Palestinian cause and its leaders such as Yasser Arafat. Yet, Reed had become a great admirer of the PLO, Arafat and their armed battle to establish a homeland in the territory now controlled by Israel.

Reed was scheduled to fly to Beirut, Lebanon, and once there to hook up with the PLO and discuss a possible movie of their struggle, and in particular, the siege of the camp Tel Zaatar. Once again, the Stasi tried to convince Reed that they were only trying to protect the PLO against attacks. But while Reed had been eager to swallow that line when it came to spying in the U.S. Embassy, he balked at reporting to the Stasi about Palestinians who would be traveling with him to Beirut or the conversations they might have. "It was evident that he likes to work against the Americans, however, what concerns the PLO he doesn't want to be noticed," Capt. Sattler wrote after their meeting.

The conversation continued, but Reed would not be swayed. Reed decided to move up the chain of command. He demanded a meeting with General Mischa Wolf, the notorious East German spymaster who had successfully planted scores of agents in the highest levels of the West German government. If Wolf could explain to him why he must spy on the PLO, an ally of the East Germans, then perhaps he would do it. Sattler told Reed he couldn't arrange a meeting because Wolf worked in a different department, but he agreed to bring along his own supervisor to a meeting in the parking lot of the Kosmos Theater on November 1.[7]

The parking lot conversation apparently eased the American's worries about spying on the PLO. He traveled to the Middle East and when he returned, he called the Stasi agents. In early December Reed again met with his handlers and talked about his trip and "enthusiastically told about his impressions of the struggle of the PLO and the planned production of a film about the fighters of the PLO." He also reported that he had invited the U.S. diplomats to the premier of his new movie, *El Cantor*, on December 11. "He expressed in no form any doubt or misgivings against the co-workers of the MfS, on the contrary, by his own initiative he left the impression that he is willing to support the MfS."[8]

But Reed was having doubts about his spying, and more important, the goals of the Stasi and the East German government. Reed, never one to mull over his thoughts in silence, was letting his Stasi handlers know of his disillusionment. Reed was planning to attend the eleventh World Festival Games in Cuba in August 1978. The games, another world gathering sponsored by the Soviet Union and designed to bring together the athletes from the Communist bloc and unaligned nations, was routinely ignored by the United States and many other Western countries. Nonetheless, the Stasi wanted to make sure Reed would present no problems. In a March memo, Stasi officials noted that the singer "has reservations about the MfS," and the state security agents should not ask him to do any work on their behalf at the games. Still, there was no reason to block his trip there either.

"Otherwise, there are no negative references about R. under discussion. He presents a clear political viewpoint, he sets himself firmly on our order of society and above all stands up for the anti-imperialistic world freedom movement. R. has a secure existence in the DDR and has not let it be known that he wants to leave our country."[9]

Reed's unease continued to grow. He accepted that the United States was a danger to the East Germans and to world peace. American foreign policy was aggressive and focused entirely on containing the spread of Communism in the world, and if possible, mopping it up and replacing it with capitalistic democracies. But why should he be spying on allies such as the Palestinians? This made no sense to him. And who else would he be asked to spy on? He traveled frequently to the Soviet Union and met with some of its most important figures. Likewise, he spent time in Czechoslovakia, Bulgaria, Hungary and was scheduled for Cuba. Would he next be asked to report back to the Stasi about these friends and allies as well? Reed's prominence continued to rise in East Germany and he had developed a relationship with the ruling Central Committee and even East German President Erich Honecker.

"I would debate with him what was going on here (in the United States)," Marv Davidov recalled. "I would be critical in some ways of Soviet policy, East German policy, Stalinism and we would debate it. And he would say, 'I can go right to the top.' Which he could."[10]

As Reed's disenchantment and questions grew about his use by the secret police, he decided to stop wrestling with his doubts alone. Reed decided to confront Honecker, himself, about the government's spy policy. What exactly happened, and when, is murky. Sometime in the spring or summer of 1978, Reed drove his car down the wide boulevards of East Berlin, darting in and out of the traffic of poorly running and ugly East German cars until he arrived at Honecker's office. He complained vociferously about the Stasi request to "work against the PLO." While the Stasi officials told Honecker that the American had misconstrued his instructions, the ruckus made him unsuitable for further spying. Major General Kratsch, a high official in the ministry of State Security, ordered Sattler and other Stasi agents to "break off the collaboration with R." The government was now worried about the hotheaded American. What would their propaganda prize do next? The worst possible scenario would be Reed packing up his things and heading back to the United States, where he would tell the newspapers and television reporters what a lousy place East Germany was and reveal what little he knew about their spying operations. They quickly moved to ban foreign travel for Wiebke, because she now possessed an American passport. Even though the couple was having marital problems, the Stasi leaders hoped enough love remained to keep him from leaving her behind.[11] The Stasi was not a timid organization. They would continue to monitor Reed's mail, follow him when they thought it worthwhile and perhaps listen in on some of his phone calls, especially his foreign ones. Somewhere in the bowels of headquarters the possibility of an untimely end to Reed's life must have been mentioned.

Reed did nothing rash. He continued to speak publicly about the glories of socialism and the evils of American foreign policy. But it was the beginning of a reevaluation of his life and his beliefs.

Fifteen

The Smell of Gunpowder

ean Reed was miserable. The end of the 1975 Christmas season found him in a Berlin hospital battling pneumonia rather than at home enjoying the last of the holidays. Lying in a hospital bed left him to his own thoughts much of the time. Frequently, goaded by a survivor's guilt, those thoughts returned to the U.S.-backed overthrow of the Allende government in Chile by Gen. Augusto Pinochet.

Allende had kept his campaign pledges. He nationalized copper mines and other industries and he pushed land reforms. But by 1973, inflation was an astronomical 500 percent, rendering paychecks almost worthless the day they were cashed. The Nixon administration withdrew foreign aid to the nation and the CIA was actively working with opposition groups to topple the Chilean president. Finally, on September 11, 1973, the army, under Pinochet's command, staged a coup. The tanks moved through the streets of Santiago and at least one plane bombed the presidential palace. At first, Allende fought back, trying to rally support. But the bombs set fire to the presidential palace where Allende was holed up and ultimately the president took his own life by putting a rifle in his mouth and pulling the trigger. Pinochet instituted a thorough and brutal crackdown. Leaders of Allende's party, unionists, anyone who was a leftist or a suspected sympathizer of the former president was rounded up. So many were snatched that the army was forced to hold them in soccer stadiums. Many were tortured. Thousands were murdered. Some just disappeared. Besides Allende, other friends of Reed's died during the takeover, including poet Pablo Naruda, although his death was indirectly related to the coup, and singer Victor Jara. Reed had watched the news reports of the army's actions, easily visualizing the tanks moving down the same streets that had once been crowded with his fans as he rode from the airport during his first tour. The deaths of his friends bothered Reed greatly but the crush of obligations from his movie-making and concert dates had prevented him from dwelling on it. Now, the lonely nights and the endless days on his back allowed the thoughts to flood over him.

"Your letter filled with fighting spirit arrived at an opportune time," Reed wrote to Marv Davidov on January 13, 1975. "For the past two weeks I have been in the hospital with pneumonia and even though I'm getting strong rapidly, hospitals in some ways resemble prisons. I have been working very hard on many projects and have been trying to do all possible for my second homeland, Chile. It was the greatest tragedy of my life the day my personal friends such as Allende, Naruda, Jara and many more just as brave and dedicated but less famous were killed. It is the first time I have known the death of friends and I still cannot sleep and have nightmares where I feel I should have been with them."[1]

Davidov suggested in his letter that Reed come to the United States and organize opposition to the Chilean dictatorship and its political support by the U.S. government. Reed quickly accepted and contacted another friend, Angela Davis, to organize concerts, meetings and film showings in Los Angeles, where she taught at UCLA. Other dates were scheduled for Seattle, Denver and New York City.

For Reed, the trip was a chance to visit old friends. There was no friction between Reed and the East German government at the time so Wiebke was free to travel with him and they stayed with Paton Price and his wife Tilly in Los Angeles. Burt Schneider, producer of *Five Easy Pieces*, *Easy Rider*, and *Hearts and Minds*, threw a party for Dave Dellinger and all the Hollywood leftists were there. Shirley MacLaine, Haskell Wexkler, Robert Vaughn,

Susan Anspach, Kent McCord and others mingled with the Vietnam War protestors, including Davidov, who flew out from Minneapolis to see his old friends. On April 30, 1975, the last of the Americans had fled by helicopter from the roof of the U.S. Embassy in Saigon, just hours ahead of the triumphant North Vietnamese Army. For those who had spent years of their lives opposing Uncle Sam's involvement in the war, it was vindication that they were right, that no amount of U.S. help would ever be able to prop up the poorly motivated South Vietnamese troops.[2]

The next day, Reed drove out to Palm Springs, alone, to visit Patricia and their daughter, Ramona. Patricia had returned to the United States about a year earlier and was now living modestly in the desert with Ramona and doing substitute teaching at a school for abused children. The three of them ate dinner together (hamburgers Patricia had picked up at a fast-food joint), and after they tucked Ramona into bed, Reed turned his full attention to his ex-wife. "He romanced me that night and we slept together," she said.

"The next morning he said what about us getting together again. I said no, I want to be a teacher. You just want a roll in bed and somebody to make dinner for you."[3] He kissed his daughter goodbye, jumped into the car and sped back to Los Angeles

A few days later, the Reeds touched down at the Minneapolis-St. Paul International Airport where Davidov picked them up and drove them back to his little apartment near the University of Minnesota's Minneapolis campus. Davidov already had organized some stops for his friend's visit and the next morning they headed out to do the rest. Davidov, after years of leading antiwar protests, was well-known among newspaper reporters and editors. He had contacted the *Minneapolis Tribune*, the state's largest newspaper, and told them Reed was coming, provided the singer's biography and said Reed would be performing to benefit Chile. An editor told Davidov to bring him by for an interview. "When I brought him over, they had just been bullshitting," Davidov said of the *Tribune's* editors. "So I said to Reed, bring your guitar. He started singing and all the work stopped and people started coming over and we got our interview."[4] Then it was on to the University where Davidov could always count on a sympathetic ear at the *Minnesota Daily*, the student newspaper. The *Daily* was housed in Murphy

Hall, about thirty yards from the centerpiece of the campus, its grassy mall. Lining the mall are stately brick classroom buildings and a library. At one end, across a footbridge, is Coffman Memorial Union. At the other end, on an elevated brick plaza looking out over the mall, is Northrup Auditorium. After his *Daily* interview, Reed walked out to the mall, turned right and strolled toward the auditorium. Summer, Minnesota's best season, had arrived and the elm trees stretched their shade over the green grass. The summer session students were tossing Frisbees or just lying in the grass talking with friends. It was also the time of year when a microphone often was set up on the plaza so anyone from student organizations to politicians to traveling evangelists could address the students. Davidov noticed the lonely microphone and suggested his friend go up and sing for the passing students and drum up some more interest. Reed did, and while the college students were mildly engaged, a small group of Soviets visiting the school were startled to see the American superstar performing not fifty feet from them. They began yelling his name and eventually, Reed walked over and chatted with them. They had to be equally surprised that they were able to get so close to the entertainer and that so few people were paying him any notice.[5]

That night, Reed performed at the University Club, a converted mansion on St. Paul's wealthy Summit Avenue. About 250 people paid to hear Reed sing. Between songs, he urged the audience to write their senators and representatives in Congress and demand they stop supporting the Pinochet dictatorship.[6] After four days in the Twin Cities, Dean and Wiebke Reed left and were soon back in East Berlin. But a few months later, Davidov received another letter.

"Dear Friend, Comrade Marv, Presently am giving a solidarity concert for Chile in USSR. But not as Soviet singer Dean Reed, but as American singer Dean Reed. Received the peace prize this year from Hungarian government and Czechoslovakian government. But best of all, Wiebke is pregnant and we shall have one more revolutionary in the world. Hope you are well and happy and fucking in the bed where Wiebke and I had the best fuck in the U.S. I love you, Dean."[7] On May 17, 1976, Wiebke gave birth to Reed's second little girl, whom they named Natascha.

A year later, Reed saw an opportunity to push the fledgling democracy in Spain down the socialist path. Along with Chile and Argentina, Spain was a country he considered a base, a home. While Reed never had the intimate relationship with that country and its people as he did with the Chileans, it had been his refuge when he fled Argentina with Patricia. He made several movies there and often spent weeks and months at time in and around Madrid. The government had made him uncomfortable, the fascist dictatorship of Francisco Franco that had been installed with the help of Nazi Germany in the 1930s and propped up after the war by the Western democracies including the United States. Surprisingly, except for the little kissing civil disobedience with Patricia, Reed had been silent about Spain, its government and its lack of freedoms. But in late 1975, Franco finally died and the monarchy was restored with King Juan Carlos. Carlos set elections in 1977 for a free and democratic parliament. Reed saw a chance for the Communists to win seats and govern the nation and he traveled south to help. He sang at Communist rallies and claimed that 200,000 appeared at a single gathering. He took his politics to the street, where trouble naturally followed.

"But the elections of course are not completely free—yet," Reed wrote to Patricia. "For example of course one does not change a policeman who has beaten and tortured his people for forty years in one day by a new law from the king. On Monday hundreds of cars passed down the main street packed with fascists who gave Hitler's fascist salute. I was walking down the street with a communist senator from Italy and we answered the fascist provocations with our fists high in the air. All of a sudden 2 jeep loads of police screeched to a halt and about 7-8 policeman [*sic*] jumped out in their uniforms for war. The chief looked at me and pointed his finger—and then screamed—hit him—hit him! One policeman came toward me and tried to smash in my skull with his club. I blocked it with my arm. By this time my Italian friend was heading in the direction of Rome! I screamed at the chief, 'but why are you attacking us—the fascists are there and they are the ones who are provoking!! The chief turned red and screamed 'harder, harder—hit him harder.' I was hit one more time before I decided I should not try to reason with the asshole fascists—

Sooo—as you can see—Elections we had—So free they were not!"[8] Reed happily reported to his ex-wife that the Communists pulled in 9 percent of the vote, 1 percent more than the fascists and called it a moral victory. The news was not all political. The American reminisced, telling Patricia that his week in Madrid brought back many memories of their time together in that country, the apartment house where they used to live, a Mexican restaurant where they used to dine. It was a sweet letter and it almost overlooked the fact that they were now divorced and Reed was remarried.

His work done in Spain, he turned his attention to the Middle East. Reed's views were evolving on Israel and the turmoil in that part of the world. In his early concert tours in the USSR, Reed insisted on playing "My Yiddish Mama," despite hostility from the anti-Semitic leadership in Moscow. He had expressed admiration for Israel and Jews in general. But his continuing drift to the left, and ultimately into a Communist country, had meant adopting a view that Israel was a war-mongering proxy of the United States and a major obstacle to peace. The Jews had been without a country until 1947 when the United Nations voted to partition Palestine into two states, one for the Jews and one for the Palestinian Arabs. However, when Britain withdrew from Palestine in 1948 in order to implement the plan, the Arab states tried to prevent the establishment of Israel. They failed, but in the process, the Palestinians were left homeless when Jordan occupied the West Bank and Egypt took the Gaza Strip. The situation only worsened after the 1967 War in which Israel was spectacularly victorious over Syria and Egypt and expanded its holdings to include the Sinai Peninsula, the Golan Heights, the Gaza Strip and the West Bank. In 1973, Reed met Yasser Arafat, the leader of the Palestine Liberation Organization. The two hit it off, not for political reasons, but cinematic. It turned out that Arafat was a bit of a movie buff and was a big fan of Reed's Italian movies. Reed was forever susceptible to a fan's praise and with Arafat lauding his work and recounting some of his favorite movie scenes, the actor was more than happy to spend time with the man many loathed. He listened to Arafat's version of the struggle between the Palestinians and the Israelis and soon Reed was firmly in the PLO camp. Where many in the West saw Arafat and the PLO as terrorists who killed innocent citizens with bombs that blew up marketplaces in Israel and airports throughout the world, Reed saw a champion of peace. "He kept telling us, Arafat is going to make it, quit sweating it," Reed's mother recalled. "He said that Arafat was a moderate."[9]

Reed became intrigued with the possibility of doing a movie about the Palestinians and their struggle. In particular, he thought a movie about two doctors who were in the Palestinian refugee camp Tel Zaatar as it was surrounded and bombarded by Israeli-supported troops during the Lebanese Civil War in 1976 would be compelling. He tried to explain his understanding of that region in a letter to his brother Vernon.

"Of course, it is a very important decision in my life—for as you may know—the zionist secret service has been assassinating our people throughout the world—and of course the one theme which is completely taboo in the USA is to talk against the racist and fascist theory of Zionism. The Zionists have made their propaganda so well, that many people have the false impression that if one is against Zionism—then one is anti-Semitic. Of course, that is a 180 degree turning of the facts. The government of Israel has become the bulwark of fascism today. Of course, someday—the Arabian nations shall rise up and throw off their own false leaders who act as prostitutes between the Soviet Union and the USA—and together with the progressive jewish people, together they shall be able to defeat Zionism."[10]

In early November 1977, Reed flew into Beirut, Lebanon. The PLO provided him with a bodyguard/interpreter. For the first few days he did research by watching films of the Palestinian struggles. Then he spent several days traveling in southern Lebanon, where the PLO Fedayeen were regularly skirmishing with Israeli troops. Reed ate with the soldiers, performed songs with them and fell silent as they listened to shelling first a couple of miles to the east and then to the west of their position. He returned to Sidon where Arafat spoke at the graduation of the new Fedayeen officers, a ceremony that ended early when Israeli warplanes flew overhead. Reed also visited the orphans of Tel Zaatar, again singing songs with them. But his anger rose at what he saw as the constant provocation of the Israelis. Fifty people died in a bombardment in a village five kilometers from Tyre. Three rescue workers were killed hours later in the same village by time bombs.

"I am supposed to leave today for Berlin, but I am so full of hate for the policy which would drop bombs on peaceful peasants that I tell Mahmoud that I do not want to go to Berlin," Reed wrote about his trip. "I want to go to the front lines—but not as a tourist. I want a uniform and weapons and I want to stay alongside my brothers in case a full aggression by the Zionists shall be made."[11]

The transformation of the one-time pacifist was complete. Reed was now carrying an automatic rifle, a Soviet Kalashnikov and a Chinese hand grenade. For three days, Reed walked around the hills, less than two miles from the Israeli border. Over his right shoulder was his gun and on his left, his guitar. "Just after lunch, war planes again can be seen and we all scatter to our positions," he recounted. "I go with the anti-aircraft gunner to the side of a hill. Our trench is dug in under some olive trees. I think of how many years the Vietnamese had to watch the skies—until they were able to live in peace in their homes. I wonder how many years it will take before these brave people shall also fight before they are allowed to live again in their homeland.

"But I truly believe that there are many ways to be a revolutionary—and to change the guitar for a machine gun is not so strange. It should be a normal procedure for any artist who calls himself a true revolutionary."[12]

Reed tried to make a distinction between Jews and the "racists and fascist ideology of Zionism," but it is not a difference he spent any time expounding. He talked about the constant attacks by the Israelis and how if the PLO retaliated to one of a dozen attacks, the Israelis used that as an excuse to justify their bombardment. "Too bad that the great majority of the press in my country is controlled by the Zionists and that my people hear and believe these lies," he wrote. After four days, Reed returned to Beirut where he performed a concert arranged by the PLO at the American University. That night, he was escorted to an apartment where Arafat was staying and writing a letter to Egyptian President An-war Sadat, urging him not to go to Jerusalem to meet with Israeli Premier Menachem Begin. Sadat would ignore that plea and his historic meeting led to one of the first breakthroughs in peace negotiations between Israel and an Arab state. Reed and Arafat talked for an hour and a half and they agreed to make the movie together and dedicate it to the people of Tel Zaatar. "He is a great leader—the most honest and brave in the Middle East," Reed concluded.[13]

The following day, Reed returned to East Berlin. In January, he traveled to Moscow to receive the Soviet Peace Prize. In March, he planned a trip to Hiddensee, a small East German Island in the Baltic Sea, to sequester himself and write the script about Tel Zaatar. But the movie was never made. He wrote the script and even recorded a few songs for the movie. But filming never occurred and Reed blamed it on the continuing fighting in Lebanon.[14] It was a weak explanation because none of Reed's other films were shot on location. Italy and East German terrain were transformed into the Old West and Bulgaria substituted for Chile in his movies. More likely, the East German artistic apparatus didn't come through with the money, either because they didn't have it to spend on him or because they were feuding with their headstrong propaganda prize. "It was one of the things they promised and didn't do," Patricia said. "When he came here in 1978, he said the committee was giving him trouble. That was when Paton gave him the riot act. 'Do you think you can do everything? Do you think you are God?'"[15]

Sixteen

Power Lines and *People* Magazine

The cell door clanged shut behind him. Reed had gone through most of 1978 without offending those in power, but now he was back in jail. This time, it was almost a party atmosphere. For one thing, this was no cold cell with torture chambers down the hall. No, this was a well-built, well-heated county jail in the good old United States of America—Buffalo, Minnesota, to be exact. And he was sharing the cell with his old buddy Marv Davidov and eight other protesters from the Twin Cities. For another, Reed was cooking up a way to bring international attention to his new cause. Still, this was a detour. He hadn't come back home intending to get locked up. He came back to be a star.

His latest movie, *El Cantor*, was a success. Reed did it all in this picture. He wrote the script, directed it and played the lead. The movie depicted the life of his good friend from Chile, Victor Jara. The film's climax comes when Salvador Allende's government is overthrown by the military and Gen. Augusto Pinochet's troops begin rounding up leftists throughout the country. Jara, a famed Chilean musician, is among a large group arrested. He is tortured and finally killed without trial, without charges. The injustice moved even cynical Eastern European audiences and the premier in East Berlin ended in a standing ovation for Reed. The ability to conceive of a story and bring it to life on film boosted Reed's confidence. He scouted locations in Bulgaria that would substitute for the Chile he knew. He shot much of the movie there. In September 1976, Reed wrote to Ramona from his concert tour in Czechoslovakia and outlined to her what his next project would be like. "It shall be very difficult for I am the author, actor and director. It is a great responsibility for the film shall cost more than a million dollars and it shall be dedicated to Victor Jara who was a singer in Chile and who was my friend. He was killed by the fascists in Chile—but he shall continue to live as a symbol for all singers who believe that their art should help liberate man and make him free."[1] While he did not mention it to Ramona, Reed was sure this showcase of his multiple talents would be more than even Hollywood could ignore.

Reed did not fly directly to California. This would be an extended trip to the West, one which began in late August 1978 and ended in November. The first stop on his itinerary was Cuba and the World Festival Games where he ran into fellow performer Harry Belafonte. The two men had met seven years earlier at the Liepzig Film Festival and enjoyed their time enough in Cuba that they agreed to met again in Los Angeles. When Reed's flight from Mexico touched down in Los Angeles, Reed was not ready to work. This was a social call, a chance to catch up with family and friends. He spent a week at the beach with Ramona. Reed was pleased with the way his ten-year-old daughter was developing into her own. They swam in the ocean, bodysurfed and looked for shells. Then it was up to Northern California where Reed hooked up with his father for four days of fishing. They were skunked, but as it was with Ramona, the important thing for Reed was reestablishing the family ties.

"The ties between us were strengthened as they have never been before," Reed wrote to Wiebke. "It was very emotional when we embraced to say goodbye. He respects me and loves me very much at the end of his life .... more than the other boys .... Strange how destiny seems to turn things around at the end."[2] In his letter to Wiebke, from whom he was recently divorced, Reed hinted at a homesickness that he rarely discussed in public.

"It is so good to speak my language again. You know, no matter how well one learns a foreign language it is never like one's own. A language is a very intimate thing....with fine differences in words and double meanings, etc. It is fun to play with my language again. It is very relaxing….and my personality is again reborn."[3]

Buoyed by his visits with his father and his daughter, Reed turned to business. He drove to the NBC Studios and met with Dick Clark. Clark had turned his pleasant personality and an early enthusiasm for rock 'n' roll into an empire. His start was with a local dance show that grew into the enormously popular _American Bandstand_, which featured teenagers dancing to the records of pop performers and then rating the songs. Overseeing the fun was the genial Clark, who would interview the kids and get the bands to perform live and plug their latest record. That initial success opened many doors for Clark. Over the years, he added game show host to his resume and soon was producing various television specials from music to television bloopers for the networks.

On successive days, Reed met with Clark and with Ed Lewis. Clark promised that he would arrange for Reed to make a guest appearance on an NBC show before he left. Lewis began his career as a script writer, then worked his way up to co-producer in the movie _The Admiral was a Lady_. He teamed with Marion Parsonnet to bring the _Faye Emerson Show_ to the young medium of television. After that, he was able to produce shows for the prestigious _Schlitz Playhouse_ and then jumped back to movies where, with John Frankenheimer, he coproduced eight films, ranging from _Spartacus_ to _The Iceman Cometh_. Not only was Lewis a major player in Hollywood, but he also was nearly as left-leaning as Reed. He had recently produced a film called _Brothers_ that he dedicated to the controversial black activist, and Reed's friend, Angela Davis. Lewis offered Reed a contract and he suggested they establish a corporation in Reed's name. He should have been ecstatic, but Reed was cautious.

"We shall see//////I know Hollywood and how easy it is to talk," he wrote to Wiebke.[4] His cynicism was hard earned. Just six years earlier, in another of his stabs at American success, Reed was sure he had made it. _Newsweek_ magazine did a piece on him and he was booked on the _Tonight Show_. Millions of Americans stayed up late every week night to watch Johnny Carson bring on performers of various stripes, have them sit on the couch next to his desk and gently prod them about their lives and their upcoming film, album, club date or television show. For visibility, the *Tonight Show* could not be beat. Carson, himself, was involved in getting Reed on the show. But the *Newsweek* piece scared some of the executives. The networks were already under attack by President Richard Nixon and Vice President Spiro Agnew for being too liberal and they were afraid Reed's radical politics would escalate the dispute. Someone in the executive suites at NBC canceled Reed's appearance and even Carson's pleadings could not sway his bosses. Instead, Reed had to settle for performing at a $50-a-plate Boy Scout luncheon.[5]

Reed's skepticism about Lewis and his offer turned out to be warranted. As Marv Davidov recalled the experience, Reed agonized for a couple of days over the contract and what to do. Reed liked Lewis and thought this could be the break he long had waited for. On the other hand, he remembered the restrictions the syndicate tried to place on him when his contract was sold by Roy Eberhard some twenty-five years earlier. When he finally decided to accept Lewis' offer, something had changed. When he called the number, the secretary said Lewis was not available.[6] He never appeared on any NBC shows either.

Reed packed up his clothes, his guitar and his movie and flew to the Twin Cities, where Davidov had been at work setting up a showing of *El Cantor* on the Minneapolis campus of the University of Minnesota. The days of antiwar protests and fascination with liberal politics were beginning to fade from the campus, but it was still a receptive place for a man who attacked policies of the U.S. government. The *Minnesota Daily*, the student newspaper that circulated among the forty thousand students and the faculty, took an interest in Reed's arrival. The paper announced that the film would be showing the following Thursday evening, October 26. On the day of the showing, the *Daily* wrote a story about Reed, in which he talked about his life and his support for farmers in Minnesota who were fighting the construction of a huge power line from North Dakota to just outside the Twin Cities metropolitan area. Reed also complained that his records were not sold in America because of his politics.

"I've crossed over the line. People will accept a Joan Baez or a Jane Fonda, even a Marlon Brando," he said, referring to three entertainers who had been publicly critical of American foreign and domestic policies. "But not a Marxist living in East Germany." Reed acknowledged it "hurts a little bit" not to find acceptance in his native country, but quickly returned to his defiant self. "I'll come to America when I can help fight for a movement that needs me. But I'm not going to come to the U.S. to sit on my ass. The FBI would love that."[7]

Now that the Vietnam War had ended, Davidov had turned his attention to other issues. The one that had his interest at the moment, and that of much of Minnesota, was the power line protests. Several electrical cooperatives concocted a plan to provide what they thought would be cheap electricity for their customers living in small towns and the outer suburbs of the Twin Cities. They would build a power plant adjacent to an open pit coal mine in North Dakota. Then, to deliver the electricity to the customers in central and east central Minnesota, they would build an 800-kilovolt direct current power line across four hundred miles of farm fields of Minnesota. It was a major undertaking with an expected cost of $1.2 billion for the power plant and transmission lines. Surveyors had to lay out the course and the enormous metal towers needed to be erected. The bulky, tall towers could be seen tens of miles away against the flat landscape and looked like science fiction robots frozen in place with their arms uplifted. What the electrical co-ops, nominally run by farmers, hadn't counted on was the opposition of the landowners whose land the line would run through. Those farmers would receive no benefit from the power, the towers took up valuable crop land and they were convinced stray voltage and electrical fields from the lines would harm their livestock and their families. When the co-ops refused to change the route or abandon the project altogether, and when the legal challenges failed, the farmers turned to direct action.

At first, they removed surveyors' stakes, but that was only a minor irritant. So, when construction crews began showing up in the bitter cold of January 1978, the farmers arrived by the hundreds and blocked their work, sometimes buzzing around the crews on snowmobiles. The Stearns County Sheriff couldn't control the situation and called on the Minnesota State Patrol, which sent troopers to help bring order. At the same time, urban activists took up the cause and tried to convince the co-ops and state agencies to end the project, arguing that it was too expensive and would provoke huge electrical rate increases. Instead, they said the companies would be better off investing in energy efficiency and alternative methods of generating electricity, including solar. When Reed arrived in Minneapolis, Davidov was planning another protest, this time in Delano, about forty miles west of Minneapolis, where the power line was to end at a substation. Davidov briefed Reed on the power line issue before he arrived in town and he was happy to participate.

"Dean was staying with me in my little apartment and we had a meeting and decided who would risk arrest in Delano," Davidov said. "When it got around to him, he said, 'I'll do it too. I've never been in jail in America. I've been in jail in Argentina and Venezuela and I've been thrown out of this and that country.' "[8]

On Sunday, October 29, about two hundred people converged on the power station. The farm leaders spoke, as did Clyde Bellecourt of the American Indian Movement and Davidov. Reed strummed his guitar and sang a few protest songs, with the crowd singing along to the ones they knew. Then the crowd walked across the road and sat down in the power station's driveway. The Wright County Sheriff's deputies told them to move and when eighteen didn't, they were arrested and hauled off to the county jail on trespass charges. Bail was set between $300 and $1,000 and ten of the protesters decided not to bail out. The seven men, including Reed and Davidov, and the three women across the cellblock hallway decided to begin a hunger strike. That would draw some media attention, which was flagging after the first day's rather modest coverage. After all, the power line controversy had been going on for more than a year and had peaked with the January protests and mass arrests. But Reed, who had been promoting himself and his ideas around the world for fifteen years, told his friend he knew a way to get all the publicity they wanted.

"Dean said to me, 'we can make an international incident,'" Davidov said. "I said, 'tell me brother.' He said, 'I can make phone calls all over the world and get pressure on this situation.' I said bring it up with the others and we'll communicate with the women. The authorities were listening in, but they didn't give a shit because it was interesting. So Dean brought it up and nobody believed it. I said, 'hey man, he ain't bullshitting.' "[9]

And he wasn't. After calling the farm leaders and getting their blessing, Reed waited for the phone cart to come around. He put down his dime and made collect calls. He called the American actress and his long-time friend Jean Seberg who was now living in Paris. The former Paton Price students chatted and she agreed to talk to Jean-Paul Sartre and others in France. Reed called John Randolph, the head of the Screen Actors Guild. He called Price, of course, the Everly brothers, the Smothers Brothers, Don Murray and Hope Lange. Then he started calling his friends in Chile, in East Germany and the Soviet Union.

The strategy worked immediately. Telegrams flooded into the offices of Minnesota Governor Rudy Perpich and President Jimmy Carter by the hundreds. Many of the telegrams, especially those from behind the Iron Curtain, played off Carter's human rights stance, which was the cornerstone of his foreign policy. Frequently, he lectured other countries or based decisions on American aid depending on how well those countries allowed their citizens to enjoy basic human rights such as free speech, public arrests and trials and honest elections. John Randolph sent a telegram to Perpich and said "as a citizen and member of board of directors of the Screen Actors Guild I am outraged at learning of arrest of internationally famous actor and singer Dean Reed and other citizens on the flimsy basis of trespassing while peacefully demonstrating in support of Minnesota Farmers. We make fools of ourselves in the world defending human rights everywhere and then we see the Sheriff of Wright County and his deputies violating those rights of fellow Americans who were involved in a nonviolent conscientious action."[10]

The calls and telegrams were news. Suddenly, not only was the power line struggle back on the front page, but Reed finally was getting some ink at home as well as the customary coverage abroad. Tass, the Soviet news agency, sent a reporter and East German television sent a camera crew. But more important, United Press International, Associated Press and *People* magazine all had reporters interviewing and photographing Reed. The coverage sent the U.S. embassies in Berlin, Moscow, and Budapest, Hungary, into action, cabling telegrams to Washington demanding information on what had happened to Reed and relating the coverage and comments in the Eastern Bloc countries.

"All GDR media are currently giving prominent attention to the recent arrest of 'Peace fighter and folk singer' Dean Reed in Wright County, Minnesota," read the telegram from the Berlin Embassy. "Reed is a U.S. citizen residing in the GDR who is active in East German and other East European agitation and propaganda efforts. He is allegedly in jail in Minnesota for participation in a farmers' demonstration and is now on a hunger strike." The telegram went on to say the arrest "has prompted a growing, well-organized reaction from various GDR organizations in support of Reed," many of whom had sent messages to President Carter demanding his release. The chief East German newspaper *Neues Deutschland* carried Reed's telegram of greeting to the people of the GDR and President Erich Honecker on its November 6 front page, according to the embassy telegram. The embassy's East German sources were interested in the story and wanted to hear the American version of events. "The attitude among the East Germans with whom we have spoken in the past few days is that the arrest is probably a publicity stunt on Reed's part and another opportunity for the GDR media to flog human rights conditions in the U.S. Indeed, several of our contacts have gone so far as to express dismay that US authorities have provided Reed with an opportunity to burnish his lackluster image as a 'Freedom Fighter.'" The telegram concluded with a request for information on what was happening to Reed and what the press was saying back home.[11]

The embassy in Moscow was even more alarmed. They noted that four leading Russian musicians had sent a letter to President Carter calling for him to secure Reed's release. "The current media attention here—which is portraying this as a major human rights issue—suggests that the Soviets could raise it during the Ribicoff/Bellmon Codel visit," a reference to an upcoming congressional delegation visit led by Sen. Abraham Ribicoff of New York. That would be potentially embarrassing for the senator, especially at a time when Soviet–U.S. relations were prickly.[12] A telegram was sent back, over the signature of Secretary of State Cyrus Vance. It detailed the circumstances around the arrest and hunger strike and concluded that "it would appear that the Soviets have made an elephant out of a flea (as the saying goes) on this one."[13]

The days in the Wright County jail settled into a routine. Every morning, about 6:30, Reed would rise and loudly sing, "Oh what a beautiful morning, oh what a beautiful day," to the dismay of the burglars, drunk drivers and other inmates who were trying to sleep. They would yell at Reed to shut up, but he would finish his song and then drop to the cold floor to do push-ups to keep in shape. Despite the hunger strike, Reed was determined to maintain his muscle tone. The ten protesters would drink their water and wait for the deputies to open their cells so they could congregate in the cell block where they would talk for hours about politics, the leftist movement in America and the world and just get to know each other. On day seven, Price arrived from California to visit his old friends Reed and Davidov. He pleaded with them to give up the strict water diet and at least drink orange and grape juices. After a group discussion, they agreed they would do that much. But the prisoners were losing a lot of weight and Price continued to worry. Finally, the day before the trial was slated to begin, the trespassers were released on their own recognizance. No money was ever posted by the ten. On that eleventh day, the Delano Ten walked from the jail and immediately met with their lawyer, Ken Tilson, to prepare for the trial. And they ate their first solid food in well over a week. Tilson, a Twin Cities lawyer who had made a career of representing the poor and protesters of every stripe, gathered his clients together to go over their testimony and the statements they would make at the jury trial.

"As we were rehearsing our testimony, everybody would give their statement and the rest of us would critique it," Davidov recalled. "I remember Dean said, 'I got a lot of criticism. Don't people like me?' That's the actor. They have to be loved. They are insecure that way. I said, 'Hey man, everybody is getting this criticism, why should you be an exception?' And then, after we were done, he would have his guitar and he would say, name a song of the '50s, rock 'n' roll, anything and he knew everything anyone would come up with, so those sessions were really joyous."[14]

The trial lasted three days before a six-person jury that included a teamster, a postman, a farmer and a woman who ran a boutique, among others. All twenty people arrested were on trial but it was determined that only eight would give testimony and make statements. Reed was selected to be one of the eight. He told the jury he was born and raised in Colorado and ticked off all the places he had lived since becoming an adult.

"Some people may try to infer that I am an outsider," he told the jury.

> But you see, I am an internationalist in that I believe in one large human family—so how could I be an outsider? I, like you, eat food (usually) so how can I be an outsider to our farmers who produce it? All of us in the world who want to keep eating and who want the millions of people who are presently dying of hunger to start eating, must be interested in the problems of the farmers of our country.

> "I have been accused of trespass, but may I say that I do not accept that accusation. I am not the defendant here. I am their accuser, and my finger is pointing at the large U.S. coal companies who plan to make huge profits through the building of these power lines. They are the trespassers! They are not only trespassing upon the land of Minnesota farmers but also upon their human rights!

> On the twenty-ninth of October, after singing for a peaceful protest demonstration, I carried a sign which read, 'Power to the People,' to a line of police where I continued singing until I was arrested. Civil disobedience is an honored American tradition of fighting injustice when all other methods have failed. Who among you are not proud of the American patriots who threw the tea into the waters at the Boston Tea Party in that historical act of civil disobedience?

> Someday the people of America will also look back with pride on the acts of civil disobedience which are now appearing throughout the United States in protest to the corporations who are polluting the environment and who value their profits far more than human lives. And that is the issue here today—not we: the rights of the large American coal companies to make their huge profits versus the human rights of the farmers.

One of your farmers told me just before my arrest about one of his neighbors who is eighty years old. The power line people came to him and told him that if he didn't sell his land to hem, they would condemn it and take it anyway. He sold his land and lost everything that, for the past eighty years, had given him strength, purpose, nourishment, health, pleasure and love."

Reed had been talking directly to the jury, but now he pivoted and bowed to the judge.

Your honor. Members of the jury. Today, millions of people from South America to Europe are watching you and your decisions. They are waiting to see if you will decide in favor of the large corporations and their profits, or in favor of the human rights of the farmers and citizens of your state and our country. I trust that you will make the correct decisions, because I respect you. That is why I am here: because I respect the rights of the Minnesota farmers and I felt that I must give to them my active solidarity.

Yes. I have faith that you shall come to a just decision and find me and my fellow prisoners not guilty. It has been one of the great honors of my life to have been on a hunger strike in my cell for the past eleven days with my friends sitting here. They are good and principled human beings and we all should be very proud of their courage and honesty. Power to the people!¹⁵

Reed sat down and listened to the other closing statements. Then the jurors filed out. Seven hours later, the jury returned with its verdict: not guilty. The defendants broke into big grins, hugged and shook hands and headed back to Minneapolis for a victory party. In many ways, it was a good verdict for Jimmy Carter. He could continue to prod other countries about providing their people with human rights and the rule of law while being saddled with one less example those countries could point to in return. Secretary of State Vance fired off a telegram to the U.S. Embassy in Moscow with instructions on how to respond to the messages of the Soviet musicians who had urged Carter to release Reed.

"I understand that you sent President Carter a telegram expressing concern over the arrest of Dean Reed," Vance instructed the embassy to reply. "Under the U.S. system of justice, to be arrested or charged is not tantamount to conviction, and in fact, Mr. Reed and those arrested with him were acquitted on November 14 by the local court having jurisdiction.

"We share your interest in human rights and believe that good people should express their concern whenever they see possible abuse of these rights, regardless of international boundaries."[16]

Reed, too, was pleased with how everything worked out. In a note scrawled at the bottom of his statement to the jury, which he sent to his daughter Ramona, Reed wrote that "it was not only a great victory for the farmers of Minnesota, but for all progressive people in America."[17] It also was a win for the singer. A jury of middle-of-the-road Americans listened to what he, and others, said. They listened to the prosecutor. When it was their turn to decide, they came down on the side of the protesters. Even better for Reed, it generated some much-needed publicity for him in American newspapers and magazines.

Reed's close-up view of American justice also gave him something to contrast to what he was seeing in Eastern Europe. It did not escape his notice that the American system he had criticized for twenty-five years had worked in favor of the little guy, of poor students and hard-working farmers. He knew that was not the case in the Communist countries, even as he tried to rationalize the harsh judicial system there by praising the overall efforts for equal treatment in food, medicine and employment. Just a couple months later, Reed was back in the Soviet Union to perform at an international youth festival and ran into a U.S. diplomat waiting for a flight at the Moscow airport. The officer, who was aware of the earlier scramble for information on Reed after his arrest, asked him about his lockup and day in court.

"Yes, I had a trial with a jury and was acquitted," Reed said, according to the diplomat's report. "Another triumph for truth, justice and the American way." Reed also pulled out photos of himself singing at the rally and shots of himself in jail. "He was generally animated and very much the star, as he told the group funny stories about his incarceration in the US jail. As he left, he gave a clenched fist salute to the giggling Intourist girls who'd gathered to see the great American singer."[18]

Seventeen

Taking a Bride (Part III)

Reed returned to East Berlin and an empty house. He had divorced Wiebke in February, 1978, but allowed her and Natascha to live there awhile longer. However, he wanted them in their own place when he returned from the United States. As Reed explained to his brother Vernon, the marriage was based on good sex because neither spoke the other's language at first. Once they did, they found they were not very compatible. He went into even more depth in a letter to Paton Price just after the divorce.

"I am so happy that I am no longer tied to Wiebke," he wrote. "She of course is now doing all that I wanted her to do before—but which before she refused to do. She is teaching and also taking part in politics—(as translator for the political song festival). We don't argue so much—and we fuck as good as ever. With part of the money that I gave her in order to get the divorce—she shall buy a house about five minutes from me—and shall move in July. It may be lonely at times living alone—but I would rather be lonely at times than living with hate toward the person one lives with. I never again want to have to go to work with hate in my heart for the woman who lives with me. I don't know why I always marry women who want to be stronger than me? I refuse to fight anymore everyday just to gain equality!!!"[1]

Reed kept up a steady schedule of touring in the Soviet Union and countries behind the Iron Curtain. He recorded albums, a mix of primarily American and British rock and his own folk and country compositions. He also was putting on yearly television extravaganzas for East German television, similar to the old Ed Sullivan show. Reed would trot out dancing girls, animal acts and singers from all over the world. To warm up the audience, Reed would revert to his college gymnastics days and walk on his hands. In 1979, his friend Harry Belafonte agreed to appear on the show. However, as the date approached Belafonte canceled. Reed, scrambling to fill the spot, decided to contact his old friend Phil Everly.

The hits started drying up for the Everly Brothers with the arrival of the Beatles in 1964, but they maintained a loyal following and continued to release albums and perform on stage. They were still enough of a draw that in July 1970, ABC TV aired *The Everly Brothers Show*, a variety program designed as an eleven-week replacement for the *Johnny Cash Show*. Still, the brothers' trademark harmonies were heard only during their performances. Off-stage, their voices were discordant with constant bickering over professional and personal decisions. It all collapsed July 14, 1973, at the John Wayne Theater at Knott's Berry Farm in Hollywood. The brothers were scheduled to perform three sets that day, but the theater's entertainment manager stopped the show midway through the second set because he was unhappy with Don Everly's performance. Phil Everly smashed his guitar in disgust and stormed off the stage and out of the theater. Don Everly agreed to perform a solo third set, where he announced the breakup by saying, "The Everly Brothers died ten years ago." Phil continued to make records, first for RCA, then with a British label. They generated little interest, but in 1978, Phil appeared in Clint Eastwood's box office smash, *Any Which Way but Loose*, singing a duet with Eastwood's co-star, Sondra Locke.

Phil Everly and Reed had not spoken in years, but Price kept them up to date on each other's activities. When Reed called him directly and asked him to perform on East German television, Everly decided it would be fun to perform with his old buddy and interesting to travel to the Communist country. Everly, a conservative Republican, was surprised by two things when he arrived in East Berlin. The economic and political situation was worse than he imagined and his friend was an unbelievably big star. "Every-body knew him," Everly recalled. "You didn't go into a restaurant without the chef coming in. Everybody knew Dean. When you stay at his house, it was hard to fathom. There were ten, fifteen girls at his driveway with flowers every day. I didn't believe it until I saw it." As he was getting ready to leave, Everly flew out of the East Berlin airport, rather than driving through the checkpoints and catching a flight from West Berlin. He and the other passen-gers flying to the West were put in a stark room with a guard tot-ing a machine gun. It was late in the day, the commissary had just closed, when airline officials suddenly announced the flight was canceled. Everly was looking at the unpleasant prospect of spend-ing the whole night there. The American had watched the guard brusquely deal with anyone who had approached him with a question in German, so Everly was reluctant to ask for a favor with only English at his disposal. After weighing the possibilities, the singer decided spending the night in that airport room was far worse than being upbraided, or even struck, by the soldier. Speak-ing English, a few words of German and pointing and gesturing, Everly was able to make the guard understand that he knew Dean Reed and had his phone number. When the guard heard Reed's name, he quickly got the commissary reopened so Everly could use its telephone. When Reed arrived a short time later, the star-struck guard, his machine gun now slung over his shoulder rather than cradled in his arm, came in and fetched Everly. Everyone else remained in the airport until the next day.[2]

While the trip confirmed Everly's suspicions of how bad life was in Communist countries, for Reed it was just plain fun. The two picked up where they had left off nearly twenty years ago. They acted like old fraternity brothers at homecoming weekend. Reed showed Everly the sights, they ate at restaurants, rehearsed for the show and laughed frequently. They also debated, Everly the Ronald Reagan Republican, Reed the Marxist American living in East Berlin. Reed was not blind to the problems. "He knew what was wrong there. I think he would have liked to have been more home than not. We were in a car in East Germany and laughing about it," Everly recalled. "If they sold oranges like these in Amer-ica, we would have gone to war. They were from Russia and it looked like they took all the juice from them."

Still, Reed would argue that the communist nations were on the right track, bad oranges and all. At least everyone had their basic needs of food, clothing, housing and health care met, even if the food was not up to capitalist standards. People weren't going hungry or living on the streets or in shacks as they were back home, Reed said. But Everly kept up the offensive. He pointed out that Reed's neighbor was a butcher who would bring him meat so the American didn't have to stand in line for an hour like most East Germans. Reed had a car, he had a nice house, Everly pointed out, two things many of the people in his new country would never see. "He said the government gave the house to me," Everly said. "I said, 'what about the guy they took it from.' He laughed and said, 'You've got a point.' "

Everly had no doubt that Reed believed the praise he heaped upon the Communist system and the scorn he professed for many of America's policies. But Everly was reassured that Reed had not somehow sold his soul to the East Germans and Soviets in exchange for a nice house and movie and recording contracts. Reed was still defying those governments when they asked him to do things he did not believe in. Everly was aware of Reed singing "My Yiddish Mama" in the USSR. Everly witnessed how Reed's popular TV specials in East Germany frequently featured performers who were out of favor with the local commissar of music, a person who had the absolute power to say who worked and who didn't. Reed paid no attention, bringing in the people he wanted, including a performer who had once fled the country for the West. "I think that was his way to maintain … he called himself a Marxist," Everly said of the defiance. "Dean had that independence from the [Communist] party and he was a powerful tool for them because he was from America."

Reed told Everly about his performances around the world, every detail, including when his jokes bombed. He was performing for the Palestinians and told one of his standard yarns about an East German plane whose wings would fall off every time it flew, sending the plane into a fatal dive. The Germans put their best scientists on it and no matter what they did, the wings would detach from the fuselage and send the plane spinning toward the earth. Desperate, the government asked everyone in the country for suggestions. A man from East Berlin told the engineers he came up with a solution while sitting on the toilet. He instructed the engineers to drill some holes in the fuselage near where the wings attach. They did, the plane took off and flew for more than hour and landed safely. The scientists and engineers ran up to the man and asked him why it worked. He said, "The toilet paper never tears on the perforations either." The joke never failed to get a big laugh, except with the Palestinians. The problem was Palestinians don't have the toilet paper the way Western countries do and the joke died, Reed told Everly.[3]

Professionally, Reed had few complaints. He traveled to Bulgaria where seventy thousand people filled a soccer stadium to hear him perform. For awhile he dated a woman that the DEFA Studios assigned to be his interpreter during his film work. The romance never became very serious and by 1980 he was still living the bachelor's life, occasionally dropping by Wiebke's house to play with his daughter Natascha. Reed also was writing another movie that he planned to direct and star in, just as he had in *El Cantor*. But this time, he wanted a lighter vehicle, a comedy set in the American West. More than that, he wanted to work with his old friend and coach, Paton Price. Late in life, Price and his wife adopted a child, their first and only. They named the boy Dean. So the elder Dean paid for the three members of the Price family to fly to East Germany. He was thrilled to spend some concentrated time with his old friend. He showed the Prices around East Berlin and put them up in his now spacious house on the lake. The home, which was remodeled by Wiebke, looked a lot like Reed's Argentina house with its white stucco and red tile roof and back patio. A large grassy backyard with evergreens and a few hardwood trees sloped down to the lake and Reed's wooden dock.

Reed took Price to the DEFA Studios and introduced him to Gerrit List. List had produced Reed's first East German movie, *The Life of a Good-for-Nothing*. They didn't see much of each other for a few years after that, but reunited three years later to do *Blood Brothers*. A professional and personal friendship blossomed and they collaborated again with *El Cantor*.[4] List was on board for the new movie and was willing to let Price be the co-director with Reed.

The movie they made, *Sing Cowboy Sing*, hit the East German theaters in 1981.

From time to time, Reed also bumped into one of DEFA's biggest stars. Renate Blume had been under contract with the studios for nearly fifteen years. Her most famous role was as Jenny Marx in a DEFA film about the life of Karl Marx. She and Reed had starred together in *Kit und Co* in 1974, and had gotten along well, even during the biter cold Russian winter when the film crew shot the outdoor scenes. Still, after the movie was completed, they had gone their separate ways. Now divorced for two years, Reed turned his attention to the long-haired brunette, romancing her with flowers, songs and conversation, just as he had with Patricia, and to a lesser extent, Wiebke. Despite his pledge never again to marry a woman who wanted to be stronger than he, Reed was falling in love with someone who was at least as well-known in East Germany as he. Price witnessed the blossoming romance while in East Berlin and he didn't like it. Price advised Reed not to marry Blume. He suggested Reed remain single a while longer. Price was dying of cancer and in 1981, Reed flew to California to visit his dear friend in the hospital. He and Phil Everly and other Price pupils gathered around his bed and the two singers serenaded him. But later the talk turned serious and Price urged his Reed not to tie himself down to another East German woman. Better to remain free, he advised and give the United States, and a career here, one more shot while he was still a relatively young man.[5]

Reed ignored the advice. On September 22, 1981, his forty-third birthday, he married the thirty-seven-year-old actress. She wore a beautiful white wedding dress. He wore a sport coat and a white, open collar shirt. They settled into his house on the lake, along with Alexander, Renate's son from her first marriage. They were a power couple, she with her following as a movie actress and he with his films, television and singing. They could exert some leverage on the entertainment bureaucrats. But surely the apparatiks were equally happy. Their propaganda prize, Dean Reed, was in no danger of slipping away from them now. Reed was a romantic. What else can you make of a man who had tried marriage twice and failed? Here he was fearlessly slipping the ring on a third time. Once more he was happy, almost schoolboy giddy over his new love and his good fortune. Reed was suffering from marriage Alzheimer's, forgetting about the first two and convinced that Renate would be his one and only.

The joy of the wedding day turned to mourning just eight months later with a call from Tilley Price. Paton Price finally succumbed to the cancer on May 3, 1982. Reed took the news calmly at first, consoling the wife of his dear friend. But after the call was complete, Reed cried hard. No man, with the possible exception of his father, ever meant as much to him as Price. The older man had taught Reed much about life, love, acting and seeking the truth. Price had flown to wherever Reed had been imprisoned, from South America to Minnesota. Even when Reed dropped Paton's pacifist philosophy and decided that guns and war were sometimes necessary, the two men would argue but tended their friendship so it would continue to thrive. The pain of Price's death was just beginning to ebb when five months later Reed's father, Cyril, died suddenly. His father, by now remarried to a childhood sweetheart, had taken one of his guns and shot himself on October 29. It's hard to say what exactly drove Cyril to pull the trigger. Reed would later view his father's death through the Marxist prism and decide it was because he could not afford a new artificial leg.

"We have other reasons to commit suicide in socialism, but not this," said the American, swiveling in a chair overlooking the wind-ruffled Zeuthener See. His motorboat was up on blocks for the winter. Did he ever think of sending his father money? "My father was very proud," he said.[6]

Reed's brother Dale explained that Cyril's leg was hurting him and doctors had found some moles on his body they said should be cut out. The cost would be covered by Medicare. But Cyril, always the conservative, said somebody would be paying for it and in this case it would be the taxpayers. "I think he thought that if he went into the hospital, he would never get out," Dale Reed said.[7]

Perhaps driven by the deaths of Price and his father, Reed exploded a week later. Reed was driving the highway from Potsdam, near his home, to Leipzig on November 5. Police had set a speed trap and were pulling people over into a parking area just off the road. It was unlike Reed to drive the speed limit, but on this day he was obeying the law. No one from the People's Police flagged him into the parking area, but he turned in anyway. He jumped out and demanded to know why the police had not pulled over the car that had just passed him far exceeding the speed limit. Reed had noticed they were government cars, driven by Communist Party leaders, and demanded to know if that was the reason the police let them sail by. The police refused to answer and ordered Reed to get back into his Lada and drive away. Instead, Reed shouted at the officers.

"Under disregard of this invitation, Reed began to make insulting and defamatory remarks, in which he characterized the members of the VK (Volkspolezie or People's Police) as hypocrites, compared the GDR to a fascist state and expressed that he, as well as the 17 million GDR citizens, have had it 'up to here.' He underlined the latter words with a corresponding hand movement. Furthermore, he called upon the VK members to arrest him, which 'was the usual thing.' For affirmation, he held his hands to the VP member," according to the police report. The police officers ignored Reed, so he sat down in front of the squad car in the parking lot. At that point, an officer asked for his identification papers. Reed, still probably hoping for an arrest, got up, jumped into his car and roared away. The officers reported it to their superiors, but no one chased him and no further action was taken.[8]

Reed was hot during this confrontation. Calling East Germany a fascist state was the worst insult that could be hurled, since that term was reserved for the United States and its allies. Reed clearly was reflecting the popular mood. The official Western policy of détente, now weakened under the Reagan Administration, had nonetheless made major inroads into the psyche of the citizens of Eastern Bloc nations. During the 1970s, with cultural exchanges, as well as the constant beaming of Western radio and television programs into their countries, East German, Polish and Soviet citizens had seen how well the West lived. Working people there had good food, better music, better movies, cars and great fitting blue jeans. Some East Germans had those things, too, but it was only the elite, the Communist Party functionaries and their families.

They received special treatment, a huge contradiction to the official party doctrine of equal treatment for everyone. It grated on the people of East Germany and provoked a national cynicism. For Reed, it was even more irritating because he was being ignored in his own country, in part because of his outspoken advocacy on behalf of the East German government and socialism in general. He wanted to believe in the Marxist principle of "to each according to his needs," and yet, the party leaders were getting favored treatment while the police picked on the little guys who were just trying to get by.

His friends back home never heard of the incident until long after Reed's death. But it did not surprise them. "That sounds like Dean," said Phil Everly. "He had influence. They used him, he used them. He stood for things."[9]

The roadside incident added to the growing pile of Reed's rashness that was making the East German officials nervous about their prize. Reed, too, was getting edgy. Not only was the situation within East Germany worsening for him, but his conscience was beginning to bother him. Living in a Communist country had made a nice statement to the world about what he believed in, but it was wearing off. People did not much care anymore where he lived and battles he wanted to fight were out there, back in the Western Hemisphere. He no longer felt like he was on the front lines.

Eighteen

Reed and the Bloody Dictator

The phone rang at the U.S. Consul General's home in Santiago, Chile. It was 6 p.m, Friday, August 19, 1983 and he was hoping to relax a little at the end of what had been a turbulent week.

"Hello, this is Dean Reed," the consul general heard on the other end. "There are sixty police officers breaking into my apartment. They are here to arrest me."

The American official could tell from Reed's barely successful effort to control his voice that the situation was serious. He also calculated that the police could just as easily have smashed the door and not given Reed a chance to make the call. That was a good sign. He decided to push the advantage and asked the singer if he could speak to a captain. One of them obliged and the two men held a brief conversation. The officer identified himself as a member of the Chilean International Police. The consul general reminded the captain that Reed was an American citizen and asked why they were arresting him.

"We only want to question him about his activities here in Chile the past three days," the captain said. "It will take no more than an hour or so."[1]

The police hustled Reed out the door and into a waiting car. At the police station, his interrogators insisted he sign a statement declaring he would leave Chile forever. Reed was scared when the officers surrounded the apartment and came through the door. He had been worried since he arrived in Santiago that something might happen to him and said as much in a letter to his daughter Ramona. But the assurance he heard the captain give to the U.S. officials put the fight back into Reed. He refused to sign any statements. The argument went on for about twenty minutes. Finally, the police gave up, led Reed to another unmarked car and said they were taking him to the airport and expelling him from the country. Reed grinned, climbed into the backseat, and enjoyed the moment. He had beaten Gen. Pinochet.

The car pulled out of the parking lot and into traffic. Reed's thoughts drifted to Renate and how good it would feel to hold her, kiss her and tell her how he had performed his protest songs under the nose of the evil general. He looked out the window to see how close they were to the airport. He bolted from his slouch and peered out intently. The car was headed away from the airport into a deserted area without houses, without witnesses. The blood drained from his face. The car pulled to a stop. The American felt cold and his stomach hurt as the muscles contracted. Quietly, now, from a mouth suddenly gone dry, Reed forced the question.

"What are you doing?"

The two police officers obviously enjoyed their passenger's distress.

"We are simply following orders, Señor Reed," one of them replied, a tight smile on his face.

Reed didn't know what to do. Like all police cars, this one was locked from the outside. No one knew where he was, he was outnumbered and he was pretty sure he was going to die. The only real question seemed to be from which direction would death come. Time became a cruel mistress for Reed, dragging out her routine interminably. After a while, and by now Reed had lost all track of minutes, the car started up and the cops drove him a few more miles before stopping in an equally secluded area. Then another wait, this one just as mysterious and just as nerve wracking. His mind raced through his options. There were none. The events of the past months flashed by.[2]

He had spent most of 1983 performing both musically and in a movie. He traveled to Belgium where he was one of the stars of a Japanese-West German film called *Races*. In it, Reed played a motorcycle racer and as he had in most of his films, Reed performed his own stunts. The publicity shots showed him in leather, with a motorcycle helmet on his head and a clear view of his unlined face. It was his fourteenth film, and as it turned out, his last.

Reed also picked up a biographer of sorts. Riding along with him and filming his every move was Will Roberts, an independent film maker. Roberts had become intrigued by Reed's life in the late 1970s and had gotten Reed's permission to make a documentary of the singer's life. He traveled with Reed to Moscow and saw him besieged by fans. He interviewed both of Reed's parents and visited Reed at his home where he interviewed the American and his new East German wife on camera. Around midsummer, Reed started talking about going to Chile again. When Roberts got wind of those plans, he called Reed and wrangled an invitation to come along. For Reed, Gen. Augusto Pinochet was the great White Whale to his Captain Ahab. It was Pinochet who overthrew Reed's friend and the country's elected president, Salvador Allende. It was Pinochet whose troops rounded up many of Reed's closest friends, including Victor Jara, tortured and killed them. Despite his fund-raising shows in the United States, Reed had accomplished little in his efforts to dislodge the military dictator. Now, in August, Pinochet was in the middle of another crackdown against dissidents demanding his ouster.

Pinochet was ruthless in holding onto power. In 1976, his secret police carried out the car bomb murder of Orlando Letelier. At one time or another, Letelier held the posts of foreign minister, defense minister and ambassador to the United States for Salvador Allende's government. After the bloody coup, Letelier fled the country and became a vocal Pinochet critic. On September 21, 1976, Letelier and an assistant were killed when a bomb exploded in his car. The audacity of the killers was extraordinary. The murder occurred in Washington, D.C., the capital of an ally. Eventually, a U.S. citizen, Michael Townley, who also was an agent of the Chilean state security agency known as DINA, confessed to the car bombing. Townley was extradited to the United

States and immediately gave American investigators the complete story on Letelier's assassination, but also details on several other cases where prominent opponents of the Chilean government were murdered or attacked. The Letelier slaying involved three other DINA agents, including its commander, Gen. Manuel Contreras. DINA, the Nation Intelligence Directorate, reported directly to Pinochet, but the dictator denied any knowledge of Letelier's murder. To deflect international outrage, he disbanded the unit. The international community was not appeased and moved to isolate Chile for its outlaw behavior. One of the few exceptions was the United States, which protested the actions of the DINA agents, but did not cut diplomatic relations.

Being an international pariah slowed Pinochet not a whit. In all, the general's regime is alleged to have killed nearly thirty-two hundred people for political reasons, including some one thousand dissidents arrested by security services and never seen again, according to reports by the civilian government that replaced Pinochet in 1990.[3] His record was so atrocious it prompted Spain to ask for his arrest, which British authorities executed in October 1998 while Pinochet was in England for back surgery. Spain wanted to try him for the presumed murder of hundreds of Chilean and Spanish citizens. The Spanish charges included numerous people who were kidnapped in Chile between 1976 and 1983 and taken to Argentina and never heard from again.[4] No one was more aware of the dictator's bloody rule than Reed. He had been sniping at Pinochet from a distance for years, but now he saw a chance to move in close and take on the general in person. In his writings, Reed explained how he used his U.S. citizenship to his advantaged because it allowed him to travel to Chile without having to obtain a visa. Reed wrote that he felt duty-bound to go there because he thought he could help.[5] But Pinochet's murderous proclivities spooked Reed. He made the arrangements like a man who was not sure he would return alive. He made out a will. And on the Fourth of July, he wrote a long letter to his daughter, Ramona, now fifteen years old.

> Dearest Ramona,
> Mother is arriving tomorrow—for two weeks—then Renate, Alexander and I shall travel to Tunis for a vacation as

guest of Arafat—and then on the 15th of August, after 10 years, I shall return to Santiago, Chile. I wanted to write you a letter, before my departure for Chile. As you probably know, Chile has lived under the brutal dictatorship of fascism since 1973 when the democratically elected president, Salvador Allende was murdered and overthrown by the fascists. The US government was responsible for his murder and for the overthrow of the democratic government of Chile. The people of Chile have now lived for 10 years under the dictatorship of General Pinochet. He has brought moral and economic ruin to his country and his people. This year, the people of Chile are rising up and are trying to take their destinies in their own hands. They refuse to live on their knees anymore. They are beginning to march in the streets and strike in their factories. It is time that I return to Chile to try to give the people of Chile courage to fight on. No one knows what will happen when I arrive in Chile or how Gen. Pinochet will react to my arrival. I know that there is some risk to my life and my well-being, but each human being must do his part as a citizen of this world. Each human being must be willing to risk something so that other human beings have the possibility to live in freedom and in peace.

I just wanted to say that I am glad that you exist in this world. I am sorry that I couldn't have made your life easier at times. I have never been so happy in my life as I am now. For that reason, I have also fear in my heart of my trip—because I have more to lose. But I have a responsibility not only to Alexander and to Renate—but also to the people in Chile. I can only be a good husband to Renate and a good father when I am also a good human being and words alone make no one a good human being.[6]

Reed and Roberts arrived in Santiago on August 15, 1983. Friends met him at the airport and briefed Reed on what had been happening. They told the actor that just four days earlier there had been mass demonstrations and the general sent thousands of soldiers to confront them. Student demonstrators at the university were tear-gassed by the troops and many were beaten and arrested. Twenty-seven people had died in the streets of Santiago so far. Reed told them he wanted to sing and speak on behalf of the demonstrators. It was what Reed's friends had hoped and expected he would say. The arrangements already were made. Reed knew he was about to challenge Pinochet's power, so he went to the U.S. Embassy the next day and registered. He and Roberts also asked for and received the home phone number of the embassy's consul general. He also informed the embassy that he was staying at the home of Maria Maluenda, a prominent member of the Chilean Communist Party.[7]

Then Reed went about his now familiar routine. He held a press conference where he denounced the Pinochet government and the U.S. support of the dictator. He reminded the press of his close ties to the Allende government and how he had washed the American flag in front of the U.S. Embassy before Allende was elected. That was brash enough, given Pinochet's control of the media and the country. But Reed was just getting warmed up. On August 17, he traveled to Rancaqua and the police were waiting for him. They showed him an official order saying he was forbidden from singing because he was in Chile as a tourist, not as an artist. Reed argued that even a tourist could sing all he wanted as long as it was with friends in their house and for no charge.

Representatives of the miners' union ran with Reed's logic. They told the police they were Reed's friends and they wanted him as a guest in the biggest and most beautiful house they had, which happened to be the union hall. They entered the hall where the Copper Union was holding a rally. The communist-influenced union had been demonstrating against Pinochet and his policies. During the rally, Reed made a short speech in which he said he believed in a democratic future for Chile and that Pinochet was an outlaw because Allende was the legally elected president. Reed grabbed his guitar and led the unionists in solidarity songs.

The risk could not have been higher for the union and the singer. Pinochet's police and soldiers were monitoring the meeting and could, at any moment, move in and arrest them. With basic civil liberties suspended by Pinochet and his secret police, those arrested could be held for days or weeks without charges and without anyone knowing where they were. The unionists made nervous jokes amongst themselves, but they had seen or heard of too many friends who had kissed their wives or lovers goodbye in the morning and never returned. Pinochet had to be stopped, but they did not relish being martyrs. Reed, too, knew he had traveled well past hypothetical danger. It was only a little more than ten years earlier that he was arrested and tortured in Argentina for similar antigovernment actions. He did not wish for a return engagement. But if he did nothing, Reed would feel responsible for the deaths and brutality directed against his friends. So he sang.

"I admit that I was afraid and got goose bumps as I started singing because in this moment I thought about the words of friends who were threatened with imminent prison, but with each word I became more confident," Reed recalled. Pinochet's agents and soldiers made no moves. The rally, though charged with emotion and ending with chants of solidarity among the workers and people of Chile and against Pinochet, ended peacefully. The price of admission was one kilogram of groceries and the rally produced large amounts of flour, bread, rice, beans, vegetables and fruit for the families of the eight hundred miners who had been fired when they went on strike. Once his fear passed, and the rally ended without incident, Reed was euphoric. He was winning. He was staring down his devil, Pinoche, and the devil was blinking. Reed was on the front line and, by god, the people were excited to have him there because he was one of them, even as he remained a revered star. The singer's joy was sustained the next day when the large Santiago daily newspaper *El Pais*, reported on the miners' rally. The general's government tightly controlled the media, but here was a report on opposition to the dictator. "The article contained no commentary, but it was commentary enough. Because the fact that the publisher had given a complete report in sobering words about my visit in the copper-mining city of Rancaqua without giving one word to the defense of the Pinochet regime was a clear sign of the mood of the country," Reed said.[8]

The next day, it was on to the Pedagogical Institute of the University of Chile and a meeting organized by the leftist students there. The scene played out almost exactly as it had with the

Copper Union. Speeches by the students and Reed, and then the American led the two thousand strong in song. Again, Pinochet's people were visible inside and out and the tension was high. This time, however, the rally ended with police charging into some of the students. They swung their billy clubs and arrested dozens. An assistant professor noticed that several of the officers were eyeing Reed. She grabbed his arm as he took a step toward the rampaging officers, pulled him into her car and roared away. Reed, after all, was scheduled to sing Sunday in a large Catholic Church in Santiago at the invitation of Archbishop Enrique Silva, a forceful Pinochet opponent. That would be a huge gathering and it would hurt the effort if something happened to the singer and he couldn't perform.

But Pinochet and his enforcers had seen and heard enough. Now here was Reed, sweating in the back of the police car. Eventually, the driver fired up the engine and the car started off again. Reed began breathing. But then the car pulled over in another remote location. Four times in all, the American could only suffer as he waited to see if this was where his obituary would be written. Only after he arrived at the airport some two hours later, just in time to catch his flight, did Reed realize that the plan was not to kill him but to keep him away from any of his supporters. The police did not want to wade into a protest on Reed's behalf on top of the anti-Pinochet rallies they already were breaking up.[9] Reed flew to Moscow, stayed about a week and then returned home to Renate who had been worrying since her husband left East German airspace.

His arrest and deportation from Chile stoked Reed's courage and his revolutionary fervor. He felt vital, he felt that he was again doing his part for the world's downtrodden. He didn't wait long to return to the fray. In Nicaragua, the four-year-old government of Daniel Ortega was battling to stay in power. Ortega, a socialist, was fighting against the Contras. The Contras were backed by the United States, first legally and then illegally, when President Ronald Reagan told his subordinates to keep arms flowing to the guerrillas even after Congress cut off their aid. Many of the leaders, and some of the fighting men, were former commanders in the army of Nicaraguan dictator Anastasio Somoza. In effect, it was a rematch of the revolution of 1979 when Ortega drove Somoza from power in July of that year.

For Reed, this was the perfect situation: a socialist leader battling the corrupt American war machine. So, in April 1984, Reed flew to Nicaragua. It was a carbon copy of his time with the Palestinians. He met Ortega and gave him his support. Then he headed off with the troops as they patrolled the fields and jungles looking for the Contras. The tour took him to the small village of Jalapa, about ten miles from the Honduras border. That evening, a stage was set up. Cars and Jeeps were parked in close so that the headlights lit up the stage for his performance. Between songs, Reed told the audience of villagers and soldiers that there were other Americans than the ones who supported the hated Contras, the ruthless Contras. As he was singing, Reed noticed a boy of about fourteen standing in the audience, armed with a pistol and an automatic rifle. After the song, Reed asked the boy if he would let the singer have his rifle for a time in exchange for Reed's guitar. The boy agreed, climbed onto the stage and strumming the guitar, sang about victory over the Contras. But it was also a song of peace. "I will never forget this evening or the other Nicaraguans I met in the past two weeks," Reed said.[10] The visit was disquieting, with occasional gun battles. Most of those, however, were some distance from wherever Reed was and he never saw any major action.

Still, Reed's bravery was not in doubt. He had put his body on the line, both in Nicaragua and Chile. At either place, he could have been captured, beaten, tortured or killed. He chose to stand with those he saw as the underdogs, the oppressed and hoped that his fame and popularity, especially in Chile, would force changes. But there was something more involved. His conversations over the years with his first wife had convinced her that he never recovered from the death of Allende, Jara and his other friends at the hands of Pinochet and his troops. He carried the guilt of the survivor and wondered why he was alive and they were dead. "Dean had a death wish," Patricia said. "He wished he had died. He thought he was in war all the time. He had a death wish, but he never thought they would ever actually get rid of him."[11]

Nineteen

Nobody Knows Me Back in My Hometown

The phone rang in Reed's lakeside house.

"Dean, this is an old friend of yours from Colorado," the delayed voice on the other end said.

"Yeah?"

"Johnny Rose."

"Who? Where do I know you from?" Reed asked, unable to place the caller.

"Dammit, Dean, we met in Estes Park. We lived in Canoga Park and…"

"Oh yeah, Johnny. Country songs."

The former roommates, who hadn't seen or heard from each other in more than twenty years, began chipping away at the barriers time and distance had erected. They chatted for twenty minutes, remembering old escapades and bringing each other up to the present. Reed mentioned that he hoped to return to Denver in 1985 to show the documentary on his life that Will Roberts was wrapping up. Rose told Reed he was now going by his real name of Rosenburg, that he was happily married with nearly adult children and invited Reed to visit them when he came to Denver. Reed said he would be delighted.

The telephone reunion of the two Colorado boys who had headed to California to make it in the music business came about through a little luck and a lot of hard work by Rosenburg. In

1984, Rosenburg was in his Loveland, Colorado, home when his brother called him and excitedly told him to turn on the *NBC Nightly News*, that they were interviewing Dean Reed. Sure enough, one of the network's foreign correspondents was doing a piece on the American singer and actor from his East German home. Rosenburg called the Denver NBC affiliate to see if anyone there could help him get in touch with the reporter. The station sent a camera crew down, interviewed Rosenburg and gave him the New York City office number of the reporter. The NBC officials, in turn, gave Rosenburg the number of a woman in London who said she would check with some people and call him back with the number. In the meantime, Rosenburg called both the Russian and East German embassies in Washington, D.C. The Russians were snotty, the East Germans were polite but unable to help. About a week later, the woman called Rosenburg from London with Reed's number.

The NBC report was not the first in the American press in 1984 about Reed. In fact, it likely was spurred by a piece by a *New York Times* reporter that ran there and also was picked up by the *International Herald Tribune*, the American paper printed and read widely in Europe by American travelers and expatriates. The *Times* piece, written by James Markham, was published in late January and Reed disliked it, for some of the usual reasons, but for some odd ones as well. The story mentioned that he was a "folk hero in Moscow, Prague, East Berlin and Sofia. In a pleasant, thin voice, he belts out peace-loving, anti-American country ballads throughout the Warsaw pact nations—though not in Poland—and writes, directs and stars in movies. He is an East Bloc superstar, the Johnny Cash of Communism." Reed talked about the need for the Berlin Wall to keep out Western agents, not to keep the people from fleeing to freedom, but when asked about the people who were shot and killed trying to go over the wall, he said, "that's a problem obviously I cannot defend. But the police of Dallas have shot more of its own people than the police of the GDR." Reed also pointed to the lack of crime in East Germany and said, "Here, I don't have to go into the street to protest. Here I can walk into the Central Committee and talk about the problems, which I do sometimes," although he conceded noncelebrities probably would not have that kind of access. He admitted to missing his homeland. "Of course I get homesick, especially at Christmas. What I miss most is speaking my own language." Markham noted in his story that Reed fumbled occasionally for the right words in English, since most of his conversation was now conducted in German.[1] Reed's trouble with his mother tongue stuck out in his letter to Markham after the story was published.

In that February 4, letter, Reed was at his exclamation point-pounding best. "You, who so hypocritically defend the role of the 'free press' in the 'free world' go on to distort the truth in such a way which here in Socialism would not be allowed. May I show you a couple of examples—just in case a part of your conscience is still functioning." Reed took issue with the idea that any of his songs were anti-American. "Obviously, your source is from the archives of the CIA—and once they lie, that lie goes into the computer for all journalists to use in the future who are too biased or too lazy to search for the truth." Reed took umbrage at the line that his father "was a roothless [*sic*] schoolteacher."

"I am sure that you have used the word 'roothless' many times in your articles against my friends who are trying to liberate their lands from tyranny and exploitation, but the word 'ruthless' is not in my vocabulary. Which journalistic god gives you the right to write your own novel concerning the life of another man? I thought journalists were supposed to search for the truth—and then to report on it. You are not supposed to write your own distortions of the truth. But it is exactly for this reason that the countries of the third world are working toward the day when they will not be any longer under the dictatorial domination of the American Propaganda machine."[2] It was a good tirade. The only trouble was, Markham had written that Reed's father was a rootless schoolteacher, a fair description of Cyril's nomadic existence throughout the Western United States. Reed, his automatic grasp of English slipping, had misread the sentence as commentary on his father's personality.

Once Rosenburg reestablished contact with Reed, they began writing each other regularly. Rosenburg was happy to hear what his old friend was up to, but became concerned about Reed's lack of comprehension of his standing back in Denver, much less the rest of the country. In one of the letters, Reed suggested a parade to the state capitol building, with the singer and the mayor riding on horseback. Rosenburg laughed out loud when he read that. He started to write back, to tell Reed that nobody knew him in his hometown. "When I wrote that, I thought 'you're a songwriter, you should write a song about it.' That's when I wrote, 'Nobody Knows Me Back in My Hometown,' Rosenburg said. "I thought if anything could get the point across to him, it would be a song. And it did. He wasn't expecting a horse parade when he got here."

Rosenburg wrote the song and accompanied himself on the guitar, singing into a cassette tape recorder. Rosenburg had not lost his touch over the past fifteen years. Even though he had given up writing and performing, he still had a good feel for a lyric and a country western melody. The song not only communicated a message to Reed, but it also spoke to his commercial sensibilities. Reed listened to the tape a few times, lined up his regular musicians and headed to Prague to record the song himself.[3]

Hearing from Rosenburg may well have been the highlight of the year for the American. Things were not going well for him in East Germany or the Soviet Union. There was less demand for his performances. Neither he nor Renate were receiving many scripts in the mail for movies in which they could star. That concerned him greatly. With fewer singing performances and even fewer acting assignments, Reed was left with more time to finish writing his script for *Bloody Heart,* a movie about the Wounded Knee takeover in South Dakota where members of the American Indian Movement were holed up for seventy-one days.

The Wounded Knee incident was a natural for a movie. On February 27, 1973, members of the American Indian Movement, led by Dennis Banks and Russell Means, rode into the tiny town and occupied it. The AIM leaders said they were taking over the town, scene of an 1890 Indian massacre by U.S. soldiers, to protest the continuing injustices against Oglala Sioux by the federal government and the tribal government on the Pine Ridge Reservation. At first, FBI agents and other law enforcement officers were content to surround the group, which lived in a few buildings, including a church. But on April 27, FBI agents and AIM members exchanged gunfire. When the shooting stopped, two Indian men were dead and two federal agents were injured. The group finally surrendered May 8.

The movie could also have included a climatic trial scene. Banks and Means were the main defendants at the U.S. district courthouse in St. Paul, Minnesota, and were represented by nationally known lawyer William Kunstler and locally renowned lawyer Ken Tilsen, the same man who represented Reed in his trespassing trial in Buffalo. After an acrimonious eight-month trial, in which Banks and Means attempted to put the federal government on trial, U. S. District Court Judge Fred Nichol dismissed all the charges against the two men as the jury was deliberating and blasted the FBI and the Justice Department for their behavior during the trial.

Reed saw the Wounded Knee incident as a perfect vehicle for him. With the shooting and the courtroom outbursts, it would make compelling drama. It was good history. And it would glorify the oppressed minority battling the misguided U.S. government. It also could get him into American theater complexes. It was no coincidence that Tilsen was involved in Reed's trespassing trial and the actor was working on a script about Tilsen's other big trial involving Wounded Knee. Prior to his trial in Buffalo, Reed and some of the other defendants were meeting with Tilsen in his law office when Reed noticed *Voices from Wounded Knee*. The book contained photographs from the standoff. "Shortly after that, he called me or wrote me and said he wanted to make a movie about Wounded Knee," recalled his friend Marv Davidov. "And from time to time, he would call me and ask me to get this or that artifact which would be useful in the movie."[4]

The research and writing was relatively straightforward. But lining up financing and actors for the movie was a strain and proving more difficult for Reed than his earlier films. Worse, his body was betraying him. Old injuries from his horse riding and a motorcycle accident in Siberia years ago were causing him periodic pain. He was hospitalized for peptic ulcers and the doctors were going to operate on him right up until the moment they found a medication that alleviated the problem. He also needed sleeping pills at night, a practice he began as a teenager, but one that had intensified in recent years.[5]

Strange and sinister things also were happening to Reed. Once, while driving to Prague on a curving mountain road, one of the wheels came off the car and bounced down the hillside.

Reed had to wrestle with the car to keep it from going out of control and following the errant wheel over the cliff. Reed and his family became suspicious because the car had been in for repairs and checkup just a day or so earlier. And it came on the heels of another accident, when a truck with a clear view of the road turned into Reed's car, crushing it. Reed was lucky, he wrote Patricia, escaping with only minor injuries. Perhaps the wheel coming off was just the result of the notoriously bad craftsmanship that had become the cliché of Communist life. But the thought crossed his mind and those in his family that the accidents were really attempts on his life.[6] Some of the weird incidents were the singer's own doing. Renate related to Patricia how she and Reed were staying in a cabin in the mountains during the winter of 1984. One night Reed started drinking, something he rarely did. Soon, he was roaring drunk. He stripped off his clothes and ran outside and stood naked in the snow, screaming at the sky, sobbing, his grief at the death of his two fathers and his other problems overwhelming him and the cold. Renate pleaded with him to come inside to the warmth of the cabin, but for a long time her husband ignored her. Finally, exhausted and his grief spent, Reed trudged back inside. Renate later viewed the incident as a turning point, the beginning of a long slide in her husband's life.[7]

With the pressure building on him, Reed did what he had often done before. He found an excuse to travel to South America. This time, he wound up in Montevideo, Uruguay. He was invited there by Frente Amplio, a grassroots movement opposed to the military dictatorship that had ruled the country for nearly ten years. In 1981, Gen. Gregorio Alvarez was installed as the country's president and he promised a return to civilian rule with elections in November 1984. But negotiations with the two civilian parties and the military collapsed in July 1983. The military used that as an excuse to crack down hard. But coordinated protests by Frente Amplio and other groups weakened the general's hold and the election was rescheduled. Frente Amplio asked, and Reed agreed, to sing at their rallies.

But Reed could not resist doing more. On October 26, 1984, he tried to meet with the U.S. Ambassador in Montevideo, but was shuffled off to the embassy information officer instead. Reed told the official that he was there to protest the U.S. government's support of the dictatorship running Uruguay. The next day, Reed returned. This time he was struck and handcuffed by local police when he entered the grounds of the ambassador's residence. Reed said he wanted to talk to Ambassador Thomas Aranda and give him a letter in which he protested U.S. support of dictatorships all across Latin America. As usual, Reed alerted the press, the police held him for a few hours, then after his release, he described for reporters what had happened and told them of his plans to travel to Buenos Aires the next day. The newspapers wrote their stories and within twenty-four hours, the entire affair was over and forgotten.[8]

Back in East Germany, Reed had another painful accident. He was at a youth function in spring 1985 when he fell from his horse, landing hard on his butt and lower back. Dr. Werner Dietz treated Reed and prescribed drugs to ease the pain and physical therapy to strengthen the back. That medication was added to the assortment of pills he already was taking. "In the conversation, he told me he had difficulty sleeping and pains in his stomach many times," Dietz said. "I think Dean had constant problems with his sleep and constant pain with his stomach. He had been diagnosed after a fall from the horse and X-rayed in the stomach without pathological changes that could be determined."[9]

Reed's friend from the DEFA studios, Gerrit List, was worried, too, about Reed's physical health and the handfuls of pills he consumed daily. The two men were collaborating again, this time in trying to pull *Bloody Heart* into a workable film. "Dean had had severe injuries to his left knee," List said. "He had constant pain in the area of the lumbar vertebrae and he often had migraine-type headaches. He had constant stomach pain. So after each one of his pains, he would take another kind of pain-relieving medicine. I warned him in this discussion that not only would the different medications relieve the pain, but they would lead to further, worse illness. Dean took this warning very seriously and he promised that even before the end of work on this movie he would have a psychotherapeutic and a general examination. In the course of the next weeks, which we worked under common difficulties, I noticed Dean was experiencing physical pain. When I talked to him about it, he would lie. He would say he comes from Colorado and a cowboy knows what pain is."[10]

Twenty

Homecoming

*R*eed was heading home. After twenty-five years of traveling and living throughout the world, he was on his way back to Denver. The movie documentary by Will Roberts, *American Rebel*, was complete. Reed enthusiastically agreed to appear at its screening at the Denver International Movie festival in October and then head to Los Angeles and Minneapolis for additional screenings and reunions with friends and family. Johnny Rosenburg was thrilled to see his old friend again. Rosenburg had been busy calling around to the newspapers and television stations, trying to get them to do a story on the returning native son. Rosenburg met Reed at the airport and a few reporters tagged along, but even Rosenburg admitted there wasn't much interest in the international star.

Reed arrived on a Wednesday. Thursday, he was a guest on a talk radio show in Denver and it went fine. Friday, he had an invitation to another talk radio show hosted by Peter Boyles. Rosenburg smelled trouble and argued with his friend not to go, saying the conservative Boyles would shred the singer on the air. "He said, 'Do you think after all the things I have been through in my life that I'm afraid of some Denver talk show host?'" Rosenburg recalled.[1] Rosenburg's instincts were perfect and the show was a debacle. Boyles quickly turned the conversation to politics, jabbing hard at Reed and his socialist views. The visitor from East Berlin at first tried to dodge and deflect Boyles' shots, telling the radio audience that "I consider myself an American patriot," and "I don't defend all the policies of the Soviet Union." But Boyles landed a blow when Reed talked about Nicaragua and the Sandinista government of Daniel Ortega.

"Peter, there are twelve political parties in Nicaragua…"

"And all have been outlawed except the Sandinistas," Boyles cut in.

That exchange hurt and Reed moved the debate from the political to the personal. Boyles had been testifying in the trial of several neo-Nazis who had gunned down a friend and radio talk-show colleague Alan Berg because he was a Jew. Boyles' grief and anger over that hate crime was raw and very near the surface, Reed knew. Boyles turned the conversation to the massive famine in Ethiopia, which was killing hundreds of thousands at the time, and blamed it on the Marxist government's unwillingness to accept food from the Western nations.

"There's a worldwide famine," Reed countered. "You're talking just like the neo-Nazis that killed Berg."

"Don't you ever accuse me of that," Boyles angrily retorted.

"That's the way you're talking," Reed said. "And I think that's very dangerous."

"Get out of here," Boyles yelled at his guest. "Get out of here. Take a walk."[2]

Reed had not lasted the planned half-hour before being kicked off the show and his insensitivity left a bad impression in the minds of most of Boyles' listeners, not the kind of publicity somebody trying to overcome his anonymity would seek.

Reed seemed nonplused by it all. He enjoyed himself at the film festival Sunday night and the festival party afterward. Plenty of people were happy to talk to the tall and still handsome star, and the documentary certainly added luster to his image. One of the people who smitten with Reed was Dixie Lloyd, a pretty woman who told Reed that they had known each other in high school, although he was a couple years older than she. Lloyd said they rode horses together when they were kids. Reed told Rosenburg that he didn't remember her at all, but he thought he could use her. She had money, had been a truck driver and knew how to get things done. They became lovers.[3]

Reed spent the next week with Rosenburg and his wife, Mona, in Loveland, outside of Denver. Reed felt down the first day. The Denver paper panned *American Rebel* and the subject of the documentary. "He was devastated," Rosenburg said. "I thought he was going to cry. I said, 'Hey Dean, that's only one review, live with it.' But he wasn't used to that stuff. He was used to being pampered."[4] It was, however, the true Reed. He had never taken criticism of himself or his work very well and this was no different. His spirits rebounded, however, as the two men hung out, played some guitar together and talked for hours. The talk always came back to Reed's return to the United States. The expatriate never came right out and said it, but he was obviously disillusioned with life in East Germany and tired of living in a foreign land. He said he could live six months in America and six months in Europe and be a real international superstar. But it was going to be difficult returning. Besides trying to rekindle a career in the United States his wife Renate did not want to follow him. And Reed was embarrassed by his two divorces and did not want to see a third marriage disintegrate. In fact, Renate was terribly upset by his trip to Denver, convinced he would never return. To reassure her before he left East Germany, Reed and some friends moved a large boulder into the yard. Reed called his wife out and said, " 'Renate, you and I will be buried under this boulder. I'll be back,' " Rosenburg said.[5]

When he talked about death to Rosenburg, it was a completely different conversation than the one he had with his wife. "It really bugged him that nobody here knew him," Rosenburg said. "That's what he wanted the most. He always talked about how he didn't want to die in a country that wasn't his own."[6] And they talked politics. Rosenburg couldn't have been more different from his friend. He was a true-blue, love-it-or-leave-it conservative American. But as he listened to Reed talk about the need for everyone to have enough to eat, shoes on their feet, a roof over their head and medical care, and listened to the tales of Reed's protests and arrests around the world, Rosenburg's admiration grew.

"Dean didn't believe politically in the things I believed in, but I'll tell you what. He went out there and stuck his neck right in the noose for the things he believed in," Rosenburg said. "Whether you agree with what he believed in or not is not the question. Most of us will sit in the comfort of our four walls and bitch about things, but we won't dare step outside and be willing to take those shots. Dean was. He believed enough in the causes that he believed in that he would have laid his life down in an eye blink and did it more than once. Pinochet could just have easily shot him between the eyes and he knew that and he went down anyway. Dean had one thing that he believed enough in he would have died for. And that was, help the poor. Socialism. He simply believed that if you had a toothache, you shouldn't have to go home and suffer with it because you couldn't afford a dentist."[7]

After a week of shooting baskets with the neighbors, riding motorcycles and just relaxing, it was time for Reed to repay his old buddy's hospitality. He agreed to put on a little show in the Rosenburgs' basement for neighbors and friends. Some fifty people crammed in and Dixie Lloyd, at Reed's invitation, drove in from Denver. Reed strapped on his guitar and sang songs for the folks, told them jokes he had picked up from around the world, and invited Rosenburg to sing along with him on several songs. It was a fun night for Reed and a fitting end to the reunion with his old performing comrade. The next day, Reed headed to Los Angeles to price houses for himself and to visit his daughter Ramona, whom he had seen during the summer when she came to East Germany and traveled with him. On a trip to Moscow, Reed introduced her to President Mikhail Gorbachev.

The time spent with Rosenburg had a bracing affect on Reed. His ex-wife Patricia said he sounded better. At one point, she gave him some pain pills and a Valium that she had for her ailments and made the comment she needed to detoxify herself and end her dependency on medication. That intrigued Reed and he questioned Patricia closely on the steps she would take. By the end of the conversation, Reed was adamant that he would follow Patricia's example. And as he had with Rosenburg, Reed said he was coming back to live in the United States. He admitted he wasn't sure if he could work in the United States, but he might go live with Tilly Price, Paton's widow, and her son. Patricia arranged a dinner party for Reed and invited some of the Russian émigrés living in the apartment complex. After dinner, Reed sang some of his songs for the guests and the Russians, in particular, were thrilled with the chance to see the superstar in person. One of the women, a Russian physician, suggested that if nothing else, Reed could give concerts for the Russian community throughout the United States. She was sure he could make a good living. Still, Patricia could see problems.

"Dean was very impressed with philosophers, Nobel Prize winners, who were for the working man and would put their life on the line and do it by the pen. He thought he could do it with the pen," Patricia said. "But he forgot about the government controlling him with the women and the medicines. He was taking so much medication and he was taking it with the alcohol. He wasn't seeing well, his eyes looked bad, his sex drive was down. They can do it all with medications. Dean was lying to himself. He told me the government wasn't paying attention to him and he was upset."[8]

Reed packed his gear and flew to Minneapolis, where his friend Marv Davidov was at work on the singer's behalf. Davidov had learned in a roundabout way that Reed was coming to the United States for a visit. "A couple of friends called me, who had been in Siberia," Davidov said. "They were in a plane from Siberia to Moscow. Suddenly, all the passengers go up to the front and they are getting autographs from somebody and it turns out to be Dean. When he heard they were from Minneapolis, he said, 'Do you know Marv?' So I learned he was going to Denver to show the film. We wrote or called and I said, 'Come here and show it.' "

Davidov put Reed up in the home of a friend and for the next thirteen days, the two men talked and worked on Reed's projects. They showed *American Rebel* at the University of Minnesota and Reed gave a short speech and answered questions. Minneapolis was home to the American Indian Movement and two of its leaders, Clyde and Vernon Bellecourt. They had been major figures in the standoff at Wounded Knee. Reed was keenly interested in talking to the two Indian leaders about his current project, *Bloody Heart*. Davidov was friends with the brothers, so he arranged a meeting.

"He had met Clyde at the power line demonstration," Davidov said. "They talked about the film. And again, Dean was very serious when it came to the business. No bullshit. Very tough. He didn't want Russell Means (another AIM leader) involved. He didn't want Russell in the GDR because he didn't think he could rely on Russell. He wanted the American Indian Movement to send a family to participate and be in the film and advise, but he told them they could only be paid in Soviet money, which wouldn't be useful here. It couldn't convert."[9]

Toward the end of Reed's stay that November, Davidov organized a party inviting members of Women Against Military Madness and other peace activists, as well as Larry Long, a local folk singer whom Reed had invited to perform in East Germany five years earlier. The party was in a private home, one of the quaint, spacious, old two-story houses near the chain of lakes in South Minneapolis. Reed was a big hit. He walked on his hands. He played his guitar and sang songs, sometimes sharing the stage with Long. "He would put out the same kind of energy for a little group that he would with a stadium filled with 100,000 people," Davidov said. "Everybody was amazed. I had so much fun with him."[10]

Davidov enjoyed meeting Wiebke ten years earlier when Reed and his second wife came through town, but he had a different reaction to Dixie Lloyd. A few days after arriving in Minneapolis, Reed told Dixie to fly in and join him. He told Davidov how he met Lloyd in Denver at the film festival and how she had made herself useful, driving him around and generally doing his bidding. She was working on developing Dean Reed fan clubs and trying to get a recording contract for Reed. But Davidov was suspicious of her from the moment they shook hands. She was always taking pictures and Davidov and some of his friends at the party jokingly referred to her as a CIA bimbo. The suspicions were strong enough that when Reed went to meet the Bellecourts, Davidov pulled Reed aside and said he would not take him if she came along. The Bellecourts, after all, were considered revolutionaries by the government and the FBI had thick files on both of them. There was no need to bring an unknown outsider into the inner circle. Davidov also was unimpressed with Lloyd's plans for Reed's return to the United States as a performer. "Had there been any chance of him coming back to live, I would have helped out," Davidov said. "Although, I don't think much could happen. I think Dixie was unrealistic because of the politics."[11]

Despite the enthusiasm Reed always displayed, the man from Colorado also confided in Davidov his frustrations and heartbreak. Davidov didn't detect any depression in his friend, but Reed freely admitted that his marriage with Renate was disintegrating. The couple had consulted a marriage counselor but Reed was uncomfortable with it and thought the secret police might be taping the sessions. According to Reed, Renate was possessive and jealous. That would be a problem for a man who was constantly besieged by women and often surrendered to them. Yet, he was not proud of the broken marriages and he tried to puzzle out why he couldn't live with just one woman for his lifetime. At the same time, he was battling professional problems. He told Davidov about censorship by the Politburo. He sang a song that the party leadership took to be a criticism of life in East Germany and for a week they wouldn't let Reed perform anywhere. Eventually, Reed convinced enough of the leaders that they were wrong and the ban ended. But it left a bitter taste. Reed also told Davidov what he had told everybody on this trip. He missed his homeland and he wanted to take another stab at living and working in the place he was born.

"I know the marital problems they were having were disconcerting and painful to him," Davidov said. "We talked at some length about that. When he was here, there were no signs of depression and I go through depression. I can spot it. The work was so important to him. And this work was political. He had written it. He had worked years on the screenplay."[12]

Reed left Minneapolis for East Berlin. Davidov was convinced *Bloody Heart* would be filmed and he would see his friend again soon. They had discussed what would happen. Reed would stage a U.S. premiere of the movie at the Pine Ridge Indian Reservation in South Dakota and then show it in Minneapolis. It was a good plan. It never happened.

Twenty One

The Decline

*V*acations are meant to revitalize the body and the mind but Reed's hiatus had altered everything. It was not quite a pilgrimage to Mecca, but the trip back to the United States touched him in ways previous trips home had not. Part of it likely was the change that age brings. But in the quiet time with friends or on the airplane between destinations, the singer had done some hard thinking. He was examining everything now: himself, his work, capitalism, Communism, friendship, love. Reed's friend and coproducer, Gerrit List, was startled by the changes in his pal upon his return to Germany.

"He appeared to me to have changed in his basic traits," List said. "For example, he longed for the American people and his homeland, Colorado, and he was making plans for a great concert tour through the U.S. after the completion of his film work. At the same time, he exercised frequent criticisms of the conditions of the socialistic system. At the same time and in shorter and shorter intervals, he complained to me of phases of deep depression of which he could name no concrete source."[1] Renate, too, noticed that besides their bickering, Reed was homesick. Well into middle age now, Reed could no longer draw his sustenance from the cheering throngs and the fight for justice in tumultuous areas of the world. He was mellowing, and suddenly the company of old friends and a good quip in his native tongue had a seductive appeal.

As it happened, the three prongs of his plan were coming together. *American Rebel* had been released in the United States, gaining him a small dose of publicity. Now, CBS newsman Mike Wallace had called and wanted to interview him for a segment of *60 Minutes.* The long-running news magazine show was a perennial Top 10 performer for the CBS television network and Reed was well aware that an appearance there would be seen by millions of Americans. Meanwhile, funding for his movie was nearly at hand and production was tentatively scheduled for June. The *60 Minutes* appearance would only be about a year old by the time he was ready to show *Bloody Heart* in the states. Reed reasoned that even the dumbest press agent would be able to remind moviegoers that the film was made by and starred Dean Reed, as seen on *60 Minutes.*

Wallace arrived in East Berlin in the winter of 1986. Reed was happy to see him, as he was any American. He escorted the reporter around East Berlin, to the DEFA studios and finally, brought the interviewer back to his home on the lake. He introduced Wallace and his crew to Renate and her son Alexander. Then they sat down for a one-on-one interview. Wallace excelled in sit-down interviews with people and since the early days of television had developed techniques that kept his subjects on point. Wallace's meticulous preparation made him adept at challenging and cutting off the little exaggerations and outright lies everybody tells about themselves. Reed was supremely confident in the message he had and the persona he would project. Viewers, he was sure, would love him and welcome him back home.

The *60 Minutes* interview was telecast on Sunday April 20, 1986. Entitled, "The Defector," it started out well enough. Wallace opened the segment saying that "when we think about Americans who defect to the other side of the Iron Curtain, we usually think about traitors or spies. Dean Reed is neither. Colorado born, America bred, he now lives in East Berlin just because he likes it better over there. An entertainer who has become the Soviet version of a superstar, he sings, he acts and he speaks with what seems to be genuine conviction the Soviet line. The Kremlin has even rewarded him with their Komsomol Lenin prize. There is just one thing missing for him. He yearns to duplicate his success behind the Iron Curtain with a similar success back home." Wallace showed a film clip of Reed singing "Rock around the Clock" and "Heartbreak Hotel," before ten thousand young Russians at the World Youth Festival in Moscow the previous summer.

Dean quickly turned on the charm, trying to explain why he wasn't known back home.

"I think there's a conspiracy of silence about me and I thank you for starting to stop this conspiracy of silence so that people will know who Dean is, what type of songs does he sing, what type of films does he make, who is he, why is he a superstar there and not here? I think I've been a very good American ambassador throughout the world. I've reached people who will never see another American, and I've shown them a side of America which I think they respect."

Eventually, the conversation turned away from tracing his life and career and turned to politics. Reed said he supported the Nicaraguans and others in Latin America fighting against the United States because they do not want to be a colony of the United States. Wallace quickly cut in, asking Reed, "East Germany is not a colony of the Soviet Union, Poland is not a colony?" To which Reed responded that they were not. Wallace ticked off other Communist countries: Romania, Bulgaria. Reed denied it.

Wallace asked why the Berlin Wall was constructed by the East German government.

"The wall was put up to defend themselves in the first place," Reed replied. "In the same—"

Wallace jumped in.

"The wall was put up to make sure that East Germans would not go to West Germany," Wallace said.

"No, that's only a half truth," Reed responded. "I'm sorry, it's not true. I do believe that the government of the East Germans have the right to defend themselves from any type of attack. It's much easier when armies come across a borderline and you can see them. And I think it's a tragedy. But I think that the responsibility for this tragedy is that the United States government does not recognize that every people on this planet have the right to decide their own fate, decide whether they want to live under socialism or whether they want to live under capitalism."

After a slight reprieve, where Reed talked about renting his house for $40 a month and the fact that Alexander would be able to attend college for free and everyone gets medical care in the socialist system, the talk returned to politics. Declining to label his friends in the Palestine Liberation Organization and Yassar Arafat as terrorists, he instead turned on President Ronald Reagan.

"I think it's terrorism when, for example, Mr. Reagan says he's going to make 'Star Wars' (an antimissile defense system) and he's going to give the military billions of dollars more to create more weapons. He's putting me in terror. Millions of people live in terror from a Third World War. That's also called state terrorism."

Wallace asked if that meant Reed equated Reagan with Joseph Stalin, the Russian dictator of the 1930s and '40s who was responsible for the death of millions of Soviet citizens. "I equate the possibilities of Ronald Reagan with Stalin. I say he has the possibilities to do the same injustices and much more by incinerating this planet through an atomic war."

Reed called Soviet President Mikhail Gorbachev a more moral man than Reagan. Reed said the gulags ended after Stalin. He concluded by saying that scientist and human rights activist Andrei Sakharov was not a political prisoner because he could travel anywhere except out of the Soviet Union.

"I don't think all of a sudden that you can make such a big thing about one man who is sitting and he can't leave his country, and all of a sudden forget about the others," Reed said. "You know, I think there are many types of human rights, Mike. I think all human rights are important, but let's make the priorities clear. I don't think that the right to travel is the main human right."

"You really buy the whole communist line?" Wallace interrupted and Reed disagreed, saying he disagreed with many things. Wallace challenged him to name three. "I don't agree with the bureaucracy here," Reed responded. "I don't agree with the fact that the—we are not open enough with criticism against the—the problems within the society here. I believe that there should be more individual freedoms in this country."

He ended by saying he wouldn't mind returning to Colorado and running for the U.S. Senate. The show wrapped up with Reed singing, "Nobody Knows Me Back in My Hometown," the tune penned by his friend Johnny Rosenburg the previous year.[2]

Back in Colorado, Rosenburg was watching with his wife and just shook his head. He tried to talk Reed out of the *60 Minutes* appearance when Reed first broached the subject. As he had when Reed went on the Denver talk radio show, Rosenburg sensed that Reed would say the wrong things, things that would hurt any chance of acceptance as a working artist in the States. Now it was playing out just as he feared.

"It was like driving a wooden stake through a vampire's heart," Rosenburg said. "I just knew he had killed himself right on the spot."

Rosenburg was equally blunt when Reed called him three days later.

"What did you think of it, Johnny?" Reed asked.

"Do you want me to tell you the truth?" his friend countered.

"I know you're going to tell me the truth. That's one of the reasons I called."

"Okay. Well, first of all, you can't defend that wall in this country, no way, shape or form."

"Well, I guess I'm going to have to come back and explain some things."

"If you're going to do that, I'd suggest you get yourself a bulletproof vest."

Reed laughed.

"No, maybe I ought to get a plot picked out in the mountains somewhere," Reed responded.

"All I know is you didn't do yourself any good with that interview, Dean."[3]

It was a surprisingly pleasant conversation, given Rosenburg's tough assessment and Reed's inability to tolerate criticism. Rosenburg concluded that Reed still didn't understand what he had done. He knew the best way to reach his friend was through song, just as he had when he wrote, "Nobody Knows Me Back in My

Hometown." So Rosenburg took his guitar and some paper and sat down to compose another tune. What he created was a catchy country ballad he titled, "Yankee Man." It was a brutal song, meant to batter his friend's confidence in the rightness of his cause.

> You traded the stars and stripes for something we don't understand. Now you say you want to come back home.
>
> But think of all the things you said against the land you said you loved. I guess you're going to reap what you have sowed. Yankee man, you walked on the wrong side of the world for too long.
>
> You chose to go behind the wall to find your fame and that's not all.
>
> You seemed to think that way of life was best.
>
> Because of this and things you've done, I'd say old friend, the time has come to lay your dreams of coming home to rest.
>
> Yankee man, you walked on the wrong side of the world just too long.
>
> (Chorus) Yankee man, you say you're proud to be an American.
>
> But you turn around and you tear your country down.
>
> If you can't find nothing good to say about the USA,
>
> Then you better stay, right where you are, in the land of the big Red Star.[4]

The song continued in the same vein for four more verses, telling Reed where he had gone wrong, how his words made him a traitor. It took a while to finish the song, but finally Rosenburg recorded it on a cassette tape and dropped it in the mail in June. The tape arrived too late for Reed to hear it.

But Rosenburg's reaction to the Mike Wallace interview was shared by many Americans who watched the show. Letters poured into CBS about the interview and they forwarded most of them to Reed in East Berlin. Many of the letters were nasty, calling Reed a traitor to his country and worse. "He assumed that the film about him and the interview would be put in place and he could work again in the U.S.," Renate Reed said. "Instead of that, the population of the U.S. gave him only words of hate. It went so far that one person demanded they take away his passport because he was no American. He was very surprised by the reaction of the American public and he couldn't understand it."[5]

Much of what Reed said in the interview was defensible, if handled skillfully. President Reagan, while slashing many social programs in his first five years in office, had pumped billions of new dollars into the Pentagon and its military programs. He had launched invasions in Grenada and, over much public opposition, had been supporting the Contras in Nicaragua. His saber-rattling and defense build-up raised new fears in the United States of nuclear war, a fear that had diminished during the days of détente. The climate was so charged that Hollywood saw a chance to cash in by making a television movie called *The Day After*. The movie begins with a nuclear exchange between the U.S. and the Soviet Union and then follows the survivors in the horrific landscape left after the bombs went off. It was Reagan, too, who rejected an offer by Gorbachev to get rid of all nuclear weapons during a summit meeting in Iceland. Reagan created another uproar when he said into an open microphone that "the bombing begins in five minutes," before the recording of his weekly radio message. Unfortunately for Reed, the revelations that the United States was trading arms to its enemy Iran in exchange for money and other support for the Contras in Nicaragua would not come out until later in the year and the Iran-Contra Congressional hearings would not happen until the summer of 1987. That was the evidence Reed could have used to support his claims against Reagan and U.S. policy. But what really appalled the television viewers was the singer's inability to admit the Berlin Wall was an abomination built to keep East Germans from escaping, that Poland, Hungary and other countries were under the control of Moscow and that Sakharov was a hero for speaking out against the human rights violations in the Soviet Union. To write off Sakharov's internal exile as light punishment was especially strange coming from a man who traveled the world and kept a bank account in West Germany as his escape hatch if things went badly in the East. By the time Reed listed the three major flaws he saw in the Communist system, it was too late. Most viewers were no longer listening, but seething, or reaching for pen and paper.

Reed's physical and mental health was deteriorating. The letters from the American viewers took a toll. His friend Gerrit List recalled that after making a television show in Leizig in early May, the performer came to him and said he was experiencing the worst depression of his life. List advised Reed to stop taking all his medications and in particular, to cut the amount of tranquilizers. List also urged his friend to seek psychiatric help. But Reed resisted giving up the medicine. His left knee throbbed from the horse-riding accident, he had constant back pain and occasional migraine headaches. His stomach always hurt and he couldn't sleep without taking his pills. At the conclusion of the conversation, Reed promised that even before *Bloody Heart* was through filming, he would go in for a general physical exam and psychological counseling.[6] Renate was blunt about the effect the physical problems were causing her athletic husband.

"I am convinced that Dean, because of his character, had a very difficult time coping with what I mentioned as his health problems," Renate said. "He had always tortured himself, he has always gone to the limits of his possibilities without giving himself any kind of mercy."[7]

World events were conspiring against Dean as well. Since taking office in 1982, Soviet President Mikhail Gorbachev had undertaken a series of reforms in the USSR. Under the broad umbrella of perestroika, Gorbachev encouraged loosening the tight central controls on the economy that had been the centerpiece of the country's policies since Stalin. Gorbachev could see that the Soviet Union's economy was crumbling and he hoped that by slowly introducing more independence to industries he could revitalize it without destroying either the nation or the communist system. Gorbachev also was convinced that there had to be a freer exchange of information and opinions, a policy known as glasnost. While the media still faced censorship, there was a noticeable shift in the way the news was presented and stories about corruption and bureaucratic bumbling suddenly made their way into print. Culturally, the prohibition against rock 'n' roll also fell away. Suddenly, the kids of the Soviet Union could get their hands on the records of Bruce Springsteen, Metallica, Van Halen, and the Eurythmics as well as Swedish and West German groups. The freedom also enticed Soviet youths to form their own bands and turn out a home-brewed brand of rock. By contrast, the soft rock and country songs of a forty-seven-year-old American, approved of by the same party functionaries they were now rebelling against, seemed staid and boring. For them, Dean Reed was yesterday's news, as fashionable as Perry Como.

Phil Everly experienced that decline in popularity. After he and his brother Don had their much publicized fight and stopped performing together in the early 1970s, they reconciled and by 1984 were making records again and touring. The albums sold moderately well, although nothing like their heyday in the 1950s and early 1960s. And they were drawing in few new young listeners. As Everly saw it, Reed's declining popularity in Eastern Europe was "an inevitability, no matter who you are. He was a young, handsome man," but that doesn't last forever. Everly assumed his friend would handle that decline the way Everly had and all stars eventually must.[8] However, it takes time and a certain maturity to surrender the joys of youth and Reed's psyche was battered. He had not yet worked through how he would deal with advancing age. The only plan he had was a vague one of conquering a new frontier, the United States. With the letters he had received from his countrymen and women, that seemed highly unlikely. One of the singer's flaws, noticed by friends in Europe and the United States, flared dangerously. Reed did not take criticism well.

"He had this very distinct need to be loved and this led him to a kind of addiction for applause," List said, echoing the observations of Davidov and Rosenburg. "He would not be looking for the thousand people who would clap at the end of his concert, but the one person who during the concert would leave the hall. That would almost lead him to a depressive condition."[9]

The power of all these forces was wearing away at the man. The question now was whether he could patch the cracks or crumble.

Twenty Two

The Last Fight

*R*eed presented the image of the perfect family man, a lucky guy with a beautiful wife and dutiful stepson. In *American Rebel* Renate sat on the couch with Reed as he spoke, but not knowing English, had very little to say.

The reality was something else again. Or more precisely, Reed was reliving some of the same problems he had in his first two marriages. The bickering between Reed and Renate was nearly constant. Renate was jealous of Wiebke and the fact that she and Reed had a daughter. Reed had been explicit that he did not want to have any more children and this left Renate feeling excluded from a part of her husband. Plus, that child kept Reed tied to the still-attractive Wiebke, who lived only a few miles away. Wiebke told the police that Renate had demanded that Reed hate her and stop seeing his daughter.[1] Renate admitted as much, saying the fights were over all the times he visited his daughter at Wiebke's, rather than having Natascha visit them at Reed's house.

"What I wished for was that she would come and visit us at our house because I had no interest in having some kind of contact between him and his divorced wife," Renate said. "He did not agree with my opinion on this or my view on this. Because of that, there was often problems and fights. From that, my husband threw out that maybe I wanted to hinder him from seeing his daughter."[2]

They also argued about how to raise Renate's teenaged son, Alexander, whom Reed was raising as his own. Reed told List that Alexander was in love for the first time and had let his school work slide. As a result, Alexander fared poorly on a final exam at the high school, an exam that would help determine what he did after he completed his secondary education. Reed wanted to visit the school administrators and use his star power to persuade them to overlook the poor test. Still the romantic, he would argue it was a one-time failing and prod them into remembering the thrill of their first loves. He would slip in a promise that Alexander's work would improve. Renate, however, objected to using influence. She argued, strongly, that Alexander would have to face the consequences and experience life like any normal person, not as the son of a famous actress and stepson of an international star. If he had to learn a trade and labor the rest of his life, well then, so did millions of other people. Reed was baffled by his wife's position, but despite several shouting matches, was unable to persuade her otherwise.[3]

All the pressures and arguments came to a head on Wednesday June 11. At about 2:20 p.m., List had just returned from Moscow where he signed the coproduction contracts with the film company there. After so many delays, the financing and most of the actors were finally in place for Reed's *Bloody Heart* movie. List was about to call his friend when the phone rang. It was Reed calling him.

"Dean, just the man I wanted to talk to. I've got great news," List started. "I just returned from Moscow and all the contracts are signed. We can start work on the movie immediately."

"I want out," Reed said, his voice flat.

"Dean, Dean, it's too late for that. You know how hard it was to get these contracts. Everybody who has ever had an idea for a movie goes to them seeking money. Once you've got it, you've got to produce—"

"I'm not talking about the movie," Reed cut in. "I want out of life. I don't want to go on anymore."

List was startled. It took him several seconds to comprehend what his star was saying and then to switch gears from an economic argument to a suicide hotline conversation.

"Dean, calm down, relax," List pleaded. "I know things have been a little rough, but we can talk this through. You're a little down right now, but really, things are looking up."

"I don't think so. This isn't some kind of mood swing."

"Listen, you're at home, right?" List asked.

"Yeah."

"Okay, here's what I want you to do. Go lie down. Don't do anything. Nothing. I can be there in less than an hour and we can talk about everything. Can you do that? Can you just sit tight?"

"Yeah, sure."

List was unconvinced. He hung up the phone and dialed the general director of DEFA Studios and related the disturbing conversation he just had. The general director agreed that List should hurry to Reed's house and in the meantime, he would have his assistant call the police station closest to Reed's place. They could check on the American and make sure nothing happened until List arrived.[4]

When the police knocked on the door, within minutes of the call, they found Renate tending to Reed's left arm. Blood was flowing from dozens of small, shallow cuts that extended from the crook of his arm to the base of his hand. Reed had been arguing with his wife and whatever the content of the fight, Renate stung him with her verbal blows. They were in Reed's upstairs study and as the hurt piled up like firewood, the actor felt suffocated under the weight. He reached for a sword hanging on the wall. It was a dull blade, but Reed started to hack at his arm, sick of the fighting, sick of life.[5]

At about the same time, at Handel High School in East Berlin, Dr. Werner Dietz was waiting with his seventeen-year-old son and several hundred other students. Dietz had met Reed a year earlier when he treated the actor for the injuries he sustained in the fall from his horse. They had become friendly and Dietz had asked if Reed might come and sing at his son's school. Reed readily agreed, since he frequently went to schools and other youth gatherings to perform for young people. When 3:30 p.m. came and went, Dietz called Reed's house and the phone was answered by a police officer. Dietz explained who he was and why he was calling. The officer told the doctor that Reed had an accident, had cut himself on a broken window. The officer handed the phone to Renate and she asked the doctor to apologize to the students and drive to the house to look at her husband.[6]

List arrived at the house about 3:30, but was forced to amuse himself on the main floor for two hours while Renate and the police stayed upstairs talking to Reed. Finally, Renate called down to List and when he reached the study, he saw an emotionally and physically drained friend. List was as good as his word. They talked about Reed's problems. The singer couldn't stop. All of his anguish cascaded out. They talked for another two hours. Toward the end, the conversation turned to *Bloody Heart*. Reed agreed to go to the hospital and List agreed to arrange an appointment with a psychiatrist. Nearly exhausted now, the danger passed, Reed caved.

"I will do as you always said, my friend, my duty, what I am supposed to do," he told List.[7]

List turned his friend over to Dr. Dietz, who in a reversal of the usual doctor-patient protocol had been kept waiting in another room. He examined the cuts and bruises and determined that they were mostly superficial and not a serious suicide attempt. To the doctor, it appeared to be a cry for help people often shout when they are at their wit's end, but not yet ready to die. Dietz worked on the wounds and then drove the singer to the hospital. Along the way, Dean told Dietz about his wife's jealousy and how she was making his life difficult. He spoke of Renate's unreasonable dislike of Wiebke and how it tortured him not to see his daughter, but he had to limit the visits or suffer Renate's rage. Renate wouldn't let him forget the fact that Reed had a vasectomy and she could not have a child by him. Despite all that, Reed loved her and didn't want to separate from her, he told Dietz. After further treatment at the hospital, the doctor drove Reed back home and was convinced his patient had buried any thought of suicide. In fact, they made a 5 p.m. appointment for the following day at Salvador Allende Hospital to take another look at the injuries.[8]

Reed kept all his appointments the next day. The previous day's gloom had lifted. He and Renate arrived at the DEFA studio in Potsdam-Babelsberg late in the morning and shot some film for the movie, wrapping up the work in the early afternoon. Reed left for the hospital and met with Dietz and they talked until 7 p.m.

"He said he had made it through the work day with his wife and he was very happy that despite the existing conflict, he could work with her," Dietz said. "He was again thinking about the future and wrote a letter to the school saying he would repeat the concert there in the next week."[9] All that changed when Reed arrived home and sat down to dinner with Renate and Alexander. Marriages can be perplexing and certainly had been to Reed. Sometimes a couple can communicate without words, can anticipate the other's moods and needs. Other times, they never see the danger. Like a well-hidden leg trap, they are oblivious until the steel jaw snaps shut. Renate, thinking only that she was showing concern, was about to be ensnared.

"I was thinking maybe you and I should see a psychiatrist," Renate said. "I made a tentative appointment for Monday."

"I don't think so," Reed replied. "We've got too much to do. We'll do it later."

"I'm not sure that's a good idea. Everything else can wait."

"No. I'm fine. We've got to start filming."

"Dean, we've waited for months on this movie, waiting for money, waiting for approvals. Putting it off one more day won't hurt anything."

"It won't be one more day, Renate. He'll want to see us again, and then again. Maybe he'll want to prescribe something, or take me off something else, and then he'll want to monitor that, make sure the dosages are right. No, the psychiatrist can wait a few more months."

"Darling, nothing is more important to me than you. You have not been yourself for weeks. You're depressed, you get upset over the smallest things, you snap at me and Alexander. You rarely smile unless there are other people around."

"I'm a cowboy. I can handle it. You don't know anything about me. I don't want to talk about it anymore."

Renate really hated that. He always thought he was the one who was in charge, that she was just to run the house and maybe act if he let her. She laid into him.

"Cowboy!! Some cowboy. Are cowboys cowards? You didn't have the balls to kill yourself. You take a dull little sword and put on a stupid show. Just stop it. Grow up and act like a man. Either kill yourself or go see the psychiatrist, but stop these pitiful little performances. I'm sick of them."

Once again, the verbal missiles found their mark as only a lover can target them. Reed, angry and hurt, didn't even bother to respond. He pushed back from the table and went to his room. He grabbed his leather briefcase with his script, documentary materials for the movie, pens, publicity photos, newspaper clippings about himself and writing paper. He picked up a smaller yellow wash bag and stuffed in his toothbrush, razor, pills, nasal spray, hair brush, baby oil and lip balm. He strode past his wife and jerked open the door.

"I'm going to people who love me," he shouted at her, climbed into his car and squealed out into the night. It was about 10 p.m.[10]

Recollections became fuzzier at this point, as they always do when people are forced to remember exact times after a lifetime of approximations. Reed phoned List sometime around 10:40 p.m., the director guessed. He did not know where Reed was when he called. The American asked a few questions about the details of List's trip to Moscow, then asked if he could spend the night at List's apartment. List did not hesitate, telling his friend to come on over. After all, Reed had done it before and it made logistical sense, because the apartment was next to the DEFA studios and they could begin work early the next morning. "You are my only friend," Reed told List and said he would be there in about an hour. There was nothing unusual in the conversation. Reed's voiced sounded normal, there was no indication he was upset. List made up a bed in a guest room and then waited for his friend to knock on the door. He never did. List waited up until 2:30 a.m., Friday, June 13. But Dean Reed had disappeared.[11]

Twenty Three

The Search for Dean Reed

*R*enate knew almost from the minute Reed left that she made a mistake. She had pushed him too hard and his ego was fragile, more so in the past few days. Within a half-hour, she made up her mind to search for him, to apologize and hold him close, to kiss him. Their fights meant nothing. She loved him. He was tender with her and told her often that he loved her and wanted to grow old with her. Renate drove to the little apartment the couple kept in the heart of East Berlin. His car was not there, so she drove to the Interhotel in Potsdam, but again, no Reed. Now scared and tired, Renate couldn't bring herself to drive back to their home, only to catch an hour or two of sleep before making the commute again. Instead, she drove to DEFA and watched the sun come up, hoping that her husband would pull up in his car, ready for work. Eventually, List arrived. Surprised to see the actress there and looking haggard, he nonetheless told her about the call he got from Reed. His own fears rising, List said he stayed awake for hours, but his friend never arrived. Renate could feel the sick knot of panic squeezing her stomach. She found a phone and called Eberhard Fench, a representative of the ruling Central Committee's Propaganda Department. Fench told her not to worry and to return home in case Reed called. Meanwhile, Fench told her he would make some calls.[1]

List, concerned about the well-being of his two stars and friends, gathered up a few personal items and drove to Reed's house to stay with Renate and await word on her husband's whereabouts. As the hours grew, so did their anxiety. List thought Reed might have tried suicide again, but kept pushing the thought out of his mind.

"It could not be, because Dean was an honorable man and had never broken a promise he had given his friend under any circumstance," List said. "Also, in his character, there is not a possibility to betray the number of colleagues through his years of experience, to betray them of the fruits of his hard work for the production of this film. While in the house, I convinced myself he had taken his washing and his razor things with him, but not his U.S. passport. So a trip out of the country was also excluded."[2]

Fench's calls started the Stasi wheels turning. Almost immediately, a new operation, code named Aster, went into effect. Aster was the secret police's efforts to monitor the search for Dean Reed and control any ramifications that might occur when the American was found. There is no indication the Stasi went looking for Reed. They contented themselves with surreptitiously tapping the telephone at the Reed home and listening into every conversation that occurred from that Friday on. Some of the calls are from List to Fench, telling him of other places Reed might have gone and Fench agreeing to have them checked. One of the calls was from a reporter from the London *Sunday Times*. List answered the phone and said Reed was in the hospital for treatment and couldn't be interviewed. The reporter said he would contact Reed in a couple weeks after returning to England. List told the reporter Reed would be traveling with his family to the Soviet Union in August. In an attempt to cover all the bases without raising alarm, List also called a drugstore and told the owner's wife that Reed was on his way back from Prague. If he stopped there to get his prescriptions filled, would she please send him to Berlin because he had an appointment with a London reporter, List requested. In a later conversation, List told the reporter that List would know Monday if the lung disease was better.[3]

Renate was losing the fight against her feelings of dread. At best, she thought her husband might be hiding, but she kept returning to the likelihood that he had driven into the woods and hanged himself or mutilated his body once more. Reed would look for someone to blame for problems and lately Renate had been the fall guy. Still, she vowed that if he suddenly reappeared, she wouldn't be upset, she wouldn't yell, she would only tell him it was wonderful to see him again. The next time he started to irritate her, she would simply call one of her girlfriends. At the moment, though, all she wanted to do was sleep. She was thinking of taking a pill to calm herself because she needed the rest. But the worry kept jolting her with adrenaline and even when she lay down, she couldn't drift off. After 9 p.m. Friday, Fench called the house and talked to Renate briefly, but then put his wife, Doddy, on the phone at Renate's request.

"Oh, Renate, I'm so sorry about this," Doddy said. "You must be feeling awful."

"I'm a mess," Renate responded. "I haven't slept for almost two days now. I can't eat. I've about cried myself out. I'm just so worried."

"Eberhard told me a little about what's been going on the past few days. Do you want to talk about it?" Renate briefly described the suicide attempt and the dinner table fight and Reed's final words about going to see the people who loved him.

"Do you think he's staying with another woman?" Doddy asked. "That might explain what he said to you."

"I know he's had other women," Renate acknowledged. "I would be so happy if that was where he is. If he walked in the door right now with his pants unzipped and carrying the smell of another woman's perfume I would hug him and kiss him until he couldn't breathe. But I don't think that's where he is."

"Well, Dean better show up pretty soon, for a lot of reasons," Doddy said. "You need him back, and, quite honestly, Eberhard has been struggling with whether he should tell his boss about Dean's disappearance. If he does, that will be bad for both of you. Everybody in the party leadership will know. He has enough enemies there who will be happy to use his behavior against him. And against you, too."

"Doddy, you are a good friend. Thank you for talking."

"I've done so little, Renate."

"No, just being able to talk to another woman is a big relief. I'm going to try to get some sleep. I'll talk to you tomorrow."[4]

The next day, Saturday, June 14, the already edgy Renate was tortured by the telephone. It rang at 10:12 a.m. and again at 2:07 p.m. Both times she picked it up, said hello, and then heard the click of someone hanging up. At first, Renate told no one. She began to hope, then desperately to believe, that it was Reed trying to make contact. "Dean told other people he wanted to go to Chile and be in the underground if he couldn't get his film made," Renate told a friend in one of the intercepted conversations. "Perhaps Dean is only pretending he killed himself. Maybe he will get his passport and disappear. Or maybe he is really sick, but the Central Committee had already passed a motion that today he should see a psychiatrist."[5]

The last statement was a telling commentary on life in the Communist country. For someone like Renate, who had lived virtually her entire existence under a system where huge chunks of a person's life was directed by the government, it was not hard to imagine the Central Committee ordering the abduction of her husband. Of course, it would be justified as being for his own good and the good of the nation. After all, a national singing and acting treasure like Dean Reed should not be allowed to self-destruct when the state had the ability to intervene and get him to a hospital for psychiatric treatment.

Eventually, Renate decided she had to tell someone about the strange phone calls. Prompted by another one late Sunday morning, June 15, she contacted Fench. He reassured Renate and said he would contact the comrades in the leadership and have them place a wiretap on the phone in an effort to hear who was on the other end and track them down. What Renate did not know, and perhaps Fench didn't either, was that the Stasi had been listening in to every phone call for at least the past two days. Just after noon, Reed's mother called Renate. She thanked her for a letter Reed sent but said her son had forgotten to enclose his passport picture so she could renew his driver's license. Renate, who spoke little English, and Ruth Anna, who spoke even less German, couldn't communicate well. Renate decided not to tell her mother-in-law that Reed was missing. Instead, she told Ruth Anna that she would pass along the need for the photos when she saw Reed.[6]

But this day also brought the first break since the American roared away Thursday evening. Fench called Renate in the early afternoon with the news.

"Renate, they found Dean's car."

"Oh God," she sobbed. "Where? Is he, is he in it?"

"I don't have many details, Renate, but no, he was not in the car. Listen to me. This is very important. Two people will be coming to your house this afternoon. One is a Stasi agent and the other one is a police investigator. I want you to cooperate fully with them. You must answer all their questions completely and honestly. Your answers will be held in strict confidence. They will not come back to hurt you or Dean. Do you understand what I'm telling you?"

"Yes," she said quietly.

"I can't stress enough how important it is that you cooperate fully. It is the only way to bring Dean back alive and healthy."

"I understand, Eberhard. I will do whatever is necessary to bring him back. I love him and am so sorry this has happened."

Reed's car had been discovered two days earlier, on Friday night, about 7:30, by a twenty-two-year-old Berlin woman who had gone to the rescue station by Zeuthener Lake, not two miles from Reed's house. The car was in among the underbrush about thirty yards behind the station. The woman didn't report it because it was an area where people often parked their cars while taking a short walk through the woods and out to a dock on the lake. But when she returned Sunday morning and it was still there, she called police. Investigators found a dent on the left front fender of Reed's car and a tow rope on the ground behind the automobile. For an hour, between 2:45 p.m. and 3:45 p.m. police brought two dogs, Cindy and Cilly, to track any scent from the vehicle. Both dogs, independently, picked up a scent that took them from the car northward along an overgrown walking path nearly 400 yards to a campsite. From there, the scent continued another 30 yards to the small boat dock. There, the dogs lost the scent.[7]

The Stasi agent and police officer knocked on the door and were ushered inside. The two men were efficient and humorless. They asked Renate what Reed was wearing and left with a couple of photos so searchers would know who they were looking for, although it seemed like an odd thing to do for one of the most recognized men in East Germany. They asked Renate what had happened the night Reed left and once more she went over the story of their fights.[8] After Renate exhausted her cooperation, she peppered the officers with her own questions. What had they found in the car? Was his kit still there? Did it look like he was hurt? Was there an accident? The officers answered in the universal language of cops, telling Renate only that they had found the car, but really, they couldn't say too much more until they had more time to investigate. But of course, they would let her know more as soon as they found anything. Thanks for your time and we should be getting back to work. They intentionally withheld critical evidence they found in the car from Reed's wife.

Renate didn't know what to think. It was reassuring that they found Reed's car and obviously he was not in it. But it answered so little and her two conflicting possibilities were still very much in play. Her husband could very well have gone farther in the woods and killed himself and they just hadn't found the body. Or, maybe he is in hiding, hoping to sneak back to their house, grab his passport and fly to Chile. Indeed, on Monday, June 16, Fench called Renate and told her the police had conducted an extensive search and found no clues. But the police were following every lead and had talked to numerous Chilean and PLO comrades staying in East Germany. They told investigators they had heard nothing from Reed, but they would watch for him and contact authorities if they heard anything.[9] Still, the past four days had drained the German actress of more emotion than any performance. Sometimes she cried, but most of the time now she was numb, her body battered by four nights with almost no sleep, and days where nothing happened and the fears were tended and grew strong in the mulch of tedium.

The discovery of Reed's car and the scent the dogs followed down to the water's edge had the local police searching both land

and water. When Officer Sven Bosener reported to work at 7:15 a.m. Tuesday, he was given details about the missing American. He was ordered to take a boat and begin a methodical search of the lake. In particular, he was to examine a weed bed near the shore. He hadn't been looking long when he spotted the body and hauled it into his boat.[10]

Investigators and Communist officials took their time once Reed's body was found. This was an American, after all, and there was no way the East Germans wanted the superpower thinking they had anything to do with Reed's death. The officials met and finally decided they would release a short statement. The popular actor and singer died in a "tragic accident," in the lake not far from his house. Fench appeared to be in on the meeting and it was left to him to bring the news to Reed's wife. Fench arrived at the Reed home six hours after the body was brought to shore. Renate collapsed in a heap, crying in loud sobs, the worry and torment of the past six days pouring out of her heart and exhausted body. At 3:25 p.m., the widow Reed was still crying and her condition concerned Fench enough that he called a doctor and asked him to come to the house and bring a tranquilizer for Renate.[11]

When Patricia's husband told her she had a call from East Germany that Tuesday afternoon, she figured it was Reed calling to tell her he was coming for Ramona's graduation from Beverly Hills High School. He had told his ex-wife earlier in the spring that he would like to surprise his daughter by showing up for the ceremony. He hadn't said anything about it when he sent Ramona a cassette with a new song and then called her on the phone the previous week. But it wasn't Reed on the other end of the line. It was someone with accented English, telling her that Reed had died in a swimming accident. She called Ruth Anna, Reed's mother, in Hawaii, who had received word from the DEFA Studios not long before Patricia. Ruth Anna booked a flight to Berlin and the two women arranged to meet there and get more details.[12] Reed's mother arrived in East Berlin on Thursday. Patricia and Ramona arrived the following day. Ruth Anna quickly learned that Reed had been missing for days and that Renate had lied to her on Monday when she said her son was out. That lie, and the story Reed had drowned in an accident, aroused the suspicions of his mother and ex-wife. Reed was an athlete, a former lifeguard, the man who once raced a mule. Death by drowning was far-fetched.

The pending arrival of the Americans worried List. He called a high-ranking communist official looking for advice. There must be something more on the death, something he could tell the women that will make sense and not look like it was a suicide. "Americans only believe in psychiatrists and autopsies," the movie producer told the comrade major. The official said not to worry, that they would believe the accident story, but he would see what he could do. But late Thursday night, List's fears proved all too accurate. List called Joachim Fiedlkorn, the communist official, and told him that Ruth Anna was unconvinced. She kept asking the same questions. Why did Dean drive to that place by the lake in the first place? Were there barbiturates in his system? List no longer knew what to say and repeatedly told Ruth Anna that her son was in the water and nobody else had a hand in his death. The American mother dug in, refusing to allow her son's body to be cremated until the toxicology reports came back indicating what was in his blood. That could take days or weeks. Yet, if Ruth Anna returned to the United States unsatisfied with the answers, the whole incident could be raised to a much higher level, one that the two East Germans didn't want to think about. List suggested the two men take Renate and Ruth Anna to the police the next day and get the facts. Fiedlkorn would then tell them that Reed's death was due to drugs. That would still leave open the question of why he was in the water, but it would have to remain a mystery since there were no witnesses, Fiedlkorn said.[13]

Heide Kuschel, a translator at the DEFA Studios, talked to List by phone on Friday and said she told Ruth Anna that tissue samples were taken from the body. List suggested, and Kuschel agreed, that the pathology report should go directly to Reed's mother. By Saturday, Will Roberts arrived. Roberts spent two years with Reed making the documentary of his life. He, too, was making trouble, pressing Renate for details and loudly proclaiming that Reed was murdered. Renate heightened everyone's suspicions by lying again.

She denied that Reed had slashed his wrists the previous week, saying he had an accident and put his hand through a pane of glass. It was only later that Renate learned that Wiebke had visited Ruth Anna and Patricia at their hotel and brought along the doctor who had treated Reed after the suicide attempt.

When Renate realized she had been sandbagged by Wiebke and the Americans, she panicked. Distraught, she called Fench and explained what had happened. Fench told her to relax, but to tell no more lies. He plotted strategy with List and the two of them worked out what they and Renate would tell, and what they would keep to themselves. So, Renate told the relatives how Reed slashed his wrists, but did not tell them she called her husband a coward. List told them about the call he received from Reed that ill-fated night, but would say only that Reed wanted to sleep over because of his appointments the next day. List counseled Renate not to tell anyone about the second fight, the one that ended with Reed storming out of the house for the last time. If she did, the relatives would make a big deal out of it in the Western press and Renate would not be able to stand it, List told her. It also was time to counterattack. List said he would tell the women he was appalled that some people were trying to dirty the proud and honorable memory of Dean Reed. What happened on that Wednesday afternoon was really nobody's business and of no importance. He hoped that chastisement would throw them off, make them feel sheepish and less willing to press their inquiry.[14]

List and Fiedlkorn finally arranged for the Americans to meet with the Berlin police investigating the death. Patricia, Ruth Anna, Roberts, Renate and Matthias Manz, a vice-counsel from the U.S. Embassy, arrived at the police station just before 10:30 a.m. Monday, nearly a week after Reed's body was pulled from the lake. Comrade Major Pohl explained, with the translation help of Heide Kuschel, what the police had discovered. They stressed that investigators had unearthed no evidence of a crime and that Reed's death was an accident. Pohl told the family that the autopsy indicated that Reed was in a state of intoxication or only semiconscious from taking a high dose of his sleeping medicine Radedorm. The investigation determined that Reed struck a tree as he came off the road into the area where the car was discovered, causing minor damage to the front bumper. However, because there were no witnesses, it was impossible to say what happened to Reed between the time he parked the car and when he drowned. The most likely scenario, Pohl said, was that the singer walked down to the dock to splash water in his face and tumbled in. The family and Roberts bought much of what the police had to say, but were troubled by two aspects. No one could explain where Reed was for nearly an hour between the time he left the house and the time he called List. And none of them were convinced that the amount of sleeping pills in his blood was enough to knock him out and cause him to slip under the water. Those two flaws in the explanation left the group still convinced Reed might have been murdered. Will Roberts was particularly vehement, accusing the Communist government of killing people as a matter of policy and then telling police not to investigate the situation but to write it off as another accident. After three hours of this, Ruth Anna asked to see the body. Police officers took most of the group to the Institute for Forensic Medicine in Berlin. There, Professor Radam explained that Reed died from a drowning complicated by a strong dose of Radedorm, making it difficult for him to swim.[15]

They laid Reed to rest at high noon on Tuesday, June 24, 1986. The family put out a simple death announcement.

> Our beloved husband, son and father
> Dean Reed
> Singer, actor and producer
>
> Born on September 22, 1938 in Denver (Colorado)
> Has died on the 13th June 1986 as the consequence of a tragic accident
>
> In deep pain
> Renate Blume Reed
> Ruth Anna Brown as mother
> Daughters Ramona and Natascha
> And son Alexander
>
> We ask you to refrain from visits of condolence.[16]

The music was by Beethoven, Haydn and Reed. Some three hundred people attended the service at Crematorium Berlin-Baumschulenweg. Many of those present were actors and directors from the DEFA studios as well as Communist officials from the Peace Council and Committee for Entertainment. Actor Jerry Wolf read some of Reed's own words about his life and convictions. The main eulogy was delivered by the Deputy Minister of Culture, Comrade Horst Pehnert. Reed's friend and video biographer, Will Roberts, spoke about his friend as an interpreter translated his words into German. Roberts said Reed once told him he wanted to be buried in Berlin, but Roberts said Reed was an international artist and proposed that his ashes be brought to the United States, Chile, Nicaragua, Italy, Argentina and Moscow. In a slight act of defiance, Roberts said he still wanted to know exactly how and where Reed died, but concluded that probably no one ever would. Roberts, though, understood Reed's greatest love. He was an entertainer and he asked the audience to give Reed one last round of applause. The three hundred strong filled the air with their clapping for the American singer and actor.

Ruth Anna was moved by the applause and by the events of the past few days. She unexpectedly asked to speak and told the crowd there was a debate about splitting the ashes between Berlin and America. Now, however, she was convinced that all of Reed's remains should stay in East Germany where he had loved two women, lived happily and where Renate, whom he loved above all else, still lived. The ashes, Ruth Anna said, should stay with her. At the end of the eighty-minute funeral, Reed's voice boomed from the speakers, singing "Give Me a Guitar." As the song ended, the mourners once again applauded and filed out. Stasi agents watched the entire service and those who attended. The agents were pleased to report "there came to be no remarks directed against the GDR."[17]

The funeral struck Patricia as odd. Where was the press, the television cameras, the fans? In the United States, when celebrities of sufficient stature die, there is press and television coverage, sometimes even live. Fans would gather as close to the ceremony as they could, even if it meant standing across the street. When Elvis Presley died in 1977, hundreds of thousands of people flocked to Graceland and stayed there until after he was laid to rest. But here, this was a prop funeral, Patricia thought. Most of the mourners filling the chapel were employed by the studio. It was hard to tell if they were truly paying their last respects or simply being paid.[18]

Renate's lies, and those of List during the first few days of Reed's disappearance were now, in the days following the funeral, resurrected as evidence that Reed was murdered. Russell Miller, the reporter from the London *Times* who had tried to contact the American after he fled the house, went to press with his bizarre tale of the conversations he had while trying to line up an interview with Reed. Miller reported that on Friday, June 13, he had called the Reed house from West Berlin and Renate told him Reed was in the hospital with pneumonia. Miller called back that evening and while he was talking to Mrs. Reed, a man took the phone from her and identified himself as Mr. Wieczaukowski, the codirector of Reed's new film. He confirmed that Reed was in the hospital. When Miller heard about Reed's death, he immediately called Wieczaukowski at the Potsdam number the reporter had for the mysterious director. A woman answered, Miller wrote, and told him no one by that name lived there. Miller also quoted Dixie Lloyd, the woman Reed met in Denver who was now calling herself his U.S. manager. She told Miller she did not believe Reed killed himself or died accidentally. He was murdered, she told the London reporter, because he had spoken openly of returning to the United States and the East Germans did not want to lose a valuable propaganda prize. Just the week before his death, Lloyd talked to Reed and he had complained about being under stress and unclear about his status in East Germany.

The unknown Wieczaukowski was, in fact, Gerrit List. Why he deemed it necessary to use an alias is a mystery. But the clumsy efforts to cover up Reed's disappearance until they knew what had happened to him now took on sinister overtones. Could it be that Stasi agents had threatened their lives unless they went along with the ruse? Fueling that kind of speculation were several stories in West German newspapers in the days immediately following the recovery of Reed's body. The stories quoted unnamed artist friends of the American performer who claimed Reed was found with a cut rope around his neck, in his car, at the bottom of the lake. Obviously he could not have hanged himself and driven the car into the water. There had to be a third party.

Reed also was the subject of as many sightings as Elvis. Both Reed's mother and Patricia learned about a shopkeeper named Mrs. Rumpf. Her little store overlooked the lake and Reed was a regular customer. Mrs. Rumpf said Reed stopped in about 6 p.m. on the Thursday he disappeared and bought several expensive ballpoint pens. But it was the next morning, when Reed already was under the water, that Mrs. Rumpf claimed to have seen him again. Reed popped into the store in late morning and said he needed ten more of the same pens. He also told her he was in a hurry, so she quickly wrapped the pens and he hustled out of the store and drove away. On the day after Reed's body was pulled from the water, Karin Davidson, an American working for a local television station in West Berlin saw Reed twice. Both times he appeared to be in a hurry, so she did not speak to him. She was certain it was him, even after she returned to her office and for the first time heard the news that Reed was dead.[19]

Family members found other oddities. Ramona checked her father's wallet. The outside was wet, as expected after several days in the lake, but the inside was dry. Reed was wearing a jean jacket, one he borrowed from Johnny Rosenburg the previous year and never returned. Yet, it was summertime and the temperatures, even at night, were too warm for a jacket, Patricia said. The lies, inconsistencies and reported sightings all added to the confusion and fueled speculation that the government report of a tragic accident was as phony as the economic reports they regularly issued. Reed's family was not buying the death by accident story.

Twenty Four

Who Killed Dean Reed?

A break in the mystery occurred in 1992. Ruth Anna had not let her son's death fade. She contacted her U.S. senator, Gary Hart, and he in turn, pushed the U.S. State Department and the Berlin embassy to obtain more information. Reed's mother also kept in touch with Wiebke and Renate. Those contacts paid off when the Soviet bloc nations were washed away by the tides of history.

Dean's old acquaintance, Soviet Premier Mikhail Gorbachev, had ignited a small fire in the USSR that he hoped would burn away the worst deadwood of the Communist system. But the freedom fire soon burned out of control, blazing through the Soviet Union and then jumping the little firebreaks of national boundaries. One of the first nations to get scorched was East Germany. In a rerun of the months before East Germany erected the Berlin Wall, East German citizens found new ways to flee their Communist paradise. Between May and October 1989, thousands traveled to Prague, Czechoslovakia, and ran to the West German embassy there. They asked for, and were automatically granted, citizenship in the Western state and provided transportation to a refugee processing station in one of the West German states. By late September, nightly protest marches began in East Germany. Demonstrators would gather at the churches, primarily Lutheran, and thousands of them would fill the streets chanting "Freedom Now,

Democracy Now." In an eerie echo of what Reed had said just a few years earlier when he confronted the police pulling over regular citizens, a commentator pointed out that the East German leaders were isolated in their country dachas and driving in Volvos with the shades pulled down.[1] The East German leaders hesitated this time. Even Erich Honecker, who ordered the construction of the Berlin Wall in 1961, seemed unsure of himself. In late October, Honecker stepped down and turned the government over to Egon Krenz, head of the Stasi. The move made no difference. In the waning days of November, the government fell. The people were in control and men and women from both East and West Berlin danced atop the hated wall, while others chipped away chunks of the most enduring symbol of the Cold War.

With the fall, and reunification of the two Germanys, came access to formerly secret records. Chief among those were Stasi files, which at first were only available to family members. Wiebke, who was always the resourceful one, got her hands on a piece of evidence police had confiscated the moment they found Reed's car by the lake. On the dashboard was a fifteen-page suicide note written on the back of the script for his new movie. "The farewell letter was submitted immediately after its discovery to the staff members of the MfS (Stasi)," according to a memo from secret police files.[2] The Stasi agent who visited Renate the day the car was found didn't mention it. When Ruth Anna, Renate, Patricia and Will Roberts received their briefing at police headquarters about the death investigation, no one mentioned a suicide note. Keeping the note secret was a deliberate decision by a member of the Central Committee—probably Fensch. "The U.S. citizens and relatives of Dean Reed who were present were informed nothing about there being a farewell letter from Dean Reed (as per the wish of the deputy leader of the section propaganda at the ZK of the SED at the inception of the investigation.)"[3]

So there it was. The crucial piece of evidence that would have answered nearly everyone's questions was officially buried. The government officials never wrote a memo explaining why they covered up the suicide. But given the near hysteria about how Reed's death would be viewed in the West, the government probably did not want to give any indication that life was anything but grand. Indeed, the East German government did not like to acknowledge that suicide occurred among even its regular citizens. After all, was not the country a worker's paradise, where everyone had a job, a place to live and free medical care? Was this not superior to the decadent West where crime, poverty and racial discord ran rampant? Why then would anyone want to commit suicide? After Reed's body was discovered, numerous orders were issued, all intended to block any potential embarrassment of the East German government by the United States. Typical was the Stasi memo the day Reed was hauled ashore. "It is proposed that a suitable staff member of the DEFA studio for feature films have conversation with Reed, Wiebke and arrange it with her so that she not allow acts directed against the GDR to be misused in connection with the death of Dean Reed."[4]

While the flamboyant and talkative Wiebke was viewed by the East German government as the loose cannon who might shoot holes through the fabric of its "tragic accident" story, she was not the only one to receive instructions on how to act. Renate was quieter and more timid than Wiebke, but she was, after all, the official widow. She also had been under more stress than anyone since Reed disappeared. Stasi officers were well aware of her state and orders came down from headquarters for someone to instruct Renate on what she "could answer to inquiries by the USA Embassy or journalists."[5]

It was six years after Reed's death that Wiebke obtained a copy of the suicide note police found on the dashboard of the American's car. She forwarded a copy to Ruth Anna, who had it translated from Reed's German to English. She read it, but did not believe it. She refused to share the note with reporters because seeing it in print gave it too much credibility, more than she was willing to extend to it. However, the full note was contained in the Stasi documents released by the German government and while his mother remained unconvinced that he wrote it, or at best, wrote it under duress, the phrases echo the words of earlier writings and thoughts. The note was a summation of the current fights with Renate, the past and his efforts to make a difference in various countries. It contained thoughts about the future and his hope that others could correct the flaws of Communism and help it reach its promise. The note was dated June 12, the Thursday night he drove away from his home.

My friend and General Eberhard Fensch—

I am sorry my friend. You are a model for me—as so many fair socialists of Chile to Lebanon. My death has to do nothing with politics. Let not our enemies, the fascists and reactionaries, explain it as such!

I wanted to [visit] you in peace with Renate on Sunday. But as I came back this evening from DEFA and sat by the TV—(Sascha—my son can confirm it) Renate started to tease me, that I am only a show man—and it was only a "show" by me.

I asked her to leave me alone, but she screamed again and again, that I was only a bad American show man. She torments me and tortures me for many years because she is sick, jealous of all the people I love or who love me. Prof. Welkonig, Cemit, Les, Marlen Hoffmann, Martin Wagner—however especially my former wife Wiebke and my daughter Natascha. I have taken her son Sascha as my son and love him like my own. But Renate, for 5 years terrorized me, if I want to see Natascha. She and Wiebke should be my enemies. I refuse to hate somebody whom I have had once as wife. I love Renate, despite her illness, but I can find no way out of my problem. I have to film a difficult important film in a week—with Renate it can't go well. If she constantly screams at me, that I am only a show man and have no courage to commit suicide. She makes me already crazy enough, must I also hear that to my death? The only way to save DEFA with the SU is if I am dead—I would much rather have died also in Lebanon or Chile—in the fight against our enemies. The criminals, who have tortured and killed my friends everywhere. But I also do not achieve that now.

My greetings to Achim and thanks for everything— don't be angry—there is no other way. I wanted to live with Renate until death separates us—however she has killed me day by day and to say today to me, that I am too cowardly to kill myself—Because she continued, Sascha came to me and said that he thought it was disgusting what she does to me. He also wanted to go away. Renate needed for her ego only the most preferred products—and she did it—Frank, Gesko and I—and then she finished us.

I believe as always in the progressive superiority—the persons of good will build a better world—a socialist world. Stay honest and open-minded like you are. Stay courageous and fight also against our own contradictions. I am so sorry that I have not fallen with my friend Victor. But each has his own fate. I have fought much and have tried to turn my power and talent to all persons who needed my help. I hope my life has had a value for my friends in Nicaragua, Chile, Argentina, Uruguay and the Palestinian people. It is the only solution for DEFA—if I die—because I cannot take the money of the people for a film which will possibly never come to an end because every day my wife will torture and torment me further— and there is not enough time to find another actor. I am sorry for Natascha, who must suffer, only through the jealousy of Renate. That was unjust and awful of my wife. I love her son, but I may not love my own daughter.

Eberhard, you were always a faithful friend—please do not hate me. I was at the end yesterday and everything would be better if Renate would have not begun to see me as a coward. She said that you have said, that that was "show" yesterday. I am sure she always lies to me if she wants me to separate myself from my friends.

My greetings also to Erich—I am not in agreement with everything, but socialism is not yet mature. It is the only solution for the main problems of mankind of the world. I love you and so many others in Chile, Argentina, Uruguay, Palestine, SU, CSSR, and the GDR, which was my second home for a short time. Let all progressive persons take the hands of each other and together you will create a better, just and peaceful world.

Send my love please to my mom whom I so love and was such a model for me. To Ramona, my daughter, to Natascha, my daughter and Sascha my son.

I embrace you–

Dean Reed 12/6/86"

[In German, the day is written first, then the month, so this was dated June 12, 1986][6]

The nearly unanimous reaction by Reed's friends and family to the suicide note was disbelief. Because the East German authorities hid it for so long, it aroused suspicions that they simply took their time and forged Reed's final words. His mother drew a parallel to the phony Hitler diaries that turned up in the mid-1970s and were believed to be authentic for months before scientists and historians were able to prove they were faked. "We're not even sure the letter was written at that time," Ruth Anna said. "Where has it been all this time?"[7]

Rationally, it did not make sense to her for another reason. Her son had worked for several years trying to pull together the financing for his movie *Bloody Heart*. Just days before his death, the joint venture between DEFA and a Soviet film company was finalized and the money was in hand. This was the film he was sure would propel him to stardom back in the United States. Why would he end that chance by taking his life, his mother wondered. So she took comfort in the ideas of others, including a former CIA agent who visited her not long after Reed's death. While not having any firsthand information on her son's drowning, he told her about "wet jobs," a common tactic among covert agents around the world, he said. Kill the victim and then make it look like an accidental drowning, the former agent explained to her.[8]

Phil Everly was surprised to hear of the suicide note. Reed was not the type to take his life and especially not at that point. He was fascinated by the prospect of returning to the United States and igniting his smoldering career. "I didn't get the impression that the break-up of a marriage would have done him in," Everly said. "Not even a third time. I got the impression he got around pretty good. It could have been a jealous husband. I prefer to think of him as laughing and a good guy who believed in peace."[9]

Reed's first wife, Patricia, was there when he was first arrested and interrogated in Argentina. She watched him face other dangers and take unpopular stands. She did not believe the suicide theory, either, but acknowledged he was suffering. When he was fighting for the poor in South America in the 1960s, he was part of a medium-sized movement that was bold, lively and fun. The poor responded with cheers and salutes and his ideological brothers bolstered his spirits when they flagged. The newspapers, especially the leftist ones, were happy to talk to Reed almost any time. East Germany offered almost none of those elixirs. "A lot of times, we would make love and I would hold him and soothe him," Patricia said. "The next morning, he would get up this energy. The reason he died is because the people around him didn't give him the lift. We had all these liberals (in Argentina) who would say, 'yeah, yeah, yeah.' We had the newspapers in our palms. He could call the newspapers, I could, and they would put it on the front page."[10]

Only older brother Dale breaks with the family line. He concedes that suicide is possible. The two men drifted apart over the years. Dale was working at the Boeing aircraft company and occasionally on Top Secret military projects. He never visited his brother in East Germany, in part because he feared it would jeopardize his security clearance with the U.S. government and curtail his work at Boeing. But Dale was a conservative, much like his father, and he was put off by Dean's radical stance. They would write each other letters, arguing about politics and both men were too stubborn to surrender any points while Dean was alive. That changed for Dale after his brother died. He pondered the things Dean had said and eventually he switched departments at Boeing, leaving nuclear weapons and transferring to commercial aviation. He also started working with Physicians for Social Responsibility, a national organization strongly opposed to nuclear weapons.

"We agree a lot more now than then," Dale said "I wouldn't admit it when he was alive. I hadn't thought it as thoroughly as I have now. I switched, in part, because of him and Mom. He changed a lot of people, the socialist countries, with his guitar and rock music."[11]

In some ways, the philosophical distance between the two brothers may account for Dale's perspective that suicide is the best explanation for his brother's death. He still disagreed with much of what his younger brother did and said and he has no interest in turning Dean into a martyr for progressive causes, a saintly man cut down in his prime by the forces of repression and evil.

"I could see he was living really high and successful," Dale said. "But he was having stomach problems. His wife wasn't going to live in the U.S. It would be easy to swim away from shore and keep going until he was too tired. My nephew committed suicide. Then Dad. It's not against our culture to do that."[12]

It's true that the Stasi could have forged the suicide note, although there is a request in their own records for a handwriting analysis of the suicide note. Why bother if your agents wrote the note? It's also true that the secret police could have purged their files of any record of orders to kill the American. However, that is even less likely than Reed having been murdered by a foreign government. First, bureaucracies universally have a need to record what they do. Some of it is for future reference and some of it is just the requirements of the bureaucrats themselves. To justify their existence, they document their actions and decisions and send it on to their superiors. Historians and reporters have made livings off that habit for centuries, pouring through official documents for insights and evidence. Rarely are they disappointed, for rarely is the record purged. Second, the Stasi might have tried to expunge some of the most damning papers, but the fall of the government came quickly in 1989. Even if they started such a review and destruction, they likely would have started with cases more significant than Reed's, cases that involved West German officials who could use the documents to harm them in a reunified Germany. Or they would have shredded the files of cases involving the deaths of hundreds of East Germans as they tried to escape the country, cases that could be bundled together and taken to court as crimes against humanity.

The rejection of the suicide explanation by the people who knew Reed best is easy to understand. They feel cheated. Here was a man who lived an exciting, almost storybook life. But instead of a triumphant ending, it is as though the author didn't know how to write an ending. It was unsatisfying, so therefore, it must not be true.

Reed's suicide is unsatisfying, but consistent with his life. Patricia saw a death wish in her husband. He kept injecting himself into dangerous situations and more than once, even before the suicide note, he lamented the fact that he had not died with his friends in Chile. His increasingly erratic behavior, the physical breakdowns and the growing pile of medications he was ingesting all are indicative of a man heading toward a crisis, one in which taking his life seems reasonable. Most telling was his confession to List that he was having ever deeper and longer bouts of depression. Only a severely depressed man would illogically write that only his death could help DEFA studios and the making of a film that was the sole creation of the actor about to take his own life. He was blind to the bigger picture and could only see his own suffering and could think of no other way to cure it than to take more pills and swim fully clothed into the middle of the lake. Focusing on the death, however, obliterates his life. Marv Davidov knew better.

"There is no other American life like this one," Davidov said. "He was an American through and through. His experience is an American experience which took twists because he was an entertainer and he became a leftist."[13]

More than that, it was a thoroughly human story. Was he self-centered? Certainly, and sometimes cruel. But he was alert to injustice and sprang into action wherever he saw it. He paid the price physically and financially. People with less talent than Reed have had good entertainment careers here, but they were not agitating for their beliefs on a weekly basis either. Stubbornly, righteously, Reed soldiered on, fighting for peace, fighting for the poor, fighting together with those seeking a better government, whether in Chile, Argentina, the United States of America or Communist East Germany. Gen. Pinochet and leaders of the other governments Reed challenged at least disliked him and possibly hated him. But they were not as powerful as Reed's own demons, which in the end did what the mighty could not do. They silenced the music.

Notes

ONE: The Body in the Water

All Stasi references are from the East German Secret Police records obtained by the author and translated into English by Gayle Carlson. The numbering system, e.g., BStU, is theirs and refers to a specific document or page of a document.

1. Sven Boesner was searching for a body… Police interview of Sven Boesner, June 17, 1986, Stasi files Vol. 4 BStU 71-73

2. American viewers were outraged… Police interview of Renate Blume Reed, June 30, 1986, Stasi files Vol. 4 BStU 98

3. He was married three times… Interview of Patricia Reed Wilson, in Los Angeles by the author, August 18-19, 1998

4. "A basic principle of Dean…" Telephone interview of Phil Everly by the author, May 31, 1996

5. During the funeral service… Stasi files, Vol. 3 BStU 138

TWO: Mobbed

1. A van from a Santiago Radio Station… From the book, *Dean Reed Tells about His Life,* as told to Hans-Dieter Brauer. Translated by Gayle Carlson (Peters: 1984), p.25.

2. The next day was more of the same…Ibid. However, some of the dialogue was created by the author based on Reed's account and others' descriptions of how he talked

3. "Every town had a dancing hall…" Patricia Reed Wilson, telephone interviews Oct. 24-25, 1996

4. Santiago's restaurants and cafes… *Dean Reed Tells about His Life,* p. 26.

5. "In person he could make…" Patricia Reed Wilson interviews, Oct. 24-25, 1996

6. "He was a cross between…" Telephone interview of Phil Everly, May 31, 1996

7. "Of course I had…" *Dean Reed Tells about His Life,* pp. 27-29

8. Dean's father, Cyril, gave his son… *Dean Reed Tells about His Life,* p. 12

9. Cyril recalled Dean on the stage… From the movie documentary *American Rebel,* produced and directed by Will Roberts, 1986

10. He wrote some of his own… *The Cold Warrior,* an unpublished script by Patricia Reed Wilson, provided to the author

11. Bill Smith was one of the wranglers…Taken from the account in *Newsweek,* August 6, 1956. The dialogue was created by the author.

12. "He was always stubborn…" Phone interview with Dale Reed, Oct. 6, 1995

THREE: Wandering the West

1. He lost a leg… Dale Reed interview, Oct. 6, 1995

2. There, Ruth Anna Hansen… Interview of Ruth Anna Brown at her home in Boulder, Colo. by the author on Oct. 18, 1994

3. "We had a lot of fun…" Dale Reed interview, Oct. 6, 1995

4. "…it's hard when you're…" Ruth Anna Brown interview, Oct. 18, 1994

5. "The only thing that this…" *Dean Reed Tells about His Life*, p. 12

6. He worked his boys hard… Dale Reed interview, Oct. 6, 1995, and Patricia Reed Wilson interviews, Oct. 24-25, 1996

7. When he looked in a mirror… Patricia Reed Wilson, *The Cold Warrior*

8. The yearbook at… Yearbook from the Dean Reed collection at the Colorado Historical Society

9. Ruth Anna made fun…Dale Reed interview, Oct. 6, 1995

10. During his sophomore…Dean Reed résumé provided by Patricia Reed Wilson

11. "He was always a ladies man…" Dale Reed interview, Oct. 6, 1995

12. His early grades…Grade transcripts from the Dean Reed Collection of the Colorado Historical Society

13. From the beginning… *American Rebel* documentary

14. A cowboy hat pushed…Dale Reed interview, Oct. 6, 1995 and Patricia Reed Wilson interviews, Aug. 18-19, 1998

FOUR: The Czech Chanteuse

1. He called his mother…Conversation recreated by author based on interview with Ruth Anna Brown on Oct. 18, 1994

2. After his first tour… "L.A. Singer makes hit with Latins," *Los Angeles Times*, Dec. 26, 1963

3. "He taught himself Spanish…" Patricia Reed Wilson interviews, Oct. 24-25, 1996

4. Dover was ten years older… Ibid.

5. "I love you…" Letter from Nyta Dover in Argentina to Dean Reed, April 17, 1962 or 1963. Letter provided to author by Patricia Reed Wilson.

6. "I remember exactly how…" *Dean Reed Tells about His Life*, p. 30.

FIVE: The Jungle and the Bomb

All U.S. State Department memos and documents were obtained by the author through the U.S. Freedom of Information Act.

1. Just as likely… *American Rebel* documentary

2. "He was always showing off…" Dale Reed interview, Oct. 6, 1995

3. The four men traveled north and east…Patricia Reed Wilson interviews, Oct. 24-25, 1996, and August 18, 1998

4. "Look guys, I think we ought to…" Ibid.. with dialogue created by the author

5. At the Buenos Aires airport… *Dean Reed Tells about His Life*, pp. 32-34

6. Number one, with 29,330... *Termometro Juvenil de Dictembre* poll from the Dean Reed collection of the Colorado Historical Society

7. Alongside a photo of himself...Copy of advertisement provided by Patricia Reed Wilson

8. Radio stations and newspapers...State Department telegram number 927, April 26, 1962

9. "Embassy attempting to locate..." Ibid.

10. One of Cole's deputies...State Department memo: Activities of Dean Reed in South America, May 2, 1962

11. "...his actions are considered..." State Department Instruction CW-8853, May 4, 1962

12. In Lima, Peru, an employee... Ambassador James Loeb, Jr., telegram to State Department, May 23, 1962

13. "Shocked by your reaction..." Telegram to Loeb from State Department files

14. The telegram also prompted... *Dean Reed Tells about His Life,* p. 36

15. "Come in Mr. Reed..." Conversation created by author based on Cole recollection in State Department Airgram A-135 from American Embassy in Santiago, June 5, 1962

16. "That impressed Dean," Patricia Reed Wilson interviews, Oct. 24-25, 1996

17. "But I think artists..." L.A. Singer makes hit with Latins"

18. By then, the story... *American Rebel* documentary

19. "Dean took a serious look," Marv Davidov interview in Minneapolis, Minn. June 1996

20. "I feel that unless..." Dean Reed speech, "Our Camouflaged Colonies," March 10, 1963, at First Unitarian Church of Los Angeles, provided by Patricia Reed Wilson

21. "If someone asks me today..." *Dean Reed Tells about His Life,* p. 36

SIX: The Everlys, Raitt, Rosenburg and Price

1. "Mom, Dad, you know the guy..." Dialogue created by the author, based on recollection of Ruth Anna Brown, interviewed Oct. 18, 1994

2. Somewhere in the middle... Ruth Anna Brown interview, Oct. 18, 1994, and *Dean Reed Tells about His Life,* pp. 15-16. Reed told that story whenever anyone asked how he got his start. He never deviated, telling it to his mother and his first wife Patricia. Only his friend Johnny Rosenburg doubts it. "I think it is a myth. When I met Dean, Roy Eberhard was his manager," suggesting it was Eberhard who was Reed's entrée to Capitol.

3. By the second day... *Dean Reed Tells about His Life,* p. 17

4. His ten minutes with... Ruth Anna Brown interview, Oct. 18, 1994 and interview of Johnny Rosenburg at his Loveland, Colo. home, Oct. 17, 1994

5. He started by renting... Johnny Rosenburg interview, Oct. 17, 1994

6. "He would spend his days..." Patricia Reed Wilson interviews, Oct. 24–25, 1996

7. More than once... Ruth Anna Brown interview, Oct. 18, 1994

8. He trained at the American Academy... Marv Davidov interview, June 1996

9. At first, he was sent... Ibid.

10. "Here's a raw young kid..." Ibid.

11. "Although there was a great difference…" *Dean Reed Tells about His Life,* p. 19-20.

12. All were current or former… Patricia Reed Wilson interview, August 18, 1998, in Los Angeles

13. "We've always just chosen…" Phil Everly interview, May 31, 1996

14. He convinced a buddy… Johnny Rosenburg interview, Oct. 17, 1994. Dialogue almost exactly as Rosenburg recounted it

15. "Johnny. Dean Reed here." Ibid.

16. His brother Dale… Dale Reed interview, Oct. 6, 1995

17. "When I met him…" Phone interview of Marge Raitt Goddard by the author, Nov. 6, 1996

18. "He was very charming…" Ibid.

19. "I never knew the reason…" Johnny Rosenburg interview, Oct. 17, 1994

20. "The buyers were part…" *Dean Reed Tells about His Life,* p. 18

21. "I borrowed …" "L.A. Singer makes hit with Latins,*"*

22. Copy of Dean Reed Passport application obtained from U.S. State Department through Freedom of Information Act

SEVEN: Taking a Bride

1. Hobbs spent some of her days… Patricia Reed Wilson, *The Cold Warrior.'*

2. She stopped in at her agent's… Patricia Reed Wilson interviews, Oct. 24-25, 1996. Dialog recreated by author based on her recollection.

3. The next night they went… Ibid.

4. The young couple were … Ibid.

5. In mid-October, Dean returned… Patricia Reed Wilson interviews, Oct. 24-25, 1996, and August 18, 1998

6. As they drove up to the trailer… Ibid.

7. "He dropped me off…" Patricia Reed Wilson interviews, Oct. 24-25, 1996

8. Before he left for Acapulco… Patricia Reed Wilson interviews, August 18-19, 1998

9. A newspaper photo… Newspaper photo, courtesy of Patricia Reed Wilson

10. "I don't want to have anything…" Patricia Reed Wilson interviews, Oct. 24-25, 1996

11. He and two of his friends… Ibid.

12. "What a triangle I'm creating…" Letter to Mae Hobbs from Patricia Hobbs, provided by Patricia Reed Wilson

13. The look had to be perfect… Patricia Reed Wilson *The Cold Warrior* and interviews, Oct. 24-25, 1996

14. The next night… Ibid.

15. The day before… Patricia Reed Wilson, *The Cold Warrior*

16. "I've traveled around this world…" song lyrics courtesy of Patricia Reed Wilson

17. "It was very romantic…" Patricia Reed Wilson interviews, Oct. 24-25, 1996

18. Reed would mount letter-writing… Patricia Reed Wilson *The Cold Warrio* and interviews, Oct. 24-25, 1996

19. Reed and Patricia would often pose... Patricia Reed Wilson interviews Oct. 24-25, 1996

20. "Down here I'm different..." "L.A. Singer makes hit with Latins"

21. The film was nearly finished... Patricia Reed Wilson, *The Cold Warrior*

22. "I want you to know..." Song lyrics courtesy of Patricia Reed Wilson

23. "Dean didn't want me..." Patricia Reed Wilson interviews, Oct. 24-25, 1996

24. "The biggest event of my life..." Dean Reed review of his year, Nov. 7, 1964, Oceanside, Calif., provided by Patricia Reed Wilson

EIGHT: Adventures in Argentina

1. He leaped for the bed and nearly slid off... Patricia Reed Wilson, *The Cold Warrior* and interviews, Oct. 24-25, 1996, and *Dean Reed Tells about His Life*, p. 44. The created dialogue is based on those sources.

2. When Dean arrived home... *Dean Reed Tells about His Life*, p. 44

3. "He took real risks..." Marv Davidov interview, June 1996

4. "Have had 2 exciting..." Letter to Mae Hobbs from Dean Reed, provided by Patricia Reed Wilson

5. Dean purchased the two-story... Patricia Reed Wilson, *The Cold Warrior* and photos; Ruth Anna Brown interview, Oct. 18, 1994

6. "As each year goes by..." Dean Reed review of his year, Nov. 7, 1964

7. "In South America there are..." Dean Reed writing, courtesy of Marv Davidov

8. "South America changed my life," *American Rebel* documentary

9. Dean was performing... Dean Reed's writing from Dean Reed collection at the Colorado Historical Society

10. Varela was an active... *Dean Reed Tells about His Life*, p. 51

11. While the Congress... Patricia Reed Wilson interviews, Oct. 24-25, 1996

12. Dean did as requested... *Dean Reed Tells about His Life*, pp. 51-52

13. A memo to FBI... FBI memo dated August 30, 1965, obtained through the Freedom of Information Act

14. "Considering the free atmosphere..." *Dean Reed Tells about His Life*, p. 45

15. After the show... Created conversation based on recollections in Patricia Reed Wilson, *The Cold Warrior*; *Dean Reed Tells about His Life*; and *American Rebel* documentary

16. When he opened the door to his house... Patricia Reed Wilson interview, August 18, 1998

17. "That was a blow to me." Ibid.

18. On one of the visits... Patricia Reed Wilson, *The Cold Warrior*

19. "So many times in my ..." Lyrics provided by Patricia Reed Wilson

20. One evening the Reeds... Dialogue created by author, based on recollection in Patricia Reed Wilson, *The Cold Warrior*

21. One afternoon, not long... Ibid.

22. He had been sleeping... Ibid. and Patricia Reed Wilson interviews Oct. 24-25, 1996. Of the four people there that night, only Patricia still is alive. It is possible Varela knew Guevera, since Varela did travel to Cuba in 1960 and wrote glowingly in *Cuba with a Full*

Beard. It also is true that one of the middle names the Reeds would give their daughter was Guevera. Still, Dean makes no mention of the visit in his book. That could be explained by the fact that in 1984, Castro was becoming sharply critical of the Soviet Union and its policies, making it impolitic for Reed to mention the incident, a view Patricia shares. However, she does not know why her husband didn't mention the incident in his writings. It's also possible it never happened. Guevera was a romantic figure to many Americans. His beret-topped face was a popular poster in college dormitory rooms throughout the United States. He was the revolutionary many young Americans, including Patricia, wanted to be. "We loved Che, we had his picture on the wall," she said. Patricia acknowledged people might not believe the story since she is the only survivor. But in repeated interviews over two years, she never wavered.

23. "Dean was very serious…" Patricia Reed Wilson interviews, Oct. 24-25, 1996

24. Again she suffered a miscarriage… Ibid.

25. On March 25, 1966… State Department cable from Buenos Aires, March 30, 1966, obtained through the Freedom of Information Act

26. On March 28, the newspaper… FBI memo, June 29, 1966, obtained through the Freedom of Information Act. There is more about Reed in the memo, supplied by "another government agency engaged in intelligence investigations," but the FBI censors blacked it out.

27. Patricia remembered that they left… Patricia Reed Wilson, *The Cold Warrior*

NINE: Conquering the Soviet Union

1. But Patricia's mood soured as… Patricia Reed Wilson interviews, Oct. 24-25, 1996

2. Still, Dean was planning… FBI memo, Dec. 19, 1966, reprinting information from the Bulletin of the World Council of Peace

3. As usual, Dean's appearances… Oct. 7, 1966 memo to State Department from U.S. Embassy in Moscow

4. "As a performer, he has…" Airgram to State Department by J. C. Guthrie of the American Embassy in Moscow, Dec. 9, 1966

5. A half hour before one of his shows… The name of the drummer was not disclosed and the dialogue created by the author is based on the report in the Dec. 9, 1966, State Department airgram.

6. "It is the embassy's conclusion…" Airgram to State Department by J. C. Guthrie of the American Embassy in Moscow, Dec. 9, 1966

7. The music had an infectious beat… Patricia Reed Wilson interviews, Oct. 24-25, 1996

8. "It was still very difficult…" *Dean Reed Tells about His Life,* p. 73

9. The soccer players never made… Patricia Reed Wilson interview, Aug. 18, 1998, and *Dean Reed Tells about His Life,* pp. 70, 76

10. The American was being paid… Patricia Reed Wilson interview, Aug. 18, 1998

11. Patricia, as she often did… Ibid. and letters from Patricia Reed to Mae Hobbs, Oct. 8 and Oct. 26, 1966, provided by Patricia Reed Wilson

12. "Patti be brave…" Telegram from Dean Reed, provided by Patricia Reed Wilson

13. "Freedom is the Word of Today…" Lyrics provided by Patricia Reed Wilson

14. "The people in Vietnam…" Dec. 6, 1966, Czech radio transcript provided to FBI Special-Agent-in-Charge of Los Angeles Office by CIA liaison and obtained through Freedom of Information Act

15. "You mention that you hate..." Letter to Cyril Reed from Dean Reed, April 22, 1968, provided by Patricia Reed Wilson

TEN: "Lights, Camera, Deportation"

1. "These are shallow people..." Interview of Patricia Reed Wilson, Aug. 18, 1998

2. In Aug. 1967... Patricia Reed Wilson interviews, Aug. 18-19, 1998

3. Not long after doctors... Patricia Reed Wilson interviews, Aug. 18-19, 1998

4. "Dear Ramona..." Patricia Reed Wilson, *The Cold Warrior*

5. "He thought the U.S...." Patricia Reed Wilson interview, Aug. 18, 1998

6. A report by the U.S. State... June 8, 1967, memo from O/Sy/L-L.E. Gruza to FBI: Subject Dean REED, Harold HUMES

7. "Finally, my belief..." September 18, 1967, memo from Legat, Bern, to Director, FBI, Subject: Dean Cyril Reed

8. One Sunday, Dean's... *Dean Reed Tells about His Life,* pp. 60-63 and *American Rebel* documentary

9. "Yurii, for many weeks now..." Dean Reed letter to Yurii, September 29, 1968, provided by Patricia Reed Wilson. It is unclear whether this is a copy or the original and thus whether it was ever sent.

10. A Buenos Aires newspaper... Memo from U.S. Embasy legat, Buenos Aires to FBI director Aug. 7, 1969

11. "A Kennedy man, a progressive..." FBI Report on Dean Cyril Reed, Aug. 22, 1969

12. "I have just received..." Aug. 21, 1969, letter from Patricia Reed, from Dean Reed Collection at the Colorado Historical Society

13. "That was scary..." Patricia Reed Wilson interviews, Aug. 18-19, 1998

14. "Do you realize that..." Letter to Cyril Reed from Dean Reed, April 22, 1968

ELEVEN: Trouble at Home, Victory Abroad

All letters and speeches in this chapter were provided to the author by Patricia Reed Wilson during a visit to her Los Angeles home in Aug. 1998.

1. "When he had these other..." Patricia Reed Wilson interviews, Oct. 24-25, 1996

2. "not good material..." Patricia Reed Wilson, *The Cold Warrior*

3. "Anyway, thank you..." Undated 1967 letter from Dean Reed in Caracas, Venezuela, to Patricia Reed in Oceanside, Calif.

4. "I go to sleep..." Undated letter from about 1964 from Dean Reed in Buenos Aires to Patricia Reed in Palm Springs

5. "Hi kitten..." Letter from Dean Reed in Cannes, France, to Patricia Reed on Jan. 23, 1967

6. "My Dearest Wife..." Letter from Dean Reed in Cannes, France, to Patricia Reed, February 2, 1967

7. "We hung out..." Marv Davidov interview, June 1996

8. "Dear fellow peace workers..." Copy of Dean Reed speech to Stockholm Conference, March 27, 1970

9. "In Santiago, Chile..." *Dean Reed Tells about His Life,* p. 88

10. "To the peoples of the World..." Copy of Dean Reed speech

11. "He was briefly..." State Department memo on Dean Reed from Korry in U.S. Embassy Chile, March 12, 1971

12. "He was in Chile to help..." Marv Davidov interview, June 1996

13. "For me, it was a piece..." *Dean Reed Tells about His Life,* p. 89

14. "booed off the stage..." State Department memo on Dean Reed from Korry in U.S. Embassy Chile, March 12, 1971

15. "I would have been proud..." Letter to Ramona Reed, Nov. 19, 1970

16. "Youth in the Struggle..." Memo to U.S. State Department from Mr. Beam, American Embassy in Moscow, February 10, 1971. Subject: Anti-American forays by US Citizen Dean Reed

17. "As an American artist..." Report to FBI Director from Special-Agent-in-Charge, Seattle, who had the letter translated. Report dated July 28, 1971, and obtained through the Freedom of Information Act.

18. It had cost the Soviets... *Dean Reed Tells about His Life,* pp. 78, 21

TWELVE: Busted

1. "Now we have to cut your..." *American Rebel* documentary

2. The kitchen was not concerned... Patricia Reed Wilson interview, Aug. 18, 1998

3. The military uniforms the boys wore... Dialogue created by author, based on interview of Dale Reed, Oct. 6, 1995

4. "As you know..." Letter to Mae Hobbs from Dean Reed, February 1, 1971, provided by Patricia Reed Wilson

5. "The hour has come..." *Dean Reed Tells about His Life,* pp. 89, 92-93

6. "There are many political..." May 21, 1971, letter from Dean Reed to Patricia Reed

7. "I have always believed..." *Dean Reed Tells about His Life,* pp. 46-48

8. A handful of other political prisoners... Patricia Reed Wilson interviews, Aug. 18-19, 1998

9. Back in Rome, Patricia... *Dean Reed Tells about His Life,* p. 49, and Patricia Reed Wilson interviews, Oct. 24-25, 1996

10. "I'm sure they thought..." Patricia Reed Wilson interviews, Oct. 24-25, 1996, and Aug. 18-19, 1998

11. "For some time now..." Letter to Mae Hobbs from Dean Reed, February 1, 1971, provided by Patricia Reed Wilson

12. They ate dinner at... Patricia Reed Wilson interviews, Oct. 24-25, 1996

THIRTEEN: Taking a Bride (Part II)

1. The chief organizer... Dean Reed resume, Stasi files, Vol. 2 BStU 25

2. A key part of détente... Stasi files Vol. 1 BStU 31

3. "The question here concerns..." Ibid.

4. Her family had been... Patricia Reed Wilson interviews, Oct. 24-25, 1996

5. She convinced him to ... Ibid.

6. As with the others... *Newsweek,* March 20, 1972, p.s 114-115

7. The fact that Dean… Dean Reed letter to Vernon Reed, February 28, 1978 from Stasi files Vol. 1 BStU 244

8. "Wiebke was a masturbation…" Patricia Reed Wilson interviews, Oct. 24-25, 1996

9. "I was very happy to come…" *Dean Reed Tells about His Life*, p. 107

10. "Well, we both begin…" Letter from Dean Reed to Patricia Reed, provided by Patricia Reed Wilson

11. "They were married…" Patricia Reed Wilson interviews, Oct. 24-25, 1996

12. "The approval of his…" Stasi files Vol. 1 BStU 29

FOURTEEN: Spy

1. "There was a lot of fear…" Phil Everly interview, May 31, 1996

2. "For the first years…" Patricia Reed Wilson interviews, Oct. 24-25, 1996

3. "Plan for the follow-through…" Memo of Capt. Hauptmann Sattler, April 20, 1976, Stasi files, Vol. 1 BStU 152

4. "Now, Herr Reed…" Dialogue created by author, based on report of Capt. Hauptmann Sattler, Aug. 23, 1977, Stasi files, Vol. 1 BStU 162

5. "What would he learn…" Marv Davidov interview, June 1996

6. Dean and his wife attended… Memo of Capt Hauptmann Sattler, September 2, 1977, Stasi files, Vol. 1 BStU 165-168

7. "It was evident that…" Report of Capt. Hauptmann Sattler, Dec. 1, 1977, Stasi files, Vol. 1 BStU 169-170

8. "enthusiastically told about…" Report of Capt. Hauptmann Sattler, Dec. 13, 1977, Stasi files, Vol 1, BStU 178-180

9. "has reservations about the …" Internal memo March 29, 1978, Stasi files, Vol. 1 BStU 249

10. "I would debate with him…" Marv Davidov interview, June 1996

11. "to work against the PLO…" Memos of Major General Kratsch of September 14, 1978, and Major Hauptmann Sattler, Nov. 24, 1978, Stasi files, Vol. 1 BStU 251, 252 and 259

FIFTEEN: The Smell of Gunpowder

1. "Your letter filled with fighting…" Jan. 13, 1975, letter from Dean Reed to Marv Davidov, provided by Davidov

2. There was no friction… Marv Davidov interview, June 1996

3. Patricia had returned… Patrica Reed Wilson interviews, Oct. 24-25, 1996

4. "When I brought him…" Marv Davidov interview, June 1996

5. It was also the time of the year… Ibid.

6. About 250 people… *St. Paul Pioneer Press,* June 19, 1975

7. "Dear friend, Comrade…" Letter from Dean Reed, provided by Marv Davidov

8. He sang at Communist… Letter from Dean Reed in Madrid to Patricia Reed Wilson, June 18, 1977

9. "He kept telling us…" Ruth Anna Brown interview, Oct. 18, 1994

10. "Of course, it is a very…" February 28, 1978, letter to Vernon Reed, Stasi files, Vol. 1 BStU 243

11. "I am supposed to leave…" Nov. 3, 1977, Dean Reed account of his trip, Stasi files, Vol. 1, BStU 174-175

12. "Just after lunch…" Ibid.

13. After four days… Ibid.

14. In January, he traveled… *Dean Reed Tells about His Life,* p. 123

15. "It was one of…" Patricia Reed Wilson interviews, Aug. 18-19, 1998

SIXTEEN: Powerlines and *People* Magazine

All letters and speeches in this chapter were provided by Patricia Reed Wilson unless otherwise indicated.

1. "It shall be very difficult…" September 21, 1976, letter from Dean Reed to Ramona Reed

2. "The ties between us…" Letter from Dean Reed to Wiebke Reed, September 17, 1978

3. "It is good to speak…" Ibid.

4. "We shall see…" Ibid.

5. Carson himself was involved… *The Hollywood Reporter,* May 5, 1972

6. When he finally decided… Marv Davidov interview, June 1996

7. "I've crossed over the line…" "Red Sinatra supports local powerline protest," by Don Clark, *Minnesota Daily,* Oct. 26, 1978

8. "Dean was staying with me…" Marv Davidov interview, June 1996

9. "Dean said to me…" Ibid.

10. "as a citizen and a member…" John Randolph telegram from the Dean Reed collection of the Colorado Historical Society

11. "All GDR media are…" Nov. 1978 telegram from AmEmbassy Berlin to SecState WashD.C. Subject: GDR Solidarity with Dean Reed, signed by Bolen.

12. "The current media attention…" Telegram from AmEmbassy Moscow to SecState WashDC Nov. 1978 signed by Toon. Subject: Request for background on Dean Reed case.

13. It detailed the circumstances… Telegram from SecState WashDC to AmEmbassy Moscow, Nov. 1978

14. Every morning about 6:30… Marv Davidov interview, June 1996

15. "Some people may try…" Dean Reed statement to Wright County Court jury

16. "I understand that you…" Telegram from SecState WashDC to AmEmbassy Moscow Subject: Reply to Soviet Artists Nov. 16, 1978

17. "it was not only a …" Note to Ramona Reed from Dean Reed

18. "Yes I had a trial…" Airgram from Mr. Toon, AmEmbassy Moscow to SecState Wash-DC Jan 20, 1979, Subject: Chance encounter with Dean Reed

SEVENTEEN: Taking a Bride (Part III)

1. "I am so happy…" Letter from Dean Reed to Paton Price, February 10, 1978, Stasi files,

Vol. 1 BStU 240

2. "Everybody knew him…" Phil Everly interview, May 31, 1996

3. "He knew what was…" Ibid.

4. List had produced… Police interview of Gerrit List, Stasi files, Vol. 4 BStU 87

5. Now divorced for two years… Patricia Reed Wilson, *The Cold Warrior*

6. "We have other reasons…" "American Folk Hero for Soviet Bloc," by James M. Markham, New York Times Service, February 1984 *International Herald Tribune*, as found in Stasi Files, Vol. 2 BStU 48

7. But Cyril, always the … Telephone interview of Dale Reed, Oct. 6, 1995

8. Reed was driving the highway… Report of General Major Leibholz, Stasi files, Vol. 2 BStU 36–37

9. "That sounds like Dean…" Phil Everly interview, May 31, 1996

EIGHTEEN: Reed and the Bloody Dictator

1. "Hello, this is Dean Reed…" Dialogue created by author based on accounts from State Department telegram from AmEmbassy Santiago to SecState Wash DC Aug. 23, 1983 Subject: Expulsion of US Citizen Dean Cyril Reed, and from *Dean Reed Tells about His Life,* p. 99

2. At the police station… *Dean Reed Tells about His Life,* p. 99

3. In all, the general's… "Career Change," by Eduardo Gallardo of the Associated Press in *St. Paul Pioneer Press,* Nov. 26, 1997

4. The Spanish charges… "Britain Arrests Pinochet to Face Charges in Spain" *New York Times,* Oct. 18, 1998, story by Clifford Krauss

5. In his writings… *Dean Reed Tells about His Life,* p. 93

6. "Dearest Ramona…" July 4, 1983, letter to Ramona Reed from Dean Reed, provided by Patricia Reed Wilson

7. Friends met him at… *Dean Reed Tells about His Life,* p. 95, and State Department Telegram from AmEmbassy Santiago to SecState WashDC Aug. 23, 1983 Subject: Expulsion of US Citizen Dean Cyril Reed

8. He held a press conference… *Dean Reed Tells about His Life,* pp. 96–97

9. Four times in all… Ibid., p. 99

10. Then he headed off… Ibid., p. 100–101

11. "Dean had a death wish…" Phone interview of Patricia Reed Wilson, July 1996

NINETEEN: Nobody Knows Me Back in My Hometown

1. "folk hero in Moscow…" "American Folk Hero for Soviet Bloc" by James M. Markham, New York Times Service in *International Herald Tribune,* February 1984, as found in Stasi files, Vol. 2 BStU 48

2. "You who so hypocritically…" Letter from Dean Reed to James Markham, February 4, 1984, Stasi files, Vol. 2 BStU 46–47

3. In one of the letters… Johnny Rosenburg interview, Oct. 17, 1994

4. Prior to his trial… Marv Davidov interview, June 1996

5. Old injuries from his... Police interview of Renate Blume Reed, June 30, 1986, Stasi files, Vol. 4 BStU 100

6. Once while driving... Police interview of Patricia Reed Wilson, June 25, 1986, Stasi files, Vol. 4 BStU 77-78

7. One night Reed started drinking... Patricia Reed Wilson interviews, July 1996 and Aug. 18-19, 1998

8. On October 26, 1984... State Department telegram from AmEmbassy Montevideo to Sec. State Wash. DC Subject: Arrest American Citizen Dean Cyril Reed, Nov. 1984, and *Dean Reed Tells about His Life,* p. 141

9. "In the conversation..." Police interview of Dr. Werner Dietz, July 7, 1986, Stasi files, Vol. 4 BStU 105

10. "Dean had had severe injuries..." Police interview of Gerrit List, June 27, 1986, Stasi files Vol. 4 BStU 90

TWENTY: Homecoming

1. Friday, he had an invitation... Johnny Rosenburg interview, Oct. 17, 1994

2. Boyles turned quickly... "The Mystery of Dean Reed," by David McQuay, *Denver Post,* Nov. 23, 1986

3. One of the people who... Johnny Rosenburg interview, Oct. 17, 1994

4. "He was devasted..." Ibid.

5. Besides trying to rekindle a... Ibid.

6. "It really bugged him..." Ibid.

7. "Dean didn't believe politically..." Ibid.

8. At one point, she gave... Patricia Reed Wilson interviews, Oct. 24-25, 1996

9. "A couple of friends..." Marv Davidov interview, June 1996

10. "He would put out..." Ibid.

11. He told Davidov how he met... Ibid.

12. "I know the maritial problems..." Ibid.

TWENTY ONE: The Decline

1. "He appeared to me..." Police interview of Gerrit List, June 27, 1986, Stasi files Vol. 4 BStU 89

2. "When we think about Americans..." Transcript of *60 Minutes,* broadcast April 20, 1986

3. "It was like driving a wooden..." Johnny Rosenburg interview, Oct. 17, 1994

4. "You traded the stars and stripes..." song lyrics courtesy of Johnny Rosenburg

5. "He assumed that the film..." Police interview of Renate Blume Reed, June 30, 1986, Stasi files Vol. 4 BStU 98

6. His friend Gerrit List recalled... Police interview of Gerrit List, June 27, 1986, Stasi files Vol. 4 BStU 89-90

7. "I am convinced that Dean..." Police interview of Renate Blume Reed, June 30, 1986, Stasi files, Vol. 4 BStU 100

8. "an inevitability no matter..." Phil Everly interview, May 31, 1996

9. "He had this very distinct..." Police interview of Gerrit List, June 27, 1986, Stasi files, Vol. 4 BStU 89

TWENTY TWO: The Last Fight

1. Reed had been explicit... Police interview of Wiebke Reed, June 27, 1986, Stasi files, Vol. 4 BStU 84

2. "What I wished for..." Police interview of Renate Blume Reed, June 30, 1986, Stasi files, Vol. 4 BStU 98

3. Reed told List that Alexander... Police interview of Gerrit List, June 27, 1986, Stasi files, Vol. 4 BStU 91

4. At about 2:20 p.m., List... Dialogue recreated by author, based on recollections of Gerrit List in police interview, June 27, 1986, Stasi files, Vol. 4 BStU 91

5. When police knocked... Police interview of Renate Blume Reed, June 30, 1986, Stasi files, Vol. 4 BStU 98

6. They had become friendly... Police interview of Dr. Werner Dietz, July 7, 1986, Stasi files, Vol. 4 BStU 103

7. They talked for another two hours... Police interview of Gerrit List, June 27, 1986, Stasi files, Vol. 4 BStU 92

8. He examined the cuts and bruises... Police interview of Dr. Werner Dietz, July 7, 1986, Stasi files, Vol. 4 BStU 104-107

9. "He said he had made it..." Ibid.

10. "I was thinking maybe you and I..." Dialogue recreated by author based on recollections of Renate Blume Reed in police interview of June 30 1986, Stasi files, Vol. 4 BStU 98 and list of items recovered as stated in Stasi files, Vol. 4 BStU 135-136

11. Reed phoned List... Police interview of Gerrit List, June 27, 1986, Stasi files Vol. 4 BStU 88

TWENTY THREE: The Search for Dean Reed

1. Within a half-hour... Police interview of Renate Blume Reed, June 30, 1986, Stasi files, Vol. 4 BStU 99

2. "It could not be..." Police interview of Gerrit List, June 27, 1986, Stasi files, Vol. 4 BStU 94

3. One of the calls was from... Stasi files, Vol. 3 BStU 1-7

4. At best she thought her husband... Dialogue created by author based on reports in Stasi files, Vol. 3 BStU 48, 11-12

5. "Dean told other people..." Stasi files, Vol. 3 BStU 19

6. He reassured Renate and said he... Stasi files, Vol. 3 BStU 16, 17, 20

7. "Renate, they found Dean's car." Dialogue recreated by author based on reports in Stasi files, Vol. 4 BStU 21, 28, 37

8. They asked Renate what Reed was wearing... Stasi files, Vol. 3 BStU 21

9. Indeed, on Monday, June 16... Stasi files, Vol. 3 BStU 23

10. When Officer Sven Bosener reported to work... Police interview of Sven Bosener, June 17, 1986, Stasi files, Vol. 4 BStU 72-73

11. The officials met and finally decided... Stasi files, Vol. 4 BStU 29, 30

12. When Patricia's husband told her... Patricia Reed Wilson, *The Cold Warrior*

13. "Americans only believe in psychiatrists..." Stasi files, Vol. 3 BStU 43

14. Heide Kuschel, a translator... Stasi files, Vol. 3 BStU 47-52

15. List and Fiedlkorn finally arranged... Stasi files, Vol. 3 BStU 56 and Vol. 2 BStU 128-131

16. "Our beloved husband, son and father..." Stasi files, Vol. 2 BStU 109

17. The music was Beethoven, Hayden... Stasi files, Vol. 2 BStU 137-139

18. The funeral struck Patricia... Patricia Reed Wilson interviews, Aug. 18-19, 1998

19. Dean also was subject... Patricia Reed Wilson, *The Cold Warrior*

TWENTY FOUR: Who Killed Dean Reed?

1. Between May and October, 1989 thousands... *Newsweek,* Oct. 16, 1989

2. "The farewell letter was..." June 24, 1986, memo from Main Section XX/7, Stasi files, Vol. 2 BStU 117

3. The U.S. citizens and relatives..." June 23, 1986, memo by Lt. Col. Hossack, Stasi files, Vol. 2 BStU 129

4. "It is proposed that a suitable..." June 18, 1986, memo from Main Section XX Stasi files, Vol. 2 BStU 98

5. Stasi officers were well....Memo dated June 17, 1986, Stasi files, Vol. 2 BStU 82

6. "My friend and General..." Stasi files, Vol. 2 BStU 63-77

7. "We're not even sure..." Ruth Anna Brown interview, Oct. 18, 1994

8. Her son had worked... Ibid.

9. "I didn't get the impression..." Phil Everly interview, May 31, 1996

10. "A lot of times, we would..." Patricia Reed Wilson interview, Aug. 18, 1998

11. "We agree a lot more..." Dale Reed interview, Oct. 6, 1995

12. "I could see he was living..." Ibid.

13. "There is no other American..." Marv Davidov interview, June 1996

About the Author

Chuck Laszewski has been an award-winning newspaper reporter for twenty-six years, most of them at the *St. Paul Pioneer Press*. While a student at the University of Minnesota in 1978, Laszewski first noticed Reed when the actor showed one of his films on campus. After Reed's death and the collapse of the East German government, Laszewski used his investigative reporting skills to acquire the secret police files on Reed.

Laszewski and his wife Cindy have two children and live in St. Paul, Minnesota.